D1598051

GOD'S BUSINESSMEN

GOD'S BUSINESSMEN

Entrepreneurial Evangelicals in Depression and War

SARAH RUTH HAMMOND

Edited by DARREN DOCHUK

THE UNIVERSITY OF CHICAGO PRESS

CHICAGO AND LONDON

The University of Chicago Press, Chicago 60637
The University of Chicago Press, Ltd., London

Published 2017
Printed in the United States of America

26 25 24 23 22 21 20 19 18 17   1 2 3 4 5

ISBN-13: 978-0-226-50977-8 (cloth)
ISBN-13: 978-0-226-50980-8 (e-book)
DOI: 10.7208/chicago/9780226509808.001.0001

Library of Congress Cataloging-in-Publication Data

Names: Hammond, Sarah Ruth, 1977–2011, author. | Dochuk, Darren, editor.
Title: God's businessmen : entrepreneurial evangelicals in Depression and war / Sarah Ruth Hammond ; edited by Darren Dochuk.
Description: Chicago ; London : The University of Chicago Press, 2017. | Includes bibliographical references and index.
Identifiers: LCCN 2017009043 | ISBN 9780226509778 (cloth : alk. paper) | ISBN 9780226509808 (e-book)
Subjects: LCSH: Business—Religious aspects—Protestant churches. | Evangelicalism—Economic aspects—United States. | Capitalism—Religious aspects—Protestant churches. | LeTourneau, R. G. (Robert Gilmour), 1888–1969. | Taylor, Herbert John, 1893–1978. | Evangelicalism—United States—History—20th century. | Christianity—United States—History—20th century. | United States—History—1933–1945.
Classification: LCC HF5388 .H36 2017 | DDC 338.092/8773—dc23 LC record available at https://lccn.loc.gov/2017009043

♾ This paper meets the requirements of ANSI/NISO Z39.48–1992 (Permanence of Paper).

FOR MARY AND STEVE HAMMOND

CONTENTS

EDITORIAL NOTE

Sarah Hammond's dissertation, completed at Yale University, has already influenced the field of American religious history. Specialists in the study of religion, politics, labor, and capitalism whose published works have appeared in recent years openly thank her for helping generate interest in this important topic, and for providing some of the impetus for the creation of a vibrant historiography. Were she still with us today, there is no doubt she would continue to be a vital presence in this ever-changing, always-important discussion about the relationship between faith and markets in the modern age. While experts are aware of her Yale study, many more students of twentieth-century US history need to be exposed to it, both because it is absolutely vital to our understanding of recent developments in the United States (epitomized by the election of a Presbyterian, Republican businessman to the presidency), and because it is a lively and enjoyable—as well as illuminating and highly instructive—read. It is for this reason that the University of Chicago Press decided to move forward with the manuscript after Sarah's death (the book was under contract at that time). Having had the privilege of reviewing the manuscript for the press, and getting to know Sarah and her work, I agreed to help guide the project to completion. My fondness for Sarah and appreciation of her sharp intellect and talent with the pen only grew deeper as I processed her prose. She was and remains so special to so many people, and it was a privilege to spend time with her in this unique way.

The process itself involved a number of tasks, which, for the sake of transparency, deserve brief clarification, as well as my own expressions of gratitude. No electronic copy of Sarah's dissertation manuscript could be located, so the first task was simply to retype the text. Providing tremendous help in this regard was Debra Dochuk, who spent considerable time putting Sarah's words down on the page. Philip Byers helped finish typing footnotes and cleaning up the original draft. Both deserve a most emphatic thank-you!

Before she passed away, Sarah had outlined a series of responses to the initial round of editorial reports, which led to the University of Chicago Press extending her an advance contract. While editing, I did my best to honor Sarah's own plans for revision. This entailed rewriting the introduction and conclusion, adding a fifth chapter (culled from material that originally appeared in the dissertation's four chapters), reorganizing the book into a chronological pattern, offering a bit more information on other evangelical executives, such as J. Howard Pew, and trimming, cross-checking, and updating the notes, Internet links included. In the process of reconstructing these sections, I also attempted to reference more recent historical work in the study of evangelicalism and capitalism, refit chapters (which tended to be quite lengthy) with section breaks and titles, and insert transitional sentences and paragraphs where I thought they were needed to promote consistency and flow. Sarah's ideas and voice remained front and center throughout, and I hope that the changes I made only serve to accentuate the brilliance of her insights and the playfulness and creativity of her style.

I would like to thank Mary and Steve Hammond for their encouragement and patience, for opening up their home for conversation, and for giving me access to Sarah's collection of archival materials. A hearty thank-you must also be extended to Timothy Mennel, who inherited this unusual project, and stayed with it, supportive throughout, even when challenges came along. I also appreciate the editorial help Rachel Kelly and George Roupe provided during the last stages of the process. I assume responsibility for any errors.

Darren Dochuk

ACKNOWLEDGMENTS

I owe an immeasurable debt to the archivists who made my research possible. Bob Shuster and Wayne Weber at the Billy Graham Center Archives know every nook and cranny of American evangelicalism. Bob's habit of staying late for out-of-towners gave me at least ten extra hours with the materials. My hosts Julie and John Worthen fed me, gave rides when I could have taken the train, and filled the evenings with laughter, talk, and movies. At the Margaret Estes Library at LeTourneau University, Henry S. Whitlow went miles beyond the call of duty by lending me volumes of *NOW*. Dale Hardy, an archive unto himself, mobilized volunteers to catalog hundreds of disorganized boxes. His tour of the LeTourneau plant was a highlight of my visit, as was staying with Lee Wilkinson, a favorite childhood babysitter. The Hagley Library awarded me a grant in aid to spend two weeks with the papers of J. Howard Pew. Phil Wade at the Christian Men's Committee headquarters not only searched for but also scanned sources that fleshed out the stories of evangelical businessmen's groups. I also thank the staff at the Library of Congress and the Franklin Delano Roosevelt Library.

I am deeply grateful to the organizations that helped fund my graduate school career. The Woodrow Wilson National Fellowship Foundation subsidized my first year with the Andrew F. Mellon Fellowship in Humanistic Studies. The Richard J. Franke Interdisciplinary Fellowship in the Humanities added three years of support. Most of all, the Lake Doctoral Dissertation Fellowship at the Center for the Study of Philanthropy at Indiana University enabled me to finish. Meeting the members of the Lake Institute board felt like being reintroduced to old friends. I thank them for their hospitality and their feedback on my research.

Many scholars pushed me intellectually. Jon Butler, Skip Stout, and

Beverly Gage, my dissertation committee, doled out precise doses of criticism and encouragement. Chapter 2 had its genesis at the Organization of American Historians (OAH) conference in 2007. I presented a paper for a panel titled "Religion, Economic Values, and Business Culture in America, 1865–1965," which also featured Jeanne Kilde, Tim Gloege, and Bryan Bademan. At OAH 2009, I joined Joseph Lowndes, Jason Morgan Ward, and Elizabeth Tandy Shermer on the panel "Grassroots Conservatism: From the Bottom Up or Top Down?" Elizabeth Fones-Wolf and Ken Fones-Wolf graciously supplied an unpublished paper on industrial chaplaincies and encouraged my work. Dr. Uta Balbier shared her 2009 Billy Graham Center Archival Research Lecture, "God and Coca-Cola: Billy Graham in Germany." The American Religious History Working Group at Yale and its counterpart at Columbia sharpened many a draft. Special thanks to Heather Rivera and the dedicated religious studies staff for smoothing bureaucratic hurdles.

Extraordinary colleagues and friends helped me think through what I wanted to say and did no small amount of hand-holding as I struggled to say it. Amanda Bell, Alexandra Block, Debbie Dinner, Jill Fraley, Brian Gold, Alison Greene, Keith Harper, Michael Jo, Geoff Kabaservice, Paul A. Kramer, Tracy Lemos, A. G. Miller, Bethany Moreton, Robin Morris, Dawn Neely-Randall, Eva Pascal, Gabby Redwine, Maria Satterwhite, Reva Siegel, Linn Tonstad, Kate Unterman, Shira Weidenbaum, and Molly Worthen were conversation partners, editors, and cheerleaders.

Infinite thanks to Mary and Steve Hammond, Rachel Ramirez-Hammond, and Grace Hammond for their generosity, faith, and love.

ABBREVIATIONS

ABC	American Broadcasting Company
ACCC	American Council of Christian Churches
AFL	American Federation of Labor
BGEA	Billy Graham Evangelistic Association
BIOLA	Bible Institute of Los Angeles
BMEC	Business Men's Evangelistic Clubs
CBMC	Christian Business Men's Committee
CBMCI	Christian Business Men's Committee International
CCC	Civilian Conservation Corps
CCMC	Charlotte Christian Men's Club
CIO	Congress of Industrial Organizations
CLC	Christian Laymen's Crusade
CMA	Christian and Missionary Alliance Church
CWF	Christian Workers Foundation
FCC	Federal Council of Churches
IER	Institute of Education by Radio
IFES	International Fellowship of Evangelical Students
IVCF	Inter-Varsity Christian Fellowship
LEF	LeTourneau Evangelistic Foundation
MBI	Moody Bible Institute
NAE	National Association of Evangelicals
NAM	National Association of Manufacturers
NEF	New England Fellowship
NYA	National Youth Administration

SBC	Southern Baptist Convention
USO	United Service Organizations
WCFA	World Christian Fundamentals Association
YFC	Youth for Christ
YMCA	Young Men's Christian Association

Introduction

It is 1920 and workers are striking in Zenith, a midwestern town whose gleaming skyscrapers give middle-class strivers a sense of the sublime. Each morning, George F. Babbitt—a forty-six-year-old realtor, Presbyterian, Republican, Elk, Zenith booster, and Chamber of Commerce member—gazes from his suburban window upon the thirty-five-story Second National Bank, "a temple-spire of the religion of business."[1] Torn between unreflective faith in unimpeded capitalism and qualms about violence both rhetorical *and* real against the workers, Babbitt goes to church to learn "How the Saviour Would End Strikes."[2] "Hope the doc gives the strikers hell!" hisses advertising man Chum Frink, who shares Babbitt's velvet-upholstered pew. "Ordinarily, I don't believe in a preacher butting into political matters—let him stick to straight religion and save souls, and not stir up a lot of discussion—but at a time like this, I do think he ought to stand right up and bawl out those plug-uglies to a fare-you-well!"[3]

Babbitt's congregation, Chatham Road Presbyterian Church of Zenith, is at this time a belligerent in a broad fight dividing white northern Protestants over fundamental beliefs about faith, economy, and political culture. The "modernists" within Presbyterianism accepted historical and scientific criticism of the Bible, emphasized human potential over innate depravity, and denounced industrial capitalism's extremes of wealth and poverty. They dismissed pietism without social reform as irresponsible, seeing inequality as a collective problem requiring collective—sometimes government—solutions. Conservative evangelicals or "fundamentalists," by contrast, conceptualized orthodoxy as adherence to supernatural doctrines that science could not explain: divine creation, original sin, the virgin birth, Jesus's atoning death and resurrection, an afterlife in heaven or hell. To them, social change was a by-product of conversion, which took place in individual hearts and trumped schemes for the common good. Trusting God to bless the righteous and curse the wicked, they defended capitalism by pointing to scriptures in which riches rewarded obedience. Making hay of communist atheism, they acknowledged no meaningful distinctions among the social gospel, socialism, and Bolshevism; all represented sedition against God's chosen nation, the United States.

Staunchly evangelical, Babbitt's minister embodies the totality of the conservative side in the debate, which is why he argues that opposing Zenith's strike is not simply a political statement but a religious duty. Unwilling to reduce the fundamentalist-modernist tensions of his church to finer doctrinal points, the pastor warns his parishioners that theirs is a culture war of ultimate meaning, waged between two completely oppositional worldviews. In his view, the labor revolt caps "a generation" of spiritual warfare between Bible-believing Christians and enemies of the gospel and the natural condition of free enterprise.[4] He mocks evolutionists and the "great poo-bahs of [theological] criticism" who "attack . . . the established fundamentals of the Christian creed." He calls labor unions "crazy systems . . . of despotic paternalism" that try to stop the invisible hand of God from regulating the marketplace. "[T]his whole industrial matter isn't a question of economics," he concludes. "It's essentially and only a matter of Love, and of the practical application of the Christian religion!" If management and labor could coexist in Christian brotherhood, "then . . . strikes would be as inconceivable as hatred in the home!"[5]

Babbitt stirs in his pew, agreeing with most of what is being said in the pulpit, yet also finding some of the reasoning unsteady. He bristles most at the pastor's talk about labor and love. "Oh, rot! . . . He doesn't know what he's talking about," Babbitt mutters.[6] With his home life faltering, his views of the striking laborers growing ambiguous (even liberal!) with each new episode of anti-union violence, and a general malaise about modern life setting in, Babbitt cannot help but voice frustration with the minister's easy solutions to complex problems. This whole industrial matter is only a matter of love? His mumbles of dissent make his Presbyterian brother Chum Frink uneasy. For the remainder of the service Babbitt grows increasingly nervous as his neighbor's glances of doubt and criticism grow more intense.

Babbitt makes others nervous as well, as his condemnations of the strikers continue to soften. After seeing marching protestors up close and identifying several respectable men among them—including the "white-bearded" "Professor Brockbank, head of the history department in the State University"—Babbitt wonders: "gosh . . . a swell like him in with the strikers?"[7] Moved by the visual, he finds himself in another awkward moment a short time later when congratulating police captain Clarence Drum for his handling of the march. "Fine work," Babbitt offers; "no violence." Rather than respond with appreciation, Drum answers with disgust:

> If I had my way, there'd be a whole lot of violence, and I'd start it, and then the whole thing would be over. I don't believe in standing back and wet-nursing these fellows and letting the disturbances drag on. I tell you these strikers are nothing in God's world but a lot of bomb-throwing socialists and thugs, and the only way to handle 'em is with a club! That's what I'd do; beat up the whole lot of 'em.

Before he can stop himself, Babbitt blurts, "Oh, rats, Clarence, they look just about like you and me."[8] Once again he feels the cold condemnation of a questioning glare.

However much he feels (and mutters) growing unease with the culture wars playing out before him and the tensions that encompass his church, business, community, politics, and family, Babbitt is eventually forced to choose sides. His would be a short-lived rebellion against the corporate, conservative, Christian establishment of his town. Two existential predicaments impel him to concede. Babbitt's outspoken doubts about his cohorts' undermining of labor rights eventually place him at odds with peers; lost business, lost respect, and isolation are the by-products of this liberal drift. Then his wife's sudden acute appendicitis drives him to a point of utter despair, making him realize that his love for her and his family is still real and his need for the support of his powerful friends (doctors, business colleagues, and church leaders) is essential to daily life.

Faced with these realities, Babbitt abandons the doubts and questioning of his middle-age crisis and, once again, he grasps tightly to the conformities, assurances, and probusiness and union-busting theology and politics that animates his peers. "I tell you, boy," he once exclaimed to his son, "there's no stronger bulwark of sound conservatism than the evangelical church!"[9] In the wake of his trials, amid the search for acceptance and certainty, Babbitt reclaims this truth, and makes it clear that his renewed faith in Christ and capitalism, the business and fundamentals of his church, are the only antidotes to the struggles of his time.

Brought to life in Sinclair Lewis's 1922 novel *Babbitt*, George Babbitt's personal journey through the culture clashes that mar his age is, of course, completely fictional. Lewis meant for Babbitt to be the centerpiece in a cynical satire of business-class America in boom times. Trapped in the class expectations and capitalist free-for-all that surround him, Babbitt is both victim of and participant in the rampant materialism, shallow spirituality, darker hypocrisies, and moral contradictions that Lewis saw plaguing society in the roaring twenties. In *Babbitt* readers are also exposed to the alliance of conservative business and evangelical interests that dominated America's heartland and helped agitate the social battles of the day. When Babbitt goes to work at the bank, he labors under the "temple-spire" of business; when he attends church on Sunday he worships at the altar of laissez-faire fundamentalism. Undifferentiated in its blend of secular and sacred imperatives, his is an all-consuming world of God and mammon.

Lewis's reading of these fused interests and his observation that "there's no stronger bulwark of sound conservatism than the evangelical church" may not have been considered noteworthy in 1922, at least in comparison to his other stinging critiques of 1920s society, but today it reads as a remarkably prescient commentary about the especially close and enduring ties that corporate capitalism and evangelical Christianity developed under the shadows of the Great Depression and global struggles during the interwar period. Lewis's charge that political conservatism's strongest base of support resided in the boardrooms and pews, and the linkages between them, would be just as true in 1932, when Franklin D. Roosevelt faced mounting opposition from fundamentalist preachers and corporate executives as he embarked on an unprecedented expansion of state power to fight the Depression, and in 1942, when critics of the "tyrannical" New Deal kept a wary eye on the wartime alliance between government and business. And it would ultimately be true in 1952 as well, when a coalition of religious and political conservative activists helped generate a right-wing insurgency within the Republican Party, then in compromised but no less potent fashion accepted the leadership of Dwight Eisenhower and rallied behind his effort to couch the nation in a civil religion of God and country. The union of evangelical and corporate conservatism between the 1920s and 1940s was indeed a staple of this period's tumultuous politics, and in Babbitt's own tortured negotiations, Lewis manages to glimpse them in provoking color.[10]

What remains clouded in Lewis's fictional account are the broader and real historical contingencies and long-term consequences that framed its colorful and biting morality tale. These larger-scale transformations deserve more focused attention, certainly for better understanding of *Babbitt* itself, but also for the purposes of a clearer rendering of American evangelical political convictions and action in the modern era. Despite its illustrative power and real insight into this essence of American life between the aftermath of the First World War and dawn of the Cold War, Lewis's observation has generated relatively little interest among students of American religion and politics. This oversight can be attributed to the hold that rise-and-fall narratives have had in the chronicles of modern evangelicalism and among the Republican right.[11] Shortly after *Babbitt*'s release, standard history texts recount, fundamentalists lost the civil war within northern Protestantism as well as a public relations battle with evolutionists and liberal modernists at the Scopes Trial. Humiliated and to a degree disenfranchised within church ranks, by the end of the decade they retrenched to develop an avowedly independent and insular religious subculture, one that would operate (and according to some historians, flourish) under the radar of mainstream culture well into the 1940s. Only in the 1950s and 1960s would they begin to thrive again in full view as a revitalized "New Evangelicalism."[12]

If accurate in some measure when accounting for internal institutional dynamics in American Protestantism, at no point along this continuum did the fundamentalist-turned–New Evangelical movement "become largely apolitical for decades," as the *New York Times* fifty years later phrased the conventional wisdom about the post-1960s "New Christian Right."[13] The horde of pundits that assumed the *New York Times'* perspective when trying to explain the long lead-up to the religious right of Ronald Reagan's era woefully shortchanged fundamentalists. Specifically, they overlooked fundamentalists' maneuverability where politics was concerned, as well as their tendency to couch political concerns in abstract moral and theological discourses—which, when taken at face value, could be read as apolitical. Indeed, like Babbitt's pastor, real-life evangelicals engaged the vital issues of the day in terms they defined as religious, not political: eternal, not temporal; spiritual, not worldly.[14] This is not to say that evangelicals did not construct spheres of the "worldly," to shun, and the "spiritual," to shelter. Rather, it is to argue that the totalizing nature of evangelical commitment could, and did, collapse such boundaries with remarkably little fuss for religionists renowned for aggressive apathy toward mortal affairs. True, historians of American religion have fared better than pundits at negotiating these complex displays of political outspokenness and power. A handful of recent studies of Protestant fundamentalism by historians such as Barry Hankins, Matthew Avery Sutton, and Daniel Williams have done much to show how the "roaring twenties" and the contentious years that immediately followed in fact laid the foundations for today's "culture wars." But while these new additions to the field have forced scholars to recognize long-term continuities in evangelical politics, most historians are still guilty of treating the marriage of theological, economic, and political conservatism like a shotgun wedding at the Reagan revolution.[15]

Pundits and historians have fallen victim to this motif in part because they have had their sights set on the usual suspects of religious authority. Clergymen, theologians, evangelists, and other full-time religious workers dominate their narratives, allowing intellectual and spiritual elites to speak for *all* laypeople, and overtly theological and ecclesiastical matters to override all others. Yet in the highly democratic evangelical movement, clerics can rarely speak so confidently or wholly for the laity, and while central to their identity and mission, theology and ecclesiology are not the evangelical constituency's only references of right belief and action or point of concern. This was particularly the case in the period between the roaring twenties and early Cold War, when no issue seemed more urgent than the economic condition for a free, prosperous, and virtuous society. Caught up in this apparent existential crisis, fundamentalist laity (as well as a notable number of clerics) joined libertarians, anti-Keynesian intellectuals, and small-government Republicans to preach and aggressively champion individual initiative in a self-regulating marketplace instead of an activist state.[16] While as small shop owners, middle managers, and bosses on factory floors they held tight to free market theologies and devised institutional mechanisms to maintain the laissez-faire character of their work spaces, through their philanthropy, lobbying, and political maneuvers a wealthier class of Christian entrepreneurs constructed sophisticated apparatuses to oppose organized labor and firmly resist—and outlaw—any inroads by radical dissent or left-leaning ideologies.

Herein lies another payoff of focused—and broader—examination of Babbitt's world. Such a perspective makes it obvious that in order to appreciate the sustained political energy of evangelicalism in the intervening years between the 1920s and late 1940s, students of history need to cast their gaze well beyond the pulpits and pews of this era's church life and into the boardrooms of corporate America. As a few recent histories of both the corporate and labor side of early twentieth-century US religious culture have demonstrated, it was an ongoing contest between competing views of Christian "labor" and the right standing of working individuals before God that provided so much of the impetus for the most serious political clashes of the day.[17] Christian businessmen played outsized roles in this battle royal. Already towering in their popular stereotypes as the perceived heroes of the booming 1920s and, conversely, prime culprits in America's financial collapse and 1930s Depression, Christian businessmen assumed equally enormous roles over the course of this entire chronology as mediators between the evangelical subculture, to which they brought money and organizational skills, and the broader business culture, to which they witnessed their faith. It is *their* biographies that deserve foregrounding, so too the particularities of their specific religious and economic sectors and the geographical space—Babbitt's middle America—that they inhabited. Indeed, while the domains and exploits of Christian businessmen have begun to receive attention from outstanding historians such as Kevin Kruse, Bethany Moreton, and especially Darren Grem, emerging study of the Christian corporate establishment has tended either to focus on the Eisenhower consensus of Judeo-Christian and free-enterprise (anticommunist) values, the post–World War II "Sunbelt South," or to paint with a wide brush the national trends that drew laissez-faire theology and devotees into Washington's inner circles. In addition to raising the profile of Christian businessmen in the story of evangelicalism's pre–World War II galvanization and politicking, a wide-angled lens onto Babbitt's cultural and political contexts also offers readers a simpler reminder not to forget a "fly-over" region that often gets left behind in scholarly accounts: the Midwest, then (and to a large degree still now) American evangelicalism's cultural and organization epicenter and most critical launching point toward national (and global) influence.[18]

Take for instance two subjects who serve as organizing threads, and whose brief introductions lend further texture to these central claims. The first is Robert (R. G.) LeTourneau. A self-taught engineer who built a manufacturing company during the Depression, LeTourneau transformed his corporate platform into a pulpit. A blunt, quick-witted tornado of a man, his head permanently tilted atop a towering frame that survived two neck-breaking accidents, LeTourneau embodied George F. Babbitt's "God-fearing, hustling, successful, two-fisted Regular Guy."[19] When evangelical businessmen stressed their status as laymen, as LeTourneau often did, it was to reject the implied mirror image of a cloistered, out-of-touch, effeminate minister. This gendering of roles, which countless collaborations and friendships belied, brought corporate divisions of labor and expertise into religious life. Just as businessmen felt unqualified to dissect biblical passages in the original Hebrew, they doubted clerical competence in the rough-and-tumble realm of public affairs.

LeTourneau had particular reason to assert his manhood, because he was both a layman and a preacher. Born in 1888, he began working after leaving school in eighth grade, owing early factory jobs to his evangelical sect's economic network. He fell in love with earthmoving equipment and began his career as manufacturer in California, moving in the mid-1930s to the Midwest, and opening up a factory in the South by the time America entered the war. A traveling evangelist, he advertised himself as "God's businessman," citing his success during the Depression as proof that servants of the Lord would prosper. "Christianity works not only for children and feeble old folks, but for a he-man, doing business, winning in the battle of life," he said. This placed an enormous responsibility on laymen "to win men to Christ and feel their responsibility for the cause of Christ just as much as the preacher."[20] He called God his "Senior Partner," and jetted around the country to bring his plainspoken testimony to church groups, Rotary and Kiwanis clubs, and Chambers of Commerce.

As with many businessmen fighting the era's cataclysmic market forces, government was sometimes LeTourneau's adversary and sometimes a silent partner. On one hand, he brought his conservative gospel to the factory floor, tapping a stable of fundamentalist ministers for weekly "shop talks" and keeping up a steady stream of anti-union invective in devotional publications. He donated 90 percent of his profits to evangelical causes, including Bible schools, a Bible camp for poor immigrant children, and an international conference center at one of his plants. He believed in Christian charity, not government handouts. On the other hand, he owed some of his millions to a wartime contract with Franklin D. Roosevelt's administration and hobnobbed with governors and senators happy to minimize taxes and regulations to draw industry to their states. The economic dyad he proclaimed between God and each individual was unstable. Sometimes LeTourneau treated government as a friendly go-between. Other times, most starkly when his workers exercised their legal right to unionize, he cast the state not as the long arm of God but as a threat to cosmic order. Sinclair Lewis would have dismissed LeTourneau's inconsistencies as simple hypocrisy, but even if they were hypocrisy, they were not simple. Other evangelical businessmen were negotiating the same dissonance.[21]

Groups such as the Christian Business Men's Committee International (CBMCI), the Business Men's Evangelistic Clubs (BMEC), and the Gideons, to which LeTourneau belonged, believed that businessmen were God's instruments to Christianize the world. As salesmen, they saw themselves a cadre of expert manipulators.[22] If they could convince the masses to buy their products, then they must try to bend them to God's will. According to the BMEC's Vernon W. Patterson, an early patron of Billy Graham,

"In business, [the layman] is accustomed to promote the sale and distribution of merchandise or commodities of all kinds. . . . [W]hy should not such systematic planning be extended to carry the gospel to the ends of the earth?"[23] Following nineteenth-century precedent, the CBMCI in the North, Midwest, and Canada and the BMEC in the South furnished money and personnel for a range of evangelistic programs. Members held daily noon worship in urban centers, sponsored interdenominational revivals, taught Sunday school, led Bible studies, and sat on charitable boards. They created USO-style "servicemen's centers" during World War II and backed a wave of youth evangelism in the war's wake. The Gideons participated in some of these efforts, but their focus, famously, was Bible distribution. By 1940, when LeTourneau served a term as president, the Gideons were amassing Bibles for public schools. The goal was to nurture a lifelong identification between Protestantism and American citizenship by countering evolutionary, Catholic, and communist influences.

The growing possibility that America would enter World War II heightened the groups' urgency. Indeed, the evangelical conviction that God had anointed America to redeem the world was one reason that men such as LeTourneau had a vexed relationship to the New Deal state. Fundamentalists took seriously the scriptural injunction to yield unto God what is God's and unto Caesar what is Caesar's.[24] During peacetime, they struggled to sort out which was which. During the war, the existential threat to the nation justified conflating the two.[25] Even before Pearl Harbor, missionary hopes began to soar. After America joined the fight, evangelical businessmen, clergy, and intellectuals joined their countrymen and -women planning for postwar citizenship in a superpower. England was in shambles, and the Soviet Union, a treacherous ally, did not have the atomic bomb. The CBMCI, BMEC, and Gideons rejoiced that God was giving America the power to evangelize every soul in the world. Their confidence was cultural, not subcultural.

Herbert J. Taylor, president of Chicago-based Club Aluminum, preferred the Rotary Club to the CBMCI. The suburb of Park Ridge, where he and his wife opened their home to youth for Sunday school every week, was two hundred miles and a white-collar culture apart from Peoria, Illinois, the smokestack city where R. G. LeTourneau built his first big plant. Five years LeTourneau's junior, but born into money and college-educated, Taylor was a different breed of businessman. He did not proselytize on the job, but he made a version of the Golden Rule the company ethos. He helped launch the career of future Billy Graham crooner George Beverly

Shea by hiring him to sing hymns on *Club Time*, a radio show otherwise devoted to advertising aluminum kitchenware. Taylor gave money to Republican candidates but was open to elements of the New Deal, even serving on a regulatory agency in Washington during World War II. He was an infrequent public speaker, and few of the thousands who cheered at LeTourneau revivals would have recognized his face.

Behind the scenes, however, Herb Taylor shaped American evangelicalism in deep and lasting ways. His philanthropy, the Christian Workers Foundation (CWF), gave seed money and more to fundamentalist individuals and organizations that he deemed capable of cultural leadership on a national or international level. He focused especially on higher education, the gateway to elite status. He almost single-handedly brought the Inter-Varsity Christian Fellowship, now ubiquitous on college campuses, to American soil. Other CWF legacies included Young Life, the *Old Fashioned Revival Hour* hosted by evangelist Charles Fuller, and the eponymous Fuller Theological Seminary. Taylor may have been less colorful than Babbitt-like businessmen, but behind his rimless glasses, he had keener vision.[26]

Taylor was the founding treasurer of the National Association of Evangelicals (NAE), formed in the early 1940s to unite fundamentalists as a political lobby and religious juggernaut to speed the evangelization of the world. The political lobby was in self-defense. Mainline Protestants had long since organized into the Federal Council of Churches (FCC) to streamline interdenominational cooperation and voice their concerns to the government. Motivated by the same wartime ideology of American "unity" that was spurring evangelicals to mobilize, the FCC campaigned for new radio regulations that would promote religious tolerance over theological specificity. The changes would all but disenfranchise fundamentalists from their most wide-reaching evangelistic medium. Foreign missionary work also suffered from government recognition of the FCC as the official voice of Protestantism. Evangelicals lacked automatic standing to receive visas, passports, and other authorization to go overseas, and the war worsened the backlog. The founders of the NAE wanted an organizational counterweight to the FCC with an office in Washington. To succeed, they had to persuade the notoriously independent factions of the fundamentalist community to accept the principle of strength in numbers and agree to a doctrinal baseline.

The NAE's first years brought both the teamwork and tensions between evangelical businessmen and clergy into sharp relief. Taylor and a handful of other laymen at the top wanted to run the NAE like a corporation, with clear, achievable, and, above all, affordable short- and long-term goals. They expected an element of risk, especially with God guiding the organization, but they also trusted God to keep his projects financially stable. Many clergymen ran their churches on the same basis, so the businessmen, though outnumbered, had allies. However, the visionary behind the NAE, a realtor-turned-preacher named J. Elwin Wright, followed the spirit first and worried about the budget later. His extravagant leaps of faith, such as abruptly announcing that the NAE would open an office for war relief without investigating the cost or the need for government certification, moved the NAE from a reactive stance to bold cultural interventions. But Wright might have bankrupted the NAE without timely funds from Taylor and his colleagues, one of whom angrily resigned. Soon, Wright stepped down to a role that required no money management. The organizational consequences of the NAE's lurching finances illustrate the most basic and powerful role of businessmen within the evangelical subculture. Any purse they opened, they could close.

Much like George Babbitt, then, Herbert Taylor, R. G. LeTourneau, and their cohort of deep-pocketed powerbrokers faced the disruptions of their day by holding tightly to the conformities, and shared faith in Christ and capitalism, that profoundly shaped their church environment between World War I and the Cold War. As in Zenith, so too in Peoria, Chicago, and emerging commercial centers across middle America: these resident corporate evangelicals' entry into the theological and economic revolutions of the local produced real and lasting political change, and the nation felt (and continues to feel) the effects.

Such change can and should be measured in stages; moving chronologically and shifting in scale, the narrative that follows will assume this type of layered approach. Chapters 1 and 2 offer biographical examinations of LeTourneau and Taylor, respectively, with detailed descriptions of how, during the 1920s and 1930s especially, their own life experiences and personal faiths determined their views of money, industry, and service. Chapters 3 and chapter 4 assume a wider stance to consider each executive's broader corporate and philanthropic reach during the Depression years and then during World War II, as well as their wider contributions to the construction of a "new evangelical" political front. Chapter 5 tracks change at the highest level by drawing these contained stories into one collective account of corporate evangelicalism's consolidation during global struggle in the guise of the NAE, whose formation at the height of World War II represented a pivot for Babbitt-styled fundamentalism out of any remaining obscurities into the cultural and political mainstream. The conclusion glances at entrepreneurial evangelicals, corporate evangelicalism, and the New Evangelical "front" as it exited World War II and began exercising its newly acquired power in the early Cold War years.

Depression

CHAPTER ONE

R. G. LeTourneau's Prosperity Gospel

On September 27, 1940, radio listeners across North America tuned in to *Ripley's Believe It or Not* to hear evangelical industrialist R. G. LeTourneau discuss the financial rewards of his faith.[1] The program opens with a fictional dialogue between LeTourneau, playing his younger self, and a colleague incredulous that God is their chief stakeholder. "The time . . . December, 1929, just after the memorable Wall Street crash," the narrator intones. "The place—the office of a small factory in Stockton, California. The owner of the plant is talking with his assistant. They face the unhappy prospect of bankruptcy." LeTourneau says that he intends to spend his last $500 on "one obligation . . . my missionary pledge." The assistant gasps, "What? Facing bankruptcy and you're going to use the last of your money for a church pledge? But we owe so much on other things." LeTourneau is adamant: "I told God that as long as I had a dime I would pay that missionary pledge."[2]

Introducing the punch line that made LeTourneau, who designed and manufactured earthmoving equipment, a minor celebrity, the assistant cries, "Why that's actually making God—your partner!!!" LeTourneau says, "Yes, I shall make God a partner in my business." He would henceforth serve both God and mammon by setting aside 90 percent of his salary and company profits for evangelical causes. "[Y]ou have made the Word of God a glorious, practical reality," Ripley tells his guest when the skit ends; then he turns to his audience with his own trademark flourish: "And of such is the work of faith . . . Believe It Or Not."[3]

"Believe It or Not" is an apt phrase for the unsung story of businessmen such as LeTourneau who financed and mobilized conservative white evangelicals during the Depression and World War II. LeTourneau's star turn on *Ripley's* challenges popular histories of fundamentalism, which focus on preachers, full-time evangelists, and theologians who drew a sharp rhetorical line between believers and "the world."[4] This scholarship depicts a vibrant, proselytizing, yet deeply insular Protestant subculture whose members viewed the public sphere—"the world" of politics and hedonistic consumption—as hostile to the religious imperatives of saving souls, enforcing doctrinal correctness, and maintaining behavioral purity. Even as they appropriated dress, slang, music, and other aspect of the broader white middle-class culture, evangelicals policed the boundaries between the heavenly and the worldly. Why, then, did a prominent evangelical executive appear on Ripley's secular and frequently scandalous program, sharing the airwaves with Siamese twins and Indian firewalkers? Stranger still, why did Ripley treat LeTourneau's faith as vital and heroic rather than a fossilized freak show?[5]

The collaboration suggests that scholars of American religion have overemphasized the parochialism of early twentieth-century evangelicals and, as a result, overlooked their participation in multifaith or formally secular public spheres.[6] Work, not church, was the site where laymen and often laywomen practiced fundamentalism within the homogenizing norms of a pluralistic society. A widely held belief in the essential Christianity of capitalism served as common ground. LeTourneau's motto, "God is My Partner," meant more than extravagant tithing. It celebrated the all-American icon of the self-made man and the conservative politics that went with it, holding individuals responsible for their fate regardless of socioeconomic circumstances.[7] To be "God's business man" was to adhere to a contractual theology as old as biblical Israel and as binding as a modern commercial agreement.[8] It required obedience to divine commands such as observing the Sabbath; tithing; volunteering for church or evangelistic responsibilities; and adopting an ethos of "fairness" that valued relationships, especially with other Christians, over competitive advantage.[9] God's businessmen maintained a "Christian atmosphere" at work that challenged the conventions of male sociability, observing, if not necessarily enforcing, evangelical taboos against drinking, swearing, smoking, and overt sexuality.[10] God, in turn, rewarded fidelity with profits and punished backsliding with losses. The divine-human dyad eliminated external causes of success or failure.[11] Ripley was no fundamentalist, but he admired the seamlessness of LeTourneau's identities as an evangelical and an entrepreneur. Quoting the Sermon on the Mount—"Let your light so shine before men that they may see your good works and glorify you Father"—he challenged listeners to emulate LeTourneau's pluck and piety.[12]

LeTourneau had a weakness for portraying himself as Horatio Alger by way of *Pilgrim's Progress*, and get-rich-quick sanctity made good radio. As evangelical fans knew from his writings and speeches, however, being God's partner was neither a simple nor a solitary commitment. Nowhere did *Believe It or Not* stretch credulity more than in the opening dramatization, which reduced LeTourneau's lifetime in evangelical circles to a road-to-Damascus epiphany. It was in 1919, not 1929, that LeTourneau declared his partnership with God after one of his missionary sisters accused him of caring more about his machines than Jesus. He sought out his pastor, who told him "God needs business men as well as preachers and missionaries." LeTourneau, according to his autobiography, responded with immense relief: "All right, if that is what God wants me to be, I'll try to be His business man."[13] He did not always keep his promise. In 1931, he diverted a $5,000 missionary pledge to his company (*Ripley's* slashed it to the less regal sum of $500), only to end the year in debt. He concluded that God was punishing his faithlessness and doubled his next offering. Although 1932 proved to be the worst year of the Depression, the business prospered, confirming his belief—ubiquitous among evangelicals—that God was chastising the nation for a collective breach of contract but still offering hope.[14] Only a revival could repair a people's broken contract with God, and it was up to those who recognized the problem to take the lead. LeTourneau settled on the 90 percent tithe of his wealth sometime between 1935 and 1940, launched a side career in preaching, and threw himself into revivalistic laymen's groups such as the CBMCI and the Gideons. Meanwhile, he cultivated local and national politicians as he opened manufacturing hubs across the country, especially in the segregated and anti-union South.

The *Ripley's* introduction shows how difficult it could be to treat faith and business as bedfellows after a decade of plummeting confidence in capitalism.[15] Setting the scene in 1929 links LeTourneau's financial dilemma to the global economic crisis, but epic individualism displaces organized religion as the way out. The script omits LeTourneau's preacher and moves the "God needs business men" epiphany from a church to an office building, sanctifying the workplace by separating it from the site of communal worship—the opposite of LeTourneau's policy in his plants, where evangelistic services took place once or twice a week.[16] By putting the spotlight on one charismatic man in a program devoted to "oddities," Ripley, with his guest's blessing, wrongly implied that LeTourneau's partnership with God was unique. In fact, it belonged to a tradition that extended at least as far back as the Second Great Awakening, when businessmen such as Charles and Arthur Tappan subsidized preachers like Charles Finney and evangelical social movements such as temperance and abolitionism.[17] A century later, LeTourneau filled auditoriums with laymen who renounced what they saw as the hubris of the New Deal and called America to humility, repentance, and conversion.

Far from abandoning a sinful and pluralistic society, twentieth-century evangelical businessmen such as LeTourneau sought to leaven it through exhortation and example. Their belief in individual redemption as the force behind social progress did not detach them from political questions; in business, private gain and public policy were intertwined with religious truth. These entrepreneurs, managers, and employers believed in the top-down marketing of ideas as well as goods to a passive and pliable population. As expert salesmen, they would help—or supplant—otherworldly clergy to win converts to fundamentalist Christianity. They knew how to think strategically, raise money, organize and publicize large events, and distill complex doctrines into compelling analogies and anecdotes. Theologically, businessmen focused on the bottom line, emphasizing common ground over sectarian conflict to enlarge the fold without compromising the "fundamentals." They demanded cost-effectiveness and strategic thinking from the religious causes they supported, often through personal or corporate philanthropies, and tended them as carefully as other portfolios. Their spiritual authority hinged on success in a marketplace in which earthly and heavenly dividends were one. "The minute I started that partnership [with God], business boomed," LeTourneau told Ripley, listing sales figures into the millions. Ripley applauded. "Mr. LeTourneau, in these troubled times, you are a magnificent example to those of little faith."[18] Poverty was an effect, not a cause, of despair.

LeTourneau was indeed a remarkable man, but he exemplified a breed of fundamentalist whose worldliness was a defining spiritual credential. The turn-of-the-century context in which he learned how to be a Christian businessman reveals abundant evidence of this. So too does his own peripatetic career path, which encompassed designing earthmoving equipment for private- and public-sector projects; building roads, bridges, and dams; and in big-picture terms, helping supply the infrastructures and connective tissues of modern industrialization. The path led him to civic engagement as well, and a politics that leaned heavily to the right.

As LeTourneau moved from California to the Midwest to the South, he cultivated powerful political allies and simultaneously benefited from and decried the growth of the federal government under Franklin D. Roosevelt. He viewed himself as a generous employer, as concerned with his employees' souls as with their standard of living, and held regular evangelistic services on the shop floor while fighting "communist" unionization efforts. By the time he appeared on *Ripley's*, most of his profits went to the LeTourneau Evangelistic Foundation (LEF), which made him a powerful fundamentalist philanthropist. Whether he knew it or not, LeTourneau was as much a "missionary" as those among his friends and family (his sisters in particular) who assumed that vocation abroad. His "mission field" was small- to midsized companies like his own, and his message was that employers and managers held the tools to build Christ's kingdom.

WORSHIP AND WORK WITH THE BRETHREN

LeTourneau's generation was a living link between culturally confident nineteenth-century evangelicalism and embattled twentieth-century "fundamentalism." Jean and Marie LeTourneau, his paternal grandparents, were French Huguenots who came to Quebec as missionaries in the 1840s. After his father, Caleb, was born, they moved five miles across the border to Richford, Vermont, where French-speaking Canadians dominated the population. Jean continued to preach while he and his wife ran a boarding school, a farm, and a sawmill. In 1881, Caleb married schoolteacher Elizabeth Lorimer, another immigrant from Quebec; three of her four brothers were clergymen. Caleb would have inherited Jean's ministry if his older brother had not lost an arm in a mill accident and been unable to manage the farm.[19] Instead he took charge of the family business and became a leader in the Plymouth Brethren Church, founded in the mid-nineteenth century by Anglo-Irish evangelist John Nelson Darby. Convinced of the literal truth of the Bible and the need for believers to separate themselves from a fallen world and apostate church, Darby developed the end-times doctrine that would come to be known as "premillennial dispensationalism." He divided world history into seven "dispensations" that began with a covenant between God and humanity and ended with humanity's rebellion. He argued that the earth was currently poised in a "great parenthesis" between Christ's resurrection and the end of the world. This "church age" offered a last chance for the unsaved to repent, and the burden was on believers to convert as many souls as possible. When the clock ran out, Christians would disappear en masse, "raptured" into heaven while everyone else endured the reign of the Antichrist. Holy wars would usher in Christ's kingdom on earth at last.[20]

Premillennialism took hold among many conservative Protestants in Europe and the Americas. Although its claim to be an essential pillar of evangelical truth sparked fierce debate, its influence gave the Plymouth Brethren pride of parentage when fundamentalism emerged at the turn of the twentieth century. Conservative evangelicals felt pressed to counter emerging theological "modernism," which treated the Bible as a human artifact instead of the literal word of God and concerned itself less with the redemption of individuals than large-scale social reform.[21] Transatlantic revivalist Dwight L. Moody was the most famous antimodernist to adopt premillennialism as an antidote to what he saw as a pernicious trend toward elevating human will over divine omnipotence.[22] Yet despite the evangelistic urgency of their theology, the Brethren did not court popularity. Like other "restorationists," they sought to imitate the early church by centering worship in the local congregation, rejecting church hierarchies, and harboring anticlericalism so deep that some churches were entirely lay run. They practiced conventional evangelical asceticism but distrusted outsiders.[23] Robert Gilmour LeTourneau, born in 1888 and named after Caleb's Brethren best friend and business partner, was the fourth of Caleb and Elizabeth's eight children.[24] As a child, he internalized the magnitude of being in covenant with God but had no idea that premillennialism made the Brethren special. Rather, he recalled visible markers of difference: in particular, the "prosperously dressed and bearded men" who gathered to talk after services.[25]

These bearded men, including Caleb, were church elders and part of a far-flung sectarian business network that took the LeTourneaus from Vermont to Minnesota and then to Oregon by R.G.'s fourteenth birthday. The Minnesota connection was familial as well as religious: Caleb's brother Joshua, a printer in Duluth, hired him and Gilmour to build a house, and the pair became full-time contractors. Joshua introduced the new arrivals to Duluth's Plymouth Brethren, which LeTourneau described as "a closely knit group intensely loyal to the church and to each other."[26] He owed the formative years of his working life to the Brethren's clannishness everywhere. An explosively energetic boy, impatient with book learning and infatuated with machinery, he quit school in eighth grade, insisting to his furious father that he was, at fourteen, a "man growed."[27] By then it was 1902, and, at the invitation of a transplanted Duluth church member, the LeTourneaus had moved to Portland, Oregon.[28] Portland was a boomtown, with midwestern farmers, German and Scandinavian immigrants, and Chinese laborers feverishly industrializing the region. Between 1901 and 1910, the city's population surged from 90,000 to 207,000. Not only was there "a shortage of carpenters" like Caleb, there was also a shortage of strong youth like R.G.[29]

Caleb yielded to his impetuous six-foot, 160-pound precocious son and conspired with Brethren elders to catapult him into adult responsibilities.[30] A "little, soft-voiced" Englishman, Mr. Hill, represented the sect's transnational corporate and religious reach and the answer to Caleb LeTourneau's challenge. Hill owned the East Portland Iron Works and hired LeTourneau to work dawn to dusk in the foundry. Another employer would have left the novice to his own devices, but as an evangelical businessman and a friend of the family, Hill adopted a paternal role. He shielded LeTourneau from workmen's vices by warning the crew that serving him alcohol was a fireable offense. Under Hill's watchful eye, LeTourneau learned to use his advanced vocabulary to "cuss harder without swear words than any man"—a boast that established his tough-talking masculine credentials within the bounds of evangelical propriety.[31] Hill even took LeTourneau on as an apprentice, allowing him to use the machine shop after hours to experiment with new metals and alloys that were transforming the industry. As LeTourneau put it, "the whole science of metallurgy . . . [was] dumped on us without warning," and he thrilled to the intellectual and physical labor of practicing chemistry on the fly.[32]

Hill's supervision and support kept LeTourneau within the Brethren fold but could not produce the conversion experience that would make the boy a true believer. He went to church with his family and Hill every Sunday, barely staying awake and typecasting himself in the role of the outwardly righteous imposter. At the age of sixteen, during a weeklong urban revival—an evangelical tradition that carried over from the nineteenth to the twentieth century—the prodigal son finally found Christ. "No bolts of lightning hit me. No great flash of awareness," he acknowledged. "I just prayed to the Lord to save me . . . [and] all of my bitterness was drained away, and I was filled with such a vast relief I could not contain it all."[33] It was Christmastime, 1904, and the teenaged convert became an active, if "awkward," church member. He sang too poorly for the choir. His three sisters played leading roles in the Young People's Missionary Society, but LeTourneau was too terrified of public speaking even to deliver an opening prayer.[34]

For work, his spiritual maturation came just in time. Fire destroyed the East Portland Iron Works at the end of 1905, putting Mr. Hill out of business. LeTourneau had not completed the apprenticeship qualifications for the iron molders' craft union, which shut him out of other jobs in Portland and may have been one source of the antilabor animus he would later harbor as an employer. When a former coworker invited him to a foundry in San Francisco, LeTourneau's parents allowed him to go. For the most part, he boarded with Brethren families, joining a church on his own initiative. He completed his apprenticeship in the aftermath of the 1906 earthquake, and his union membership made him employable despite the disaster.[35]

LeTourneau's religious and business ambitions, like those of many British, Canadian, and American evangelicals, were bound up in missionary work—especially to China, to which California was the port of call. Having displaced native peoples and foreign colonizers to establish its continental borders, the United States at the turn of the century was an imperial power in its own right. The annexation of Hawaii and the Samoan Islands was relatively peaceful, but only war with Spain could win political control over Puerto Rico, Cuba, and the Philippines. While some Americans contested the strategic and moral value of conquest, white Protestants across the theological spectrum could embrace a justifying ideology of racial superiority and Christian progress. The fast-growing foreign missionary movement interpreted unprecedented American access to dark-skinned and "Oriental" lands in light of the Great Commission to "go ye into all the world and Preach the gospel."[36] Undeterred by the 1900 Boxer Rebellion, an anticolonial revolt that targeted foreign proselytizers and Chinese converts, LeTourneau's sister Sarah was studying Chinese and raising money for the journey across the ocean.[37] LeTourneau toyed with the idea of joining her and building a foundry that would expose its workers to evangelicalism. He owed this dream to Elmer Jones, one of his friends in the San Francisco Brethren. Jones had been born in China to a businessman-cum-missionary who, in retirement, served as a Chinese interpreter in American courts. Elmer continued the family tradition by entering the international oil trade and becoming a zealous advocate of "improv[ing] the living standards of the Chinese" by giving them "the word of God."[38]

LeTourneau credited Jones with inspiring him "to do something for the lot of underprivileged people."[39] Significantly, neither man believed that conversion automatically improved living standards, although both rejected the "social gospel" of Progressive-era mainline Protestantism as they understood it. The social gospel argued that Christians must look beyond unsaved individuals to the problems of industrial society. Poverty, dangerous working conditions, unsanitary housing, and juvenile delinquency warped souls as surely as original sin, a concept some but not all adherents minimized or rejected for environmental explanations of crime and disorder. Indeed, many social gospelers saw themselves as deepening, rather than departing from, the evangelical tradition.[40] More conservative evangelicals such as Jones and LeTourneau were adamant that the only way to make a Christian world was to make more Christians; their faith would guide their behavior. In fact, the differences between the camps were less stark than the same combatants would be willing to admit during the fundamentalist-modernist wars twenty years later. The quarrel over whether to transform persons or society often came down to prioritizing, rather than opposing, individual responsibility and social circumstances.[41] While LeTourneau shared Elmer Jones's assumption that Christian conversion led to Western civilization, he was equally certain that missionaries should improve material conditions before bombarding "the natives" with scripture. He doubted that "a lot of heathens have been converted to Christianity while slowly starving to death." Seeing "[God's] power in better housing, food and medical care" would bring them "eagerly" to Christ.[42]

MOVING MOUNTAINS

If LeTourneau sometimes sounded like the theological modernists he despised, it was because his faith in God was inseparable from his faith in technological modernization and progress. However pessimistic premillennialism should have made him about a world that would deteriorate until the rapture, he was enthralled by the seemingly unlimited power of manufacturing. "We mechanics are blessed because all fields of science are constantly discovering new theories and products that open new worlds for us to conquer," he avowed.[43]

His years in California, from 1906 to 1935, put him in the forefront of new technologies and dramatic changes in the physical landscape. He helped build a bridge from San Francisco to Stockton after the 1906 earthquake, then crossed it to become a car mechanic in 1909, thirteen years into the mass production of motorized vehicles in the United States and only months after Henry Ford introduced the Model T.[44] With the exception of wartime service as an electrical machinist in the navy yards (a poorly healed broken neck from a racing stunt disqualified him from combat) LeTourneau spent his first ten years in Stockton fixing automobiles. When his alcoholic business partner put the garage in debt, LeTourneau went to work for two brothers who sold engine-powered, rather than mule-driven, farm machinery. This innovation made California's postwar irrigation and highway-building projects possible, as well as LeTourneau's career.[45]

LeTourneau did harbor theological concerns about his enthusiasm for his work, but not the work itself. "I feared my love of machines was becoming an obsession that was taking me away from my love of God," he explained.[46] "Love" was not too strong a word; he coaxed, praised, and bullied his bulldozers as if they were children, not iron mules. He dismissed one invention as "the dumbest brute of a machine I ever made. No life or responsiveness. Loading, emptying, or hauling, it didn't seem to care. I didn't bother to name it."[47] By contrast, he refused to recognize the flaws in another experiment even after a colleague pointed them out. "I looked at my machine as a perfect baby, and didn't mind when it cried."[48] Was his passion a form of idolatry, valuing his creations over God's? During the war, he had settled the question by seeing himself as a tool in the Master's plan. "I was just a mechanic striving to translate [God's] laws in terms of machinery, and as long as I . . . didn't get thinking I was operating under my own head of steam, I was on the right track."[49] Yet he remained conflicted about his place in the evangelical hierarchy of "spiritual" over "material" matters. It was then, in 1919, that LeTourneau prayed with his pastor, learned that God needs businessmen, and brought the spiritual and material together by making God his partner.

What partnership meant would evolve over time, but LeTourneau felt on firm ground translating his faith into business terms. "I like my machines and they work," he analogized. "And the Gospel of Jesus Christ works too."[50] To "work" was to produce measurable results, and with religion as with machinery, LeTourneau was willing to try new approaches if the yield was poor. Because Stockton's Plymouth Brethren community was too small to sustain a church, LeTourneau and his young wife, Evelyn—the daughter of a Brethren family that regularly hosted them during their courtship before the pair finally eloped—followed Elmer Jones's urging and joined the Christian and Missionary Alliance (CMA). Founded in 1887 by the Canadian-born preacher A. B. Simpson, the CMA walked a hazy line between conservative evangelicalism and the social gospel. Simpson was a premillennialist and had ties to early Pentecostalism, both of which led him to contend that supernatural forces governed everyday life. His zeal for world evangelicalism, however, grew out of his ministry to immigrants and the poor in New York City.[51] Jones, the world-traveling businessman, made the case for the LeTourneaus to change denominations on pragmatic rather than dogmatic grounds. "Ours is a working religion," he told them. "We work for Christ, and Christ helps us." He convinced the couple that the Stockton CMA offered more opportunities for Christian activity than the Brethren. Soon, LeTourneau found himself banging the drum in an outdoor gospel band and hauling homeless alcoholics off the streets to the CMA mission house.[52]

His partnership with God outside the church seemed off to a good start in 1920, a year after he had left his employers to become an independent contractor. At the top, LeTourneau, Inc., was largely a family affair, including his father Caleb, brother Bill, wife Evelyn, and assorted in-laws.[53] In his work crews, LeTourneau made an effort to "attract a good Christian element," believing that Christians worked harder than "your toughest redneck[s]" and might even convert them.[54] While he insisted that he never discriminated against nonevangelicals because he hoped to save them, he sentimentalized faith as a bond between management and labor that served as an example for the church. "I had a mighty loyal bunch of men," he said. "If all Christians could unite like that in their loyalty to the Lord"—an inadvertently revealing image of power and subordination, not equality—"this world wouldn't be in the mess it was in."[55]

LeTourneau's first big break came in 1926, when West Coast developer Henry Kaiser hired him as a subcontractor on a series of projects (the Philbrook Dam in the Sierra Mountains and the Southern Pacific Railroad freight yard in Fresno) and bought the patents to virtually all of his designs. Kaiser used LeTourneau's equipment for a $75 million contract in Cuba and continued to throw work his way. As his contracts multiplied, LeTourneau joined the rush to build California's gleaming future.[56] Second, and more importantly, he designed what *Time* later called "the chief reason for [his] phenomenal success," a "power control unit" to propel his scrapers. This was his own patent, not Kaiser's; according to some accounts, including *Time*'s, the inspiration came in a flash after LeTourneau reluctantly attended a revival meeting he had been tempted to skip so he could worry over the design.[57] His cable-operated motor made scrapers dig up more dirt faster, with fewer equipment failures; a historian of the industry calls it his "single most important contribution to the field of earthmoving equipment."[58]

With the exception of the 1931 loss that he blamed on his disloyalty to the Lord, LeTourneau made his national name and fortune during the Depression. His signal event of 1929 was not the stock market crash, which looked then like a short-term cyclical correction, but the legal incorporation of LeTourneau, Inc., with twenty employees and a product request from "backward Russia." His brother Louis crowed, "We're in . . . world finance now!"[59] In 1931, LeTourneau became the indirect recipient of federal money when a Kaiser-led consortium called the Six Companies won a government bid to build the Boulder Dam (later the Hoover Dam). The Six Companies subcontracted LeTourneau to clear a highway from Boulder City, Nevada, to the dam site.[60] Upon finishing, he tried his hand at dam building in Orange Country, California. Despite a confrontation with a creditor who believed in a seven-day workweek, after troubling over it in anxious prayer, he held to his policy of honoring the Sabbath. "I was sincerely trying to work with [God] as a partner, and it was His company, too."[61] After restoring the withheld missionary pledge, LeTourneau made $207,237 in sales in 1932, almost doubling his total of $110,800 in 1930. In 1933, sales shot up to $379,100 and came close to tripling to $929,860 in 1934.[62] It was not LeTourneau's construction jobs that were pushing him ahead but sales from his increasingly sophisticated designs. His business was small by comparison with industry giants such as Caterpillar, Inc. The product of a 1925 merger, Caterpillar sold $45 million in earthmoving equipment in 1930 and dwarfed LeTourneau even at its 1932 nadir of $13 million.[63] Still, its executives took notice of their up-and-coming rival and agreed to be LeTourneau's nationwide distributor if he went into manufacturing full time. In April 1935, LeTourneau left the Stockton plant in the hands of "the relatives"—Louis LeTourneau, Evelyn's brothers Ray and Howard Peterson, and another brother-in-law—to build a factory close to Caterpillar's new headquarters in Peoria, Illinois.[64]

After almost thirty years away from America's industrial and agricultural centers, LeTourneau wasted no time moving his partnership with God to a bigger stage. Peoria was about 130 miles from Chicago, making it a satellite of the nation's "second city" of manufacturing and finance after New York.[65] Though dwarfed by Chicago's population of 3,380,000, Peoria's 105,000 residents made it the second-largest city in Illinois. In marked contrast to Chicago's immigrant cosmopolitanism, they were 93.6 percent "native born," a statistic that the Chamber of Commerce cited as evidence of a culturally homogenous and harmonious workforce.[66] The city bordered coal-mining country, and the Illinois River and a railroad hub made for easy shipping and transport. Farm machinery had been a manufacturing specialty since the early nineteenth century, in tandem with substantial grain and livestock markets and distilleries that recovered swiftly from Prohibition.[67] The enormous Caterpillar factory, which employed four thousand workers before the Depression, would dominate the local economy for decades to come.[68]

FIGHTING DEPRESSION AND THE NEW DEAL

Following in the footsteps of Christian entrepreneurs before him, LeTourneau saw his growing wealth as a platform that made evangelism more than a personal or business commitment; it became for him a civic responsibility. His was now the responsibility, he believed, to use his success to show Depression-era America that partnership with God was the only road to recovery. Between 1935, when he arrived in Peoria, and 1938, when he made an even more pivotal expansion to Georgia, LeTourneau reinterpreted his role as an evangelical businessman in three career-defining ways: becoming a public speaker, institutionalizing conservative Protestantism in the labor-management relations of welfare capitalism, and establishing the LeTourneau Evangelistic Foundation through which he could apply most of his profits to Christian work. As skyrocketing sales cemented his faith in the free market and antagonism toward the New Deal, he mixed increasingly overt politics with his preaching.

It was only fitting, then, that LeTourneau launched his lay preaching career in neither a church nor on a revival stump but at the Peoria Chamber of Commerce, which invited its new member to join a roster of speakers in late 1935. As he tells it, God freed him that very day from a lifetime of paralyzing shyness before an audience. He probably exaggerated the miracle story—it strains plausibility that he came unprepared, or was later able to repeat word for word the supposedly spontaneous outpouring of the spirit—but there is no doubt that his "torment of self-consciousness" was real.[69] As proud as LeTourneau was of being a self-taught engineer—after dropping out of eighth grade, he became an avid consumer of correspondence courses—he was acutely aware that high school and college graduates knew more about the refinements of language.[70] Praying for help after hearing "the experienced speakers ahead of me," he "felt a desire to give a few words of personal testimony" to "a business crowd." Despite his long experience combining evangelicalism and business, he worried that Peoria's leading citizens would tag him as "a crackpot."[71]

To the contrary, his blunt pitch for an all-encompassing religion with conservative political consequences struck a powerful chord. He had asked God "to give him the words," and God obliged with well-worn nostalgia for a golden age of American Christianity and entrepreneurship. "You may wonder what religion has to do with business, and I used to wonder about it myself," LeTourneau began. "Now I know that it was our forefathers' faith in God that made out country great. . . . I believe we need to get back to that faith, and when we do, God will lead us out of the depression we've been in." Since Franklin D. Roosevelt's election in 1932, the national Chamber of Commerce had played tug-of-war with the administration and Congress over the New Deal, parts of which it was willing to support in practice, but most of which it opposed in principle.[72] The contractual theology that enabled LeTourneau to solve the Depression in a word, "faith," was both familiar and invigorating to this "business crowd," as was his American exceptionalism. The pilgrims "seeking freedom to worship God" understood that religion and business worked together and reminded themselves every time they made a transaction. "They put on our coins the words, 'In God We Trust,' and God blessed this land above all others."[73] That it was Lincoln, not John Winthrop, who stamped God on the currency, was irrelevant to the mythology that LeTourneau repackaged with indomitable zeal. The "forefathers" had made God their partner, and their descendants—there in that room—could renew the contract on behalf of their countrymen.

Having called on businessmen to redeem the nation, LeTourneau argued that they must simultaneously redeem the church. Echoing his discussions with Elmer Jones, he continued, "We know as business men that when we have a product that won't work, it won't sell. . . . Now, I ask you, what's the use of having a religion that won't work?" LeTourneau had no use for a faith that "worked only on Sunday, or while you're in church." He envisioned "a new model that worked seven days a week, that would work when I was at church, in my home, or out at the plant." Finally, he challenged laymen to take their rightful place beside clergy to make abstract truths concrete. "The preachers can tell us that Christianity works. They are God's salesmen, selling Christianity and the Christian way of life. But unless we business men . . . testify that Christianity is the driving power of our business, you'll always have doubters claiming that religion is all talk and no production."[74] Clergy in the audience who struggled to get men involved in the religious sphere were thrilled, rather than offended, by LeTourneau's call to arms. Perhaps this self-described graduate of "the school of hard knocks" could lend masculine credibility to the pews.[75]

Along with the Chamber of Commerce, the evangelical churches of Peoria gave LeTourneau a springboard to a nationwide bully pulpit. He repeated the speech to local congregations and then gave other talks. His reputation spread to churches and business groups out of town, so he hired a gospel quartet and drove to engagements on weekends. Most of his topics were inspirational—sermons, "funny stories," or bootstraps-and-Bible tales of how to succeed in business. Titles included "Mental Attitude,"

"Sinners in Heaven," "Right Religion," "Devil Power," "Conference with the Lord," "Morale," "Mechanical and Spiritual Progress," "Run God's Business," and "School of Hard Knocks." Less often, but no less ardently, LeTourneau preached conservative politics. He attacked the New Deal's Works Progress Administration, which regulated hours and wages, gave the government the power to force competing companies into cartels, and enshrined the right of workers to collective bargaining. Along the same lines, he excoriated "Higher Taxes and Redistribution," "Socialism—Theory," and "Class Hatred"; called "Labor Union[s] a Religion"; warned against "Dictators and Propaganda."[76] In his text for "Comm[unist]—Hate" he described communism as "a doctrine of hatred" and Christianity as "a doctrine of love." The former "teaches us that we are not getting what is coming to us and we ought to fight for it," he explained, while the latter "teaches us to love God and love our fellow man and try to help him." LeTourneau opined, unoriginally, that everyone who "doesn't like our way of doing business, and wants to teach us a new social order" should be thrown "by the seat of his pants . . . on a boat bound for a land he does like."[77] Christianity and patriotism were, unquestionably in his estimation, synonymous with capitalism.

One more reason for LeTourneau's rapid ascent as an evangelical speaker is that by 1936 he was preaching to employees on the same themes and publicizing these "shop talks" as a sign of labor-management harmony. As early as his work on the Boulder Dam, he had welcomed a visiting evangelist to the worksite. He formalized the practice in Stockton, asking guests to speak to both the day and night shifts. Declaring that attendance was voluntary, he paid everyone who came on the clock. In Peoria, he continued to bring in outside speakers, aided by the proximity of Chicago's fundamentalist strongholds. Creationist Harry Rimmer and Christian Business Men's Committee leader William E. Pietsch made appearances, along with Marion Reynolds, the evangelist from the Boulder Dam who had introduced LeTourneau to the idea of industrial evangelism.[78] Sarah LeTourneau spoke to women employees about her missionary career.[79] LeTourneau handled the rest of the meetings when he was in town, leaving tantalizing notes for 1937: "Comm[unist] Hate Christ Love" (again), "Business Help of God," "L[eTourneau] Shop Temporal—Christ Eternal," "II Cor. 4:18" ["the things which are seen are temporary, but the things which are not seen are eternal"], "You Picked Me God." Just as he told the Chamber of Commerce, he told his workers "Life is What You Make It" and "[You] Get What You Put In." One newly recurring theme, however, showed LeTourneau using his religious platform to deal with business problems: "I Thank You for Your Loyalty," "Loyalty Means Sacrifice" (twice), "Loyalty Beautiful," "Loyalty Is a Force," "Compel [Not] I Nor Christ," and "30 Pieces Silver."[80] Individually, these snippets could mean anything; together, they suggest that like most manufacturers in 1937, LeTourneau feared that worker loyalty was very thin indeed.

As his lecture notes demonstrate, LeTourneau believed that the real-world opposite of "Christianity," from the global red menace to potentially his own plants, was "communism." The word carried a string of interlocking associations: atheism, arrogance about human potential to improve society, and replacing the individual with the collective. All these philosophies culminated in tyranny, most saliently, the mob rule that political conservatives had long attributed to labor unions.[81] For premillenialists such as LeTourneau, the stakes for humanity were even higher. In their interpretation of the Bible, Russian aggression was an early sign of the end times, and international politics was God's map to impending apocalypse.[82] Europe in general and Rome in particular also had roles to play in the divine drama, and Jews, God's chosen people, were at the center. Before most Americans were paying close attention to Germany and Italy, then, conservative evangelicals were conflating communism, fascism, and violent anti-Semitism into a single satanic enemy.

While in California, LeTourneau and Evelyn had taken time off to study at the premillennialist Bible Institute of Los Angeles (BIOLA), where they first met Marion Reynolds. Like the Moody Bible Institute in Chicago, BIOLA provided interdenominational vocational training to fundamentalist Christian workers, from preachers and Sunday school teachers (such as Evelyn) to laypeople seeking biblical instruction (such as LeTourneau, who did his best, but leaped at a contract from Kaiser that would deliver him from "the confinement of a classroom"). BIOLA's monthly magazine, *The King's Business*, had the New Deal in its sights from the start of Roosevelt's first term, and its perspective was global. The editors culled dire warnings from mainstream publications and the *Congressional Record* in 1933 to identify the new president's platform with international communism and fascism: "Russia has her Stalin . . . Germany has her Hitler; and impossible as it may seem, the United States of America has her Roosevelt!"[83]

Conservative evangelicals were only one group raising the alarm over concentrated political and economic power. Former president Herbert Hoover and Republican senator Robert Taft both predicted that Roosevelt was leading the nation the way of Italy and Germany.[84] BIOLA's teetotaling Protestants were in accord with the free-market militants of the American Liberty League, which the Catholic DuPont family organized in 1934 from the same ultrarich contacts they had mobilized against Prohibition.[85] While fending off a congressional investigation of right-wing dissidents in America that circumstantially linked league members with an unlikely fascist coup, the group churned out "educational" propaganda meant to mobilize the masses: *Government by Busybodies*; *Will It Be Ave Caesar?*; *The Way Dictatorships Start*; and other titles.[86] Oil magnate J. Howard Pew, then a trustee of the mainstream Presbyterian Church, was a founding member. Catholic politician Al Smith, formerly the progressive Democratic governor of New York and an erstwhile Roosevelt ally, supported Republican Alf Landon in the 1936 election. In a preelection address to the league, he accused Roosevelt's advisors of "disguis[ing] themselves as Karl Marx or Lenin," adding, "There can only be one flag, the Stars and Stripes, or the red flag of the godless union of the Soviet." Congressional Republicans defended Smith from his own party's attacks, and that fall more than a third of the electorate voted for the moderate Landon in spite of, or because of, such anticommunist tirades.[87]

Radio star Father Charles Coughlin was another of LeTourneau's strange political bedfellows. Coughlin grew wildly popular blaming the Depression on bankers and Wall Street "plutocrats" like Pew, whose vast power, he argued, only the state could contain. Yet soon he saw the New Deal state itself as a "dictatorial" and "communistic" threat to the livelihood of ordinary citizens. In 1936, his followers deserted him in droves when he backed an ineffectual third-party challenge to the president. A brief comeback in 1937 and 1938 careened into anti-Semitism but stayed on message regarding Roosevelt, whose "radicalism" Coughlin now blamed on the "Marxist atheism" of "communistic Jews."[88] Whether "free enterprise" meant the American Liberty League's *laissez-faire* or Father Coughlin's government shield against "money-changers" who thwarted upward mobility, these divergent anti–New Deal voices agreed that if it lost the battle with "communism," religious and other freedoms would go down with it.

All but Coughlin followed nineteenth-century precedent in viewing labor as one of the front lines of battle. Conservatives were right about the influence of Marxism on some intellectuals and activists in the movement, but they painted a broad red brush over the deep ideological and status divisions among workers. *The King's Business* told a story about a "member of the employing class" who encountered a "militant" supporter of labor's "extreme socialistic aims." On a train ride, he converted her to the belief that Christianity, not communism, was responsible for "every step in moral progress and social advancement."[89] When the National Labor Relations Board accused a business of union intimidation or strikebreaking, the Lawyer's Committee of the American Liberty League rushed to the defendant's side. By "plunder[ing] the rich to purchase the poor," league documents complained, the New Deal was igniting class warfare that could only end in "a common ruin of dissent, bankruptcy and revolution."[90] After John L. Lewis formed the Congress of Industrial Organizations in 1935, Roosevelt had to navigate between the demands of a fractured labor movement and anti-union white southern Democrats, both crucial to his coalition. "John Lewis and his Communistic cohorts" had better not try "a second-hand 'carpetbag expedition' . . . under the banner of Soviet Russia," Georgia congressman Edward E. Cox futilely advised, conjuring images of rapacious Yankees storming the South after the Civil War.[91]

EVANGELICAL WELFARE CAPITALISM

LeTourneau arrived in Peoria at an unpropitious time to be a full-fledged "member of the employing class." Nineteen thirty-five marked the third year of a nationwide strike wave that had taken a heavy toll on manufacturing and culminated in the Wagner Act's protection of workers' right to organize. In Illinois, he was the CEO of a four-hundred-strong hierarchy of skilled foremen and largely anonymous shop floor workers ranked and paid by specialization.[92] Across the country, his deputies ran the Stockton plant, distancing him from emerging grievances. One management strategy would be to treat management and labor as inherently hostile and boost profits by paying as little as possible for long hours of punishing work. History and common sense showed that this was a recipe for union organizing and a poor advertisement for evangelicalism. Another possibility, paternalism, bound employer and employees together as a symbolic family in which the corporation determined its dependents' best interests. LeTourneau preferred a progressive third choice, welfare capitalism, which posited a mutually beneficial relationship between employer and employee on more equal ground than paternalism and with better working conditions than the autocratic model. Adopted by many employers after violent strikes in the wake of World War I, welfare capitalism combined competitive pay, benefits, and opportunities for advancement with company-sponsored grievance channels, socializing, and recreation.[93]

LeTourneau's evangelical version of welfare capitalism co-opted the familial imagery of paternalism, casting him as an avuncular patriarch devoted to employees' spiritual and physical well-being. The "shop talks" he delivered and sponsored were no mere ruse to pacify the workers with visions of heavenly instead of earthly rewards. He believed that his partnership with God required him to proselytize to the people God had put under his care, and he viewed the in-plant services as the most important benefit he provided. Like sick leave or safety inspections, which also encouraged allegiance to the company, communal worship was both the right and the pragmatic thing to do. LeTourneau candidly stated that he thought "a genuine Christian was apt to be a better workman than one who is not," and described "better morale" as a "by-product" of the overriding goal "to get men to believe in Jesus Christ."[94] His blind spot, evidenced with his first work crews in 1920, was his unwillingness to recognize that the power he held over his employees made some see shop talks as less than voluntary. "[W]hat would be the use of this company's trying to *force* salvation on anyone?" he demanded when rumors flew around Peoria that professing Christians won more promotions than non-Christians, talk he found dangerous enough to warrant a response. "Unless you fall in love with my Savior, the Lord Jesus Christ . . . He will never intrude himself on you." More to the point, it would be un-Christian for him to be anything but "fair and square" in work evaluations or for employees not to distinguish between the company and the church. "There is a difference between loyalty to the organization you work for and loyalty to Christ. . . . You who are not Christians, please don't get confused, thinking that because you are not devoted to Christ you cannot be loyal to this corporation."[95] Loyalty, that recurring subject of shop talks, was what LeTourneau as a manger had most to lose.

To publicize all of LeTourneau, Inc.'s, good works and bring Stockton and Peoria closer in spirit, he established a company magazine, *NOW*, published in the Peoria plant and named after 2 Corinthians 6:2: "Behold, NOW is the accepted time; behold NOW is the day of salvation." LeTourneau imagined the four-page weekly newsletter as "[n]ot just a house organ to express my own views and company policy, but one that would also voice the message of the Lord I was trying to serve as a partner."[96] He took the title and the concept from its original publisher, an evangelical who "used . . . current news as a vehicle for presenting the Gospel message" and promoted it as a free Christian magazine for readers outside the company. His sister Marie's husband, tract writer Tom Olson, spun biblical allegories from inspirational anecdotes or current events in a two-page spread that comprised more than half of the written content. By 1938, there were ten times more issues of *NOW* than there were employees, and countless articles were reprinted as tracts and mailed to evangelical organizations and households. Funded not by the corporation but by the LEF, *NOW* was R. G. LeTourneau's all-encompassing public relations program.[97]

The cover of *NOW* usually displayed a machine at work or in progress, while the back page, "Plant Life," compiled personnel and business updates to make the company feel like a family. For example, "Larry Alvarez, yoke dept., has bought a new Studebaker" counted as news. Such squibs burnished LeTourneau, Inc., by showing that lower-ladder employees could afford their own cars. The "Proud Papa department" and "Bridal Bureau" tracked the births and marriages. Employees informed *NOW* about sick relatives; how they spent their company-bestowed vacation time; off-the-clock socializing (one pair of newlyweds returned from their honeymoon to "20 or 30 of the boys who presented a combination waffle iron and sandwich toaster"); and, of course, religious activities. *NOW* chronicled LeTourneau's evangelistic traveling schedule and worker initiatives such as the Bible study organized by men on Peoria's night shift. Welfare capitalism's paradigmatic leisure-time offering, team sports, was a regular feature. Business updates, though often mundane ("New 20-inch Monarch engine lathe ordered for Peoria"), drew attention to other employee benefits: arrangements for workers disabled on the job, "schooling" of foremen and subforemen in management techniques, stock options, and home rentals.

NOW even chronicled criticism and labor trouble, which were usually related. Peoria's *Labor Temple News* charged LeTourneau with publicity-seeking "religious spectacularism," sniping that "Christ probably never intended that His teachings should help advertise road graders." If LeTourneau wanted to show "a Christian spirit," he could start by "meeting his workmen on a collective bargaining basis, where duly elected representatives of his laborers can voice their needs through spokesmen of their own choice." Olson, the unnamed author of full-length articles, dodged the specific complaint and blasted "religious leaders," presumably like those at Labor Temple, who "never have appreciated the preaching of the gospel . . . [and] delivered up the Lord Jesus Christ to Pilate to be crucified and then persuaded the people to demand his death."[98] This last clause took a clear shot at unions as mobs whipped into frenzy by their "leaders," not representative democracies depicted by the *News*.

Meanwhile, LeTourneau warded off a threatened strike at Stockton by establishing another talismanic feature of welfare capitalism, a company union. He agreed to raise wages across the board by 10 percent, and the newly minted "LeTourneau Employees Union" vowed to protec[t] employees against irresponsible picketing or sit-down by minority groups"—that is, independent organizers who rejected the premise of labor-management comity.[99] The Peoria plant formed a copycat union, whose members explained their intentions in superlative tones: "We know we have the best jobs, the best Boss, and the best Company, and we intend to keep them. We, therefore, pledge our loyalty to you in any and all of your undertakings."[100] The union's president, Mark Starr, had worked for LeTourneau since 1929 and accepted Christ at Stockton in 1933. He followed LeTourneau's example and became "an earnest soul-winner" on the job and a lay preacher in his spare time until his death in 1939.[101] As a mechanic, Starr was a craftsman and likely a supervisor with a vested interest in the existing plant hierarchy. He was by no means the only LeTourneau employee, however, who shared his boss's vision of industrial evangelism as defined, in part, by an open shop.[102]

For this reason, the heart of *NOW* was its evangelistic message. The October 23, 1936, issue was a characteristically imaginative Olson production. The first long piece began with a quote from a *Time* article about "a mob of miners, maddened by labor grievances," which had started a coal fire in 1885 that was still burning. "Similarly," Olson preached, "by one man's act of disobedience sin entered into the world . . . burning its slow but relentless paths of destruction unseen." Fond of such parallelisms, he quoted *Time* again: "'Attempts have been made . . . to head off the fire by sinking cement walls, by forcing steam underground, by diverting a creek into the shaft. All failed.'" Likewise, said Olson, "[a]ttempts have been made to halt sin by reform, by education, by drastic law enforcement. All failed."[103]

Having dispatched with the social gospel and the power of the state to change behavior, Olson found his next parable in *Newsweek*. A pastor had offered a prize to the parishioner who could "name the most horrible sin in the world." He accepted "Rejection of Jesus" as "the nearest to his own, 'The abuse of high privilege.'" Olson ignored the second phrase's political implications, commenting only that Jesus was indeed "the highest privilege accorded an unsaved sinner." He skirted closer to commentary with the headline "President's Voice Used to 'Prove Broken Pledge.'" The reference to a recent Republican broadcast assumed that *NOW*'s readers listened to secular as well as evangelical radio, just as they read *Newsweek* along with *The King's Business*. "Whatever the merits or demerits of the [Republican] charge," Olson hedged, "the incident calls to mind that God has a record of every word that we say." He aimed a series of Bible verses at those without "the word of faith," leaving open the possibility that they also applied to Roosevelt: "[W]ith their tongues [sinners] have used deceit; the poison of asps is under their lips, whose mouth is full of cursing and bitterness." The closing quote, from Romans, was an altar call: "[I]f thou shalt confess with thy mouth the Lord Jesus, and shalt believe in thy heart that God hath raised him from the dead, thou shalt be saved."[104] Later, in "President's Popularity Sliding, Says Writer," Olson used a similar device: quoting three damning paragraphs before observing that whether or not the critique was correct, Christ never became "over-confident"—or unpopular.[105]

By defining Christianity in the individualistic and pietistic terms of conservative evangelicalism, LeTourneau and his mouthpiece, Olson, also ventured into conservative politics. Without question, both men cared more about saving souls than about current events per se. But Olson was invoking worldly as well as spiritual conflicts when he used striking coal miners to illustrate original sin and publicized Republican accusations that Roosevelt was a liar. Other articles in *NOW* explicitly connected theology and politics. "A few days ago President Roosevelt proposed to Congress for himself something of the reorganization of government that Jethro, the priest of Midian, proposed for his son-in-law [Moses] 3400 years ago," Olson wrote after Roosevelt's second inaugural address in 1937. The mistake, in both cases, was to increase the number of government departments to be supervised, only to put "the burden of all Israelites" on the leader (and, Olson added, provide an administrative template for Catholic "intermediaries" between people and God). During the court-packing controversy, Olson defended Chief Justice Hughes against charges of tyrannical ambition that one of his favorite sources—the *Literary Digest*, red-faced after predicting an electoral landslide for Republican Alf Landon—dismissed as the rantings of "[m]any an ardent pro-Roosevelt paper." Olson compared the alleged misquoters of Hughes to "opponents of the gospel" who, "[s]eizing onto . . . 'God is love,' or some similar passage," went on to deny the necessity of salvation. Sneering at Roosevelt's off-the-record disclosures to journalists, he pointed out that every word in scripture "can be directly attributed to God," for whom "[t]here is no danger of . . . ever being embarrassed by His own utterances."[106]

As a premillennialist, Olson often commented on international affairs, such as the British mandate in Palestine that might fulfill the prophetic requirement that all Jews regather in Israel. He pitted Hitler and Mussolini against the Apostle Paul, who "establish[ed] the civilization that the world's dictators are seeking today to destroy."[107] All told, Olson dogged sifting through any source that might yield a timely sermon illustration and gave *NOW* subscribers a highly slanted, but informative, smorgasbord of popular journalism. Like *The King's Business*, *Moody Monthly*, and other fundamentalist outlets, *NOW* ensured that conservative evangelicals read what other white middle-class Americans were reading. This was not only to highlight the differences between the subculture and "the world" but also to rally the subculture to bring its weapons of gospel truth, prayer, and conversion to a common existential fight.

NEW FOUNDATIONS

Both LeTourneau's speaking career and *NOW* evolved rapidly over the same trajectory, from a small start in Peoria to an ambitious campaign for a national audience. So did the LEF, which began as a hazily planned depository for "God's share" of company wealth and soon funded the other two endeavors on a grand scale, buying private planes that multiplied LeTourneau's preaching opportunities, and mass-producing *NOW* and its accompanying tracts.[108] In 1935, R. G. and Evelyn LeTourneau and V. R. Edman—future president of evangelicalism's intellectual flagship, suburban Chicago's Wheaton College—formed the nonprofit corporation with 70 percent of LeTourneau, Inc.'s, common stock shares. Knowing that the company was likely to clear over $2 million in profits that year, the LeTourneaus wanted to formalize a means of giving half of it to God, the "Senior Partner." Foundation philanthropy had been interwoven with Christian capitalism since the late nineteenth century, with the growth of a finance economy based in high-risk, high-yield stocks and bonds.[109] Gilded Age businessmen and society women transformed urban charities from providers of "direct personal service" to centralized bureaucracies that mirrored the economic ideology and practices of their wealthy directors.[110] It is easy, however, to overstate a linear development from amateur "charity" to professional "philanthropy." Nouveau riche businessmen and blue-blooded patricians alike inherited an antebellum ethos of Christian stewardship. Based in the biblical parables of the talents, in which a master gives three slaves an equal amount of money to invest and rewards the one who earns the most, the commandment carried the same weight in 1935 as in 1850: "For unto whomsoever much is given, of him shall be much required: and to whom men have committed much, of him they will ask the more."[111] In that spirit, LeTourneau dubbed his foundation "The Lord's Treasury" and soon raised his commitment from 50 to 90 percent of company profits and salary.[112]

By relieving government of some burdens of social welfare, foundations hoped to gain control of public policy, often to promote a social "revival" with implicit or explicit religious motivations.[113] Legally, a foundation was a trust fund whose tax-exempt status hinged on the donor's explicit restriction of the money's use for charitable intent. Ideologically, foundations emphasized self-help while retaining paternalistic supervision and control, offering a welfare-style safety net whose success would be judged on efficiency, cost-effectiveness, and short-term assistance rather than long-term dependency. Multimillionaires such as Andrew Carnegie, whose "gospel of wealth" called on private citizens to stabilize industrial capitalism by mitigating its harsh inequities, and John D. Rockefeller, a devout Baptist who believed that "[t]he Lord gave me the money," exchanged their wealth for power in many social sectors, from the arts and education to medicine, science, and religion.[114]

The LEF was less ambitious than these predecessors, because it was more of a personal fiefdom, yet less hands on. LeTourneau's evangelistic expenses were the foundation's top priority; other causes received support more on a case-by-case basis than according to a strategic plan. LeTourneau delegated the management to Harold Strathearn, a fiery Baptist preacher he met through J. Palmer Muntz, director of the evangelical retreat center established by Billy Sunday at Winona Lake, Indiana. The British-born Strathearn ran the Interstate Evangelistic Association, a fundamentalist Baptist coalition based in Rochester, New York. The LEF set up shop in Rockefeller Center, that citadel of American capitalism, and by 1940 Strathearn ran both groups from the same office. Strathearn's wife, Dorothy, a popular Christian singer known as "the Gospel Nightingale," performed frequently on LeTourneau's itinerary. *Joyful News*, the Interstate Evangelistic Association's newspaper, became by far the most militant of LeTourneau's publicity outlets, with puff pieces on "God's business man" sandwiched between denunciations of modernism.[115]

True to LeTourneau's long-standing interests, missionary work was the foundation's first purpose: "[t]o teach, promulgate and disseminate the Gospel of Jesus Christ throughout the world." Second, the LEF aimed to "unite in Christian fellowship . . . the various Evangelical Churches," in order "to appoint and engage ministers, evangelists, [and] missionaries."[116] Both goals put the foundation in the mainstream of conservative evangelicalism in the mid-1930s urban North. The Great Commission was the top priority, and ecumenical cooperation was required to storm the barricade of heathenism, liberalism, communism, and fascism. (White southern evangelicals, particularly Baptists, shared the same fears but drew firmer denominational boundaries.)[117] Again, however, the LEF's beneficiaries bore the distinct stamp of its founder. The CMA, an evangelical youth program for which Evelyn had volunteered in California, and Sarah LeTourneau's China mission received the first bequests, followed shortly by *NOW* and Tom Olson's tracts.[118] Plant productivity quickly filled the foundation's coffers. In 1935, Stockton and Peoria netted almost $600,000 in profits. In both 1936 and 1937, LeTourneau, Inc., cleared over a million, with annual sales reaching $5,500,000.[119]

LeTourneau was ready to expand his business again, and just as the Plymouth Brethren had kept him employed as a young man, the Christian and Missionary Alliance turned out to be the network he needed. In 1936, LeTourneau had attended a missionary convention in Omaha at CMA radio personality R. R. Brown's Gospel Tabernacle. One of the speakers was R. A. Forrest, the founder of a coeducational Bible and vocational school in Toccoa Falls, Georgia. Evangelical businessmen had helped sustain Forrest's dream to survive. California oilmen Lyman and Milton Stewart, who copublished *The Fundamentals*, paid off a $20,000 debt in 1915 after fire swept through the four-year-old institute. Lyman endowed a women's dormitory in 1917, and a few years later, Milton's wife sent the money needed to complete a group of half-built classrooms.[120] Nineteen thirty-six marked Toccoa Institute's twenty-fifth anniversary, and Forrest was traveling the world to meet his graduates in the mission field. Impressed that the institute taught scripture and occupational skills to rural whites in Georgia's hill country, LeTourneau sent a $1,000 check from the foundation to Forrest's mailing address in Japan. Months later, Forrest surprised him by sending back "a bale of receipts" accounting for every penny. When they finally met in person, LeTourneau increased his support for the institute to $10,000. He enrolled his son Donald at the institute. In 1938, after preliminary scouting, he proposed that he build his next plant in Toccoa Falls with the institute as a feeder school for workers. Forrest embraced the collaboration, and construction began that November.[121]

The story of Toccoa Falls and the attraction it held for LeTourneau is more complicated than the encounter of two evangelical entrepreneurs, one a layman in business, the other a preacher in education. Like other manufacturers, LeTourneau already had his eye on the underindustrialized South. High poverty rates, a Jim Crow work force that held wages down, and anti-union state governments guaranteed a cheap labor pool. Yet even as he prepared to build not only a factory but a full-fledged company town, Toccoa Falls was reaping the benefits of the New Deal. The Civilian Conservation Corps (CCC), one of Roosevelt's first and most acclaimed initiatives, paid young men to work on civic safety and other improvement projects. A CCC camp established itself in Toccoa Falls in 1933 and 1934, replanting trees in deforested land, building picnic sites, and clearing a path to the falls. Campers donated surplus food to the institute, and when they left, the government gave the institute $4,000 worth of lumber. The institute wasted no time converting the CCC barracks into a dormitory.[122] In 1938, the National Youth Administration (NYA), which offered part-time jobs to students, settled on campus. Participants, including local teenagers who otherwise would have had to work full time, took institute classes, including Bible courses, if they wished. Following the NYA's architectural blueprints, they built a radio center, an agricultural space, shops for machinery and woodworking, and a home economics building complete with a floor for women's dorms.[123]

LeTourneau might have protested such a thorough government presence on the turf now neighboring his, but instead he took advantage of what was, by 1938, a paradoxical political battle over the economic future of the South. On one side stood conservative southern Democrats who argued that minimal regulation, subsistence wages, and resistance to unions were the region's best chance of drawing private industry away from the North. On the other was evidence of the New Deal's utility: the CCC camps, for example, and the Tennessee Valley Authority, generating hydroelectric power vital to industrial development.[124] In 1938, Roosevelt signed the Fair Labor Standards Act that enacted a national minimum wage targeted specifically at the South, which he called "the Nation's number one economic problem." He barnstormed through the region during the summer, trying to rouse voters against recalcitrant congressmen he called the "Copperheads." These legislators resisted government intervention that, to Roosevelt's mind, would end the South's economic isolation and, to their minds, would trample southern independence. Georgia's senator Walter George appealed to regional pride by waving a bloody shirt, sneering that Roosevelt's tour was nothing less than "a second [Yankee] march through Georgia." In November, when LeTourneau arrived in Toccoa Falls, southern voters—which is to say, white voters—overwhelmingly reelected the Copperheads, including George.[125] From the North, *NOW* offered a detailed assessment of the Republican Party's concurrent midterm comeback, hoping it would yield "a tax bill less onerous than expected, railroad legislation more helpful to owners" and make Congress "once again a deliberative body instead of a rubber stamp for the Chief Executive."[126] Yet repudiating the president did not mean rejecting the inroads the New Deal had already made in the South. LeTourneau contracted with the NYA to build an airport in Toccoa while he created an aviation-training program at the institute.[127] In doing so, he tacitly acknowledged what pro–New Deal businessmen had contended since the end of the Hoover administration: that working with, rather than against, a powerful federal government could be the best way to navigate the Depression.

Cooperation among church, business, and state (though not Roosevelt's state) was the theme of the four-day revival LeTourneau staged in 1939 to consecrate the Toccoa Falls plant. It was a practice he had begun in Peoria, where he had recapped the themes of his Chamber of Commerce speech: "I believe that a factory can be dedicated to [God's] service as well as a church, and that it can be the means of saving many souls."[128] In Georgia, apolitical fundamentalism was nowhere to be seen. An all-star cast of public figures joined LeTourneau in insisting on the unity of theological and political conservatism. Crowds of three to five thousand enjoyed free barbecue while LeTourneau introduced them to his contractual creed.[129] "My faith in God has brought blessings on my business," he said. By contrast, "[m]ultitudes are starving" because "the average man today" lacks initiative and faith. The solution, he explained, was a Christ whose heroic masculinity and expert authority matched businessmen's image of themselves: "a man big enough, who [knows] enough to lead us." Governor Eurith D. "Ed" Rivers boosted his region and evangelical religion by attacking labor unions. "Mr. LeTourneau had the means to go anywhere else in the nation with his business," Rivers said, but instead, he chose "Georgia and the southland. He's not going to find Communists and sit-down strikes in the south!" The governor added the evangelical refrain that "a spiritual revival is needed if the nation is to climb out of the present crisis." Joining Rivers on the platform were Senator Richard Russell, a Roosevelt ally, and three state and local officials. "[W]e have . . . evidence that he is a generous man," Russell said of LeTourneau, "and the fact that he is dedicating this plant with [revival] meetings starting today, we recognize as an answer to the power of God." The CMA's R. R. Brown, who had brought LeTourneau and R. A. Forrest together, directed a seventy-five-person choir.[130]

Preston Arkwright, president of the Georgia Power Company, and R. W. Wirt, vice president of the Southern Railway, made sure that big business was represented. Arkwright reiterated the anti-union message by praising welfare capitalism. About LeTourneau Wirt offered, "This man is not starting a sweat shop. He pays better wages than the average employer. He works his labor reasonable hours. He needs no regulation. His employees need no protection." Furthermore, Arkwright inaccurately asserted, LeTourneau needed no New Deal: "All this we see here today is individual enterprise." While the *Atlanta Constitution* did not quote the three clergymen on the bill, it noted that an evening service would "be dedicated to the factory workers of north Georgia and . . . centered about wholesome, friendly relations between employer and employe [*sic*]."[131] LeTourneau was already barricading himself against the union sentiment whose existence his fellow speakers were taking such pains to deny. When he took the podium, he went so far as to criticize capital as well as labor for relying on human institutions rather than the Lord. "[T]he Capitalists instead of trusting in God, are trusting in capital; the laborer today is trusting in his labor organization instead of his God—that's what's the matter." Jesus "came down to this sin cursed world . . . [and] for our sakes became poor that we might become rich" in everlasting life, and in this life too. "[B]y the Grace of God, I am still trying to be His business man," LeTourneau shouted. "I thank my Lord and Saviour for what he has done for me and I want to present Him to you." Two thousand people stayed for services the first night.[132]

By the time he welcomed luminaries and the curious masses to his Toccoa Falls plant, LeTourneau's reputation as "God's businessman" was soaring beyond his impressive, if revised, self-presentation on *Ripley's Believe It or Not*. He had always divided his calling into two parts: bringing religion into business and bringing business into religion. Having made contacts with fundamentalist businessmen in Peoria, he crossed the Mason-Dixon line into Georgia eager to work on the second goal. In 1940, when Ripley interviewed him, LeTourneau was president of two predominantly northern organizations: the Christian Business Men's Committee International, founded in Chicago in 1930 as a revivalistic response to the Depression, and the Gideons, famous for placing Bibles in hotel rooms for traveling salesmen since 1899. Both groups (the membership overlapped) were white, mostly Protestant, nominally all male, and comprised chiefly of white-collar workers, middle managers, small-business owners, and entrepreneurs like LeTourneau.

At his inaugural speech for the Gideons, entitled "Let's Have a Sixth Column," he articulated more fully than he had at the Peoria Chamber of Commerce the leadership role of businessmen in the church. "Just as God called the men of old to do certain things, I believe He is today making that call more especially to commercial men to witness that the Gospel is still the power of God unto salvation," he began. "We commercial men have no conflict with the preachers"—a denial which implied the opposite—but "when we laymen who rub shoulders with people in the world every day tell them that Jesus Christ is the solution to all our problems . . . they can't say of us as they sometimes say of the preachers, 'They get paid for it.'" This astonishingly blunt rephrasing of his characterization of ministers as "God's salesmen" transformed the church into a marketplace in which businessmen, for once, had no ulterior motives. However, "us laymen" alone possessed the expertise "to show . . . that [the Gospel] is practical," not "only a theory"—a faith whose power stemmed from deeds, not words.[133]

As LeTourneau discovered when he moved to Toccoa Falls, the South had its own evangelical businessmen's groups with much the same philosophy. He would soon begin to work closely with two leading laymen. Vernon Patterson was a Charlotte-based southern Presbyterian salesman who headed the Business Men's Evangelistic Clubs and acted as an early mentor to Billy Graham. Rolan R. Stoker was a Baptist dentist in charge of the Atlanta BMEC; LeTourneau lured him to Toccoa Falls to set up a Christian conference center on site. The next chapter of LeTourneau's story would play out in the context of these interregional webs of evangelical businessmen. In merging their religious and commercial lives, thousands of men across the United States and Canada placed themselves at the head of the national revival. To them, LeTourneau's "practical" gospel was as transparent and reliable as Adam Smith's invisible hand. God could be trusted to reward correct doctrine, earnest faith, and righteous living with happiness and financial success. By virtue of their worldly achievements, then, they claimed the authority to diagnose the causes of personal and social crises. Like mid-twentieth-century businessmen of all political and religious stripes, they were confident that with the right marketing techniques, they could tell people not only what to buy but what to believe. Joining LeTourneau and this army of corporate types was another industrious individual whose devotion to 1930s evangelicalism's prosperity gospel, and all of its marketing dexterities and political promises, was every bit as fierce.

CHAPTER TWO

Herbert J. Taylor, Rotarian Fundamentalist

Around the same time R. G. LeTourneau was broadening his vision of business and evangelism, the president of Club Aluminum Company was widening his. Forty-nine-year-old Herbert J. Taylor had established himself as a business leader by rescuing the cookware manufacturer and retailer from bankruptcy in 1932, the worst year of the Depression.[1] A devout Methodist who believed that God called laymen as well as clergy to Christianize the world, Taylor, like LeTourneau, started to devise a system of philanthropy through which he could change his society and nudge his nation back to God. In 1938, with 25 percent of Club Aluminum stock as his financial base, he created the nonprofit Christian Workers Foundation.[2] The philanthropy would provide seed money for evangelical causes that Taylor judged capable of national and international impact. Insisting that *anyone*, regardless of vocation or status, could be a "Christian worker," Taylor set out to recruit other professionals who would put their worldly experience and skills to work for his enterprise and for God's kingdom. He did so with a vocational verve, and sense of purpose and urgency, that was infectious and endemic within his enlivened sector of corporate Christianity.

The effects of Taylor's ambition were on full display on February 5, 1942, when the Club Aluminum CEO gathered Chicago's evangelical elite for a celebration of past progress and a look ahead to next evangelistic steps.[3] Everyone he invited to the meeting at the Windy City's Sherman Hotel represented an organization the CWF had funded. Not only was the setting businesslike, but only three of the twenty-three attendees were church pastors. In tribute to Taylor's networking prowess, the group formed a cross section of his philanthropic interests and a who's who of fundamentalism's midwestern base. Taylor built the CWF's influence by requiring that either he or a surrogate serve on each beneficiary's board, giving him a voice not only in individual ministries but also in the centrifugal growth of interwar evangelicalism. At the meeting, the presidents of Wheaton College, Moody Bible Institute, Northern Baptist Seminary, and the Chicago Evangelistic Institute represented Taylor's interest in "youth work" and Christian higher education. The schools granted a spectrum of professional credentials, from Wheaton's liberal arts BA to the vocational training of the Bible institutes and the seminary's curriculum for aspiring clergy. The name "Moody," in particular, drew disparate and often quarrelsome factions together around the legacy of turn-of-the-century evangelist Dwight L. Moody, a lay preacher and former shoe salesman whose message of Christian individualism had resonated with wealthy sponsors such as J. Pierpont Morgan and Cornelius Vanderbilt.[4] Dr. Harry S. Ironside, pastor of Moody Memorial Church; Wendell P. Loveless, director of radio station WMBI; and Moody musical supervisor Dr. Homer Hamontree rounded out the spokesmen for Moody's posthumous empire.

Businessmen and professionals were equally prominent on Taylor's guest list. Shoe store owner C. B. Hedstrom and fellow evangelical Frank Sheriff, two local leaders in Christian corporate circles, were there. So was Vaughn Shoemaker, the Pulitzer Prize–winning cartoonist for the *Chicago Daily News* who created "John Q. Public" to speak for the woebegone American taxpayer; at the Sherman affair he chaired a Rotary-style lunch group called the Gospel Fellowship Club.[5] William McDermott, a *Daily News* reporter and head of the Family Altar League, and publisher and Club Aluminum board member Robert C. Van Kampen also appeared at the deluxe hotel, eager to provide leadership in Taylor's quest for spiritual comradeship among like-minded men.[6] Taylor brought in the heads of other local missions as well, all CWF supported, such as the Chicago Bible Society and the Great Commission Prayer League.

Associated if not affiliated organizations were also proudly represented. Lawyer Paul Fischer arrived as a delegate for the group Child Evangelism with director Gwendolin C. Armour, widow of the grandson of famous, or infamous, meatpacking entrepreneur Philip D. Armour.[7] The working conditions in her late husband's family's stockyards had helped inspire Upton Sinclair's exposé *The Jungle*, but like Morgan and Vanderbilt, Philip D. Armour was also a Christian philanthropist.[8] He sponsored his brother's progressive, interdenominational Armour Mission for children. The pastor of Armour's upscale church moved him to establish the coeducational Armour Institute of Technology by preaching what wags dubbed "the Million Dollar sermon," extolling the ways a million dollars could improve education in Chicago. Armour chose the minister to head the institute, and they collaborated until the tycoon's death in 1901.[9] Using her married name, and continuing the Armour philanthropic tradition, Gwendolin managed her fortune and contacts to become a singularly powerful woman in otherwise all-male evangelical circles. She was the only person at the Sherman Hotel with ties to big business; J. L. Kraft, the processed-food mogul who conceived the Laymen's Crusade for Christian Education, declined to come.[10] Finally, there was special guest J. Elwin Wright. A former businessman who ran the New England Fellowship, an influential regional node of fundamentalism, Wright was working with Taylor, among others, to conceptualize an umbrella organization that could serve as a clearinghouse for evangelicals of all denominational stripes who sought to influence American civic culture. That organization would soon come to fruition, bearing the name of the National Association of Evangelicals.

But while all these special guests collected themselves in downtown Chicago to anticipate a near future of greater evangelism and more unified religious service, a prevailing spirit among them was that 1942 was the culmination of one man's special work as much as it marked the onset of a new unified vision and coordinated action. Taylor, the builder of the sprawling ministry to which they owed and eagerly gave their service, deserved their highest praise. Yet Taylor himself—always looking ahead, never pausing for glances back—had neither the time nor patience for such praise; much work remained. In his mind, the illustrious citizens before him were present for one thing only: to figure out how to deliver, better, "the Gospel of Jesus Christ to men and women throughout the Chicago area" and to learn about "the part we and the organizations we represent might play in making this evangelistic project count for the Lord."[11] His "we," once again, meant a fundamentalist elite in which Taylor, the business executive, was as much an agent of God as the ordained ministers and Christian college presidents who sat beside him. More than that, it reflected Taylor's conviction that corporate strategies designed in boardrooms and ballrooms, of the kind enjoyed at the Sherman, as much as (indeed, more than) church outreach thought up in pulpits and pews would be the key to making ministry "count for the Lord." No forced impetus, this was the philosophy that had fueled his career up to that point and made the CWF a central player in American evangelical culture.

In the process of building the CWF empire, Herbert "Herb" Taylor brought his faith into the world and the world into his faith. He worked with other self-identified "Christian businessmen" to build and sustain networks that toiled for revival during the Depression and World War II and that would continue toiling during postwar reconstruction. These businessmen, their uncredited female support staff, and like-minded clergy poured money, time, and expertise into projects they hoped would launch a fundamentalist, interdenominational, lay-led revival that would start in North America and eventually span the globe. They never doubted that this revival would be top-down: as in business, they identified and groomed leaders who would restore the evangelical brand from its subcultural status to the cultural dominance they insisted it had held until twentieth-century apostates snatched it away. Following a long tradition of business patronage of talented "Christian workers," Taylor was one of evangelicalism's corporate sponsors in a period that, contrary to influential opinions of the time and prevailing historiographical assumptions today, saw conservative Protestants as energetic civic actors instead of demoralized remnants.[12]

Since the 1920s, when half a century of theological warfare came to a head in the urban North, the terms "evangelical" and "fundamentalist" had distinguished orthodox Protestants like Taylor from "modernists" who treated the Bible as a human and historically contingent document rather than the infallible and timeless word of God.[13] "By 'evangelical,'" Taylor wrote in the CWF's charter, he meant a "New Testament . . . interpretation of [C]hristianity which emphasizes man's fallen condition, the atonement of Christ, necessity of new birth, and redemption through faith."[14] This lowest-common-denominator statement welcomed all who believed in the Bible's divine authorship; the doctrine of original sin ("man's fallen condition"); Christ's death and resurrection ("the atonement"); a personal conversion experience ("a new birth"); and the early church as a model for communal worship ("New Testament" was code for Protestantism's *scriptura sola,* not the extra- and antibiblical canon of Catholicism).

Like generations of evangelical laymen before him, Taylor drew the boundaries of Christian fellowship as broadly as possible within these limits, subordinating internal controversies to the common task of conversion. He took care to distinguish his philanthropy from the progressive social gospel that cooperated with the state to battle poverty and other problems that evangelicals viewed as symptoms of unbelief and that businessmen, in particular, feared as breeding grounds for socialism. All the while he concretized his firm conviction that business had to be equally about the pursuit of profit and godly stewardship, and that businessmen, redeemed by Christ, could stand out and apart in society as architects of a social order organized around what the masses truly needed, what the

Bible truly endorsed, and what the divine wished for in the earthly and heavenly pursuits of his flock.

"GOD HAS A PLAN FOR YOU"

Herbert John Taylor was born in Pickford, on the upper peninsula of Michigan, to Frank and Martha Ellen Taylor on April 18, 1893. The fourth child of seven, he inherited his business acumen and religious commitment from a large, close-knit family. His paternal grandparents came to Pickford from Ontario in 1882, five years after another group of Canadians lay claim to the land.[15] Taylor would cross the Canadian border many times as an adult, in the transnational spirit that wove American evangelicalism into a wider world of Anglophone Christianity.[16] Patrick Taylor, the clan's patriarch, established homesteads for his sons to inherit upon his death in 1884. They helped build Pickford from a settlement into a small commercial center. Frank Taylor, Herb's father, founded the electric and telephone companies and managed a lumber-supply interest, a dairy, and a bank.[17] Growing up, Herb also learned from his entrepreneurial uncles: "Uncle Fred ran the hardware store; Uncle Ed the grocery; Uncle Andrew the shoe store; Uncle George the dry-goods store."[18] Fred and John were lay leaders in the Pickford Methodist Church, which Herb's family also attended.[19]

Of the second-generation Taylor siblings, Frank left the largest mark on Pickford. In addition to his wide-ranging contributions to the local economy, he made time for public service. During his tenure as the town's third supervisor, he expanded its landholdings and named three new streets after the middle names of his sons. He groomed the boys to inherit his businesses or establish their fortunes elsewhere. As an adolescent, Herb acquired an early appreciation for advertising by hawking the Taylor dairy. He also raised sheep and sold the wool to finance his education.[20] Pickford was too small for a high school, so as a teenager, he moved to the county seat, Sault Ste. Marie, not far from the Canadian border. He took classes by day and worked for Western Union by night, spending summers in Soo Junction as a railroad relief officer.[21] "[M]y mother was determined that we have a good education," he remembered. Six college-bound children—the seventh went to a two-year technical school—cost more than even the largest businessman in a remote Michigan village could afford.[22]

While Herb Taylor spent little time in Pickford as a teenager, he often came home for weekends, worshiping Sunday mornings in the crowded Taylor pews at the Methodist Church. He did not consider himself saved, however, until he was seventeen, when a visiting evangelist brought him to the altar. Taylor's retrospective conversion narrative is characteristically crisp: "I became convinced, stepped forward, and accepted Jesus Christ as my personal Saviour and Lord. I don't mean to record that moment casually, but it was just that simple and straightforward."[23] It was, in a word popular with evangelicals and businessmen alike, a *transaction*, in which Taylor pledged his faith to Jesus and Jesus his fidelity to Taylor. In principle, the agreement made Jesus responsible for Taylor's achievements and Taylor responsible for his failures. In practice, it fit comfortably with the American notion of the self-made man, with Taylor's religious choices determining his earthly and heavenly fate. In his study of spirituality in nineteenth-century New England, Richard Rabinowitz links the development of a market economy to precisely such entangling of commercial and religious language. Divine grace was a spiritual commodity akin to the products in the Taylor family's stores, characterized by "instrumental use" and "exchangeability." In a religious and financial ideology centered on rewards and punishments for individual actors, "[c]ommerce supplied key metaphors to enrich the language of moral experience—terms like investment, contract, and credit."[24] Methodists, whose theology held individuals responsible for their own conversion, had been promoting industry and profit as by-products of Christian commitment for decades before Taylor claimed the faith.[25] The message that hard work transcended "sacred" and "secular" callings, however, had much broader appeal than one Protestant denomination. LeTourneau, who was five years younger than Taylor and from a different tradition, would preach transactional theology to great effect.

Although Taylor framed his salvation in the unemotional terminology of exchange, he soon showed his religious fervor. Not long after declaring himself a Christian, he enrolled in Northwestern University, which a group of Chicagoans—six businessmen and three pastors—founded in 1850 as a place of "sanctified learning . . . under the patronage of the Methodist Episcopal Church."[26] By the time Taylor entered the class of 1917, Northwestern, like other sectarian universities, had deemphasized its religious origins in pursuit of growth and academic respectability. It added several graduate schools, including a school of commerce funded by Chicago businessmen. Enrollment in the College of Liberal Arts, which Taylor attended, leaped from 603 in 1900 to 1,469 in 1917.[27] While a private college education was, by and large, an upper-middle-class luxury, Taylor again had to work through school. Two of his sisters were also in college, and Frank could not afford three tuitions. On top of classes and the track team, Taylor telegraphed for Western Union and wrote about sports for two Chicago newspapers.[28] He made a career-minded move to become business manager of the yearbook. Finally, as if he was not busy enough, Taylor started courting his future wife (and future Northwestern student), Gloria Forbrich, during his sophomore year, while she was still in high school. Her father was a Chicago-based advertiser and industry journalist, and the family claimed a lineage of American heroes that included the Methodist temperance and suffrage advocate Frances Willard.[29] By all accounts, both families approved of the match.

Yet notwithstanding his crowded schedule and Northwestern's drift from its Methodist roots, Taylor's most formative undergraduate experience was the Young Men's Christian Association (YMCA). A popular extracurricular activity since students founded Northwestern's chapter in 1880—by the 1890s, 30 percent of the campus belonged to the men's or women's group—the "Y" combined aggressively evangelical Christianity with a social gospel that preached economic and racial justice.[30] The polarization around "fundamentalism" and "modernism" that would fracture northern Protestantism in the 1920s was only brewing during Taylor's college years. In 1915, oilman Lyman Stewart finished publishing *The Fundamentals*, twelve paperbacks in which leading evangelicals denounced biblical higher criticism and centered their own theological core on a personal relationship with Christ, proselytizing, and prayer.[31] Meanwhile, the Northwestern YMCA focused on the religious and humanitarian crisis of World War I. After graduating, Taylor and other members of the class of 1917 went to France as YMCA relief workers. When America entered the war, they were already on the battleground.

Taylor's three years in France secured his future in the business world. He temporarily left the Y to join the naval reserve, which took advantage of his skills as an aid worker and assigned him to direct the distribution of food and clothing to US sailors near Brest.[32] At the Armistice in November 1918, the navy allowed him to go on leave and accept a position as the regional director of the YMCA. Hundreds of thousands of servicemen passed through Brest to return to the United States, and twenty-five-year-old Taylor's job was to keep them out of what the Y considered trouble—drinking, prostitution, brawling, and other time-honored entertainments for battle-scarred men far from home.[33] Taylor tackled the challenge with his first large-scale merger of evangelicalism and entrepreneurialism. Taking advantage of what one Northwestern history describes as "a scheme to exchange dollars for francs at an exorbitantly favorable rate," he bought French pubs that were popular with Americans and converted them into "dry" hotels. "So unusual has been Mr. Taylor's businesslike efficiency," the *Chicago Daily News* reported, "that many of his large staff assistants outrank him in point of seniority."[34]

The *News* staff members were not the only people monitoring Taylor's work. Taylor's YMCA service in France introduced him to the men who would launch his business career and, in some cases, remain friends and networking contacts for decades. Maurice Karker, Taylor's naval commander, considered Taylor his protégé.[35] Senator Robert L. Owen of Oklahoma heard about Taylor's managerial gifts and arranged a job interview with constituent Harry Sinclair, president of the Sinclair Oil Company. George Perkins, the YMCA's chief fund-raiser in France and partner at J. P. Morgan, advised Taylor to take the position instead of another offer he found more tempting: that of associate general secretary of the YMCA.

According to Taylor's autobiography, in which God directs every event into place, the conversation with Perkins laid out his future and philosophy of life. "You think I'm going to tell you to go with the YMCA, don't you?" he quotes Perkins as saying. "Well, that's not what I'm going to tell you. I'm going to suggest you go into business. You have a considerable amount of God-given business talent." Over the long term, he argued, that talent would enable Taylor to do more Christian work with youth than joining the YMCA bureaucracy. Perkins predicted that Taylor would someday have his own company, "where you can influence the making of policies. You'll be able to take time away . . . for your youth activities. By the time you're forty-five, you'll be spending more of your long time on young people's projects than on your business." Taylor concluded in hindsight that "Mr. Perkins was the vehicle through which I'm certain God presented me with a plan—His particular plan for me. . . . From the moment I left Mr. Perkins' office, I knew the course of my life." In the first edition of his memoir, Taylor would cast himself in Perkins's role as the voice of experience for confused young Christians. The title: *God Has a Plan for You.*[36]

Taylor saw nothing unusual in finding his divine calling at J. P. Morgan instead of a church. He had spent his life around pious businessmen. Prayer, he wrote, had "clearly led" him to Perkins, a spiritual authority with one foot in business and the other in the Lord's work.[37] If Taylor also spoke to a pastor, he did not report the conversation. As much as he respected clergymen, he gravitated to people and organizations that shared his assumption that only fellow businessmen could give him practical spiritual guidance. No less importantly, for a young man on the make, confidants such as Perkins and Karker introduced him to business, social, and religious networks that would at once advance his career and bring him closer to the executive level that Perkins said would free him for evangelical philanthropy.

FROM PAULS VALLEY TO CHICAGO

Step one in the plan was for Taylor to accept the position Senator Owen had arranged with Sinclair Oil. He returned to the United States in 1919, married Gloria Forbrich, and set out for Pauls Valley, Oklahoma, fifty-three miles south of Oklahoma City.[38] He was entering a frenetic growth industry. In the late nineteenth century, white settlers swarmed into the Creek- and Cherokee-dominated land, which Andrew Jackson had designated as "Indian Territory" for the survivors of the Trail of Tears before the Civil War. Salt prospectors had discovered oil as early as 1859. In 1897, commercial drilling began in earnest, prompting the federal government to grant Oklahoma statehood in 1907, while Taylor was in high school. Twelve years later, when he and Gloria moved to Pauls Valley, Oklahoma led the world in oil production.[39]

Henry F. Sinclair, a Kansas druggist's son, had jumped into the turn-of-the century oil boom. In 1907, his Oklahoma holdings made him Kansas's wealthiest man. He and his brother ran a bank in Tulsa, and in 1913 Sinclair registered as the city's first citizen. In 1916 he established the Sinclair Oil & Refining Corporation on Wall Street. Not yet forty, he controlled fifty million dollars' worth of oil wealth and other assets. Woodrow Wilson's administration chose him to serve with eleven other petroleum magnates on the World War I War Service Committee, which is most likely when Senator Owen sought to link Sinclair with promising young men such as Taylor. In September 1919, around when Taylor arrived at Pauls Valley as a short-term assistant to the general manager—"just enough time to learn the pipeline end of the business"—Sinclair consolidated his United States, Mexican, and postwar European holdings into the Sinclair Consolidated Oil Corporation. That move, and the ambitious expansion that quickly followed, made Sinclair the tenth-largest oil company in America, and with his eye on the gasoline-powered automobile market, Sinclair was looking for more profits and more growth. Taylor was exactly where he wanted to be, on the cutting edge of the postwar economy with a promise of promotion.[40]

Yet after the training year with Sinclair Oil, Taylor saw a brighter future as an independent operator and submitted his resignation. Business conditions had changed suddenly when a "wildcat outfit" set up the first oil well near Pauls Valley "and local interest in oil really took a jump."[41] Now that land was in demand, Taylor established what he later described as "a combination lease-brokerage, insurance and real estate office." Each service had ready customers in the oil prospectors who swarmed into the area. Taylor expanded his base in Pauls Valley, the county seat, and claimed plausibly to have become "involved in every phase of the county's life."[42] He and Gloria moved from the Methodist Church to the Presbyterian Church, not to change denominations, but to encourage other well-off couples to rebuild the Presbyterians' dilapidated building out of community spirit. The project exemplified Taylor's commitment to the evangelical heritage of interdenominational cooperation for the common good. Soon he was teaching the Presbyterian men's Bible class and chairing the finance committee. Under his direction—or, as he put it, "[t]hanks to the Lord, and many enthusiastic church members"—the congregation raised $65,000 for a new church.[43] Taylor also returned to youth work. He established the first Boy Scout troop in Paul's Valley. More significantly for his future, he started a branch of the YMCA's nonsectarian civic club, "Hi-Y," at Pauls Valley High School. Among other activities, the group sponsored a Boys' Work Council aimed at deterring juvenile delinquency, a cause long dear to middle-class Americans and especially evangelicals.[44]

None of this religious and community service would have been possible if Taylor had not risen to the top of Pauls Valley's business and civic world. Although the oil lease brokerage took off after Taylor left Sinclair, his insurance business faltered until a conversation with Gloria sparked an insight that he retold for the rest of his life as a road-to-Damascus experience akin to his meeting with J. P. Morgan's George Perkins. In a rare scene portraying Gloria as a businesswoman in her own right (albeit over a dinner she had cooked), Taylor spoke petulantly of a resistant insurance prospect. Gloria replied with two questions. "First, does the man really need insurance?" Taylor said yes. Second, "Does he have enough money to pay for the premium?" Again, yes. "You know what I think?" Gloria said. "I think you're to blame for not selling him the policy. It's not his fault for not buying." According to Taylor, "That straight answer changed my entire outlook on selling"—and, he might have added, on evangelism. It was transactional theology in action, with faith and hard work rewarded or rebuffed depending on the intensity of his commitment. He hounded the man until he bought a policy, sextupled his sales "after that quiet talk with Gloria," and became one of Travelers Insurance Company's biggest sellers in Oklahoma.[45]

With success came responsibility. Taylor served as secretary of the

Chamber of Commerce "to give the town back some pride so that useful projects could be started," taking no salary until the chamber was out of debt. He spearheaded a bond issue to rescue the county from "an unhealthy backwoods image" by paving roads to enter the automotive age. To his delight, the *Daily Oklahoman* headlined its coverage of the 1924 campaign "Sign 'Em Up Taylor of Paul's Valley."[46] Pauls Valley residents, he imagined afterward, likely "remembered me best as a young man with a petition in his hand."[47]

It was in Pauls Valley that the relentlessly civic-minded Taylor made what would be a lifelong commitment to the Rotary Club. Founded in 1905 by Chicago attorney Paul Harris to "make social friends of his business friends," the club began as a networking fraternity that invited leading men from different professions to mingle with others at different locations (hence "Rotary").[48] Within ten years, Rotary had spread to cities nationwide and spawned copycats such as Kiwanis and the Lions. After World War I, in which Rotarians volunteered as idealistically and efficiently as the YMCA, the movement became international. It provided local hubs for a national and global marketplace, appealing to "smaller business men and independent professionals" with a stake in luring other investors to town, or extending their markets beyond their base.[49]

Rotary had always been religiously ecumenical, admitting Protestants, Catholics, and Jews (at least in principle) from the start. By the early 1920s when Taylor joined, it represented a right wing of progressivism, combining faith in humanity's improvement with suspicion toward the state as the source of uplift.[50] At the first national convention in 1911, Rotarians adopted "He Profits Most Who Serves Best" as their motto.[51] Members expounded on the mission in a familiar mix of commercial and religious terms that charged laymen, not politicians or clergy, with expanding Christian civilizations. "[T]he church has so many concerns in mind that it has made poor progress," a speaker argued at the 1925 convention. The Rotarian message dealt with "the real problems of life" and avowed, "The men who are doing the work of the world are the men best capable to lead in spiritual as well as in material things."[52] For example, Pauls Valley vied with nearby Wynnewood to host the area farmers' market. Taylor thought that Rotary's business elites could resolve the tensions "for the common good of both cities."[53] Since Pauls Valley already had a Rotary Club, he established one in Wynnewood, and members worked out the disagreement. In addition to encouraging economic cooperation between the cities, Taylor steered the Wynnewood group toward the youth work he was already doing.[54]

Taylor needed to ensure his legacy, for he had promised Gloria that they would only stay in Oklahoma five years before returning to her hometown of Chicago. Between 1919 and 1924, he had established a template for his professional life, which mirrored that of his father and uncles on a larger and industrial-age scale. He had also cemented his religious identity, which carried forward the irenic and cooperative legacy of nineteenth-century evangelicalism that he had first absorbed in Pickford. In 1924, Baptist and Presbyterians in northern urban centers were splintering along fundamentalist and modernist lines. Taylor gives no indication that the turmoil reached his own Presbyterian church or disturbed him as a Methodist. "The fundamentals," which other conservative evangelicals defined as battle lines, Taylor could take for granted. No modernist faction in Pauls Valley was challenging "(1) the inerrancy of Scripture, (2) the Virgin birth of Christ, (3) his substitutionary atonement, (4) his bodily resurrection, and (5) the authenticity of [biblical] miracles," as one scholar has summarized fundamentalism's doctrinal core.[55]

With no need to be on the attack or the defensive—a position that suited Taylor's temperamental aversion to conflict—his religious and business concerns were local, inclusive, and practical.[56] Much like the "Presbygationalists" who cooperated to evangelize the frontier in the generation after the Revolutionary War, Taylor and Gloria concluded that the Pauls Valley Presbyterian Church must survive because Methodists could not reach the community alone.[57] The business world was just as eager to prevent competitive impulses from thwarting mutually beneficial cooperation. Taylor's assumption that business success carried the responsibility of public service started in Pickford, grew in the YMCA, and found its apotheosis in the Rotary Club, which, in principle, subsumed personal differences into the brotherhood of businessmen. Either Taylor saw no conflict between Rotarian optimism, on one hand, and evangelical belief in original sin and human inadequacy to improve a fallen world, on the other; or he perceived a conflict but considered it negotiable, like the differences between Presbyterians and Methodists; or he simply lived with the tension, equally confident that Rotary and evangelicalism were forces for good, and exercising his prerogative to define their mission based on his reading of scripture and experience of the world. "Fundamentalist Rotarian" was not an oxymoron but an identity, which Taylor brought back to Chicago—the center of both movements.

Going from Pauls Valley to Chicago was going from the American hinterland to its central metropolis. Rotary International's icon was a wheel with hundreds of spokes flaring from its Illinois hub. Chicago in the mid-1920s still lived up to its old boast of being the "city of the century," a financial, manufacturing, agricultural, and transportation crossroads. In 1893, barely twenty years after the great Chicago fire decimated the city, raw capitalism rocketed it into international, yet peculiarly American, fame as the host of the World's Columbian Exposition celebrating the quadricentennial of the New World. Observer after observer echoed the sentiment of local writer Henry B. Fuller, who called Chicago "the only great city in the world to which all citizens have come for the one, common, avowed object of making money."[58] By the end of World War I, the majority of these citizens were European immigrants; native-born whites comprised little over 20 percent of the population but a huge share of employers.[59] Chicago's Christians tended toward polyglot extremes as well. Contending ethnic ghettos of Catholics collectively outnumbered similarly diverse and divided Protestants. White fundamentalists aligned with Moody-founded institutions clashed with mainline Protestant modernists at the University of Chicago; African American congregations swelled with migrants from the South; and Sunday services took place in a cacophony of Scandinavian, German, and other northern European tongues.[60]

By virtue of birth, education, and connections, Taylor, Gloria, and their baby daughter Beverly arrived poised to join the middle- to upper-class echelons of the native-born minority. Taylor had already lined up a job with his former navy commander, Maurice Karker, now the president of Jewel Tea Company, who "told me he'd take me into his company and move me along as fast as I was able to move," Taylor wrote. Although Travelers Insurance, his Paul's Valley employers, offered to transfer him at a high salary, Taylor "prayed about the matter, and . . . had a definite leading to go with Mr. Karker." His sense of God's will either confirmed, or was confirmed by, Taylor's feeling that he "liked the man, knew his reputation and had a lot of confidence in him."[61] The trust was mutual, and Karker kept his promise of rapid advancement, whisking Taylor up the ranks to executive vice president by 1930. During these years, Gloria gave birth to a second daughter, and the family marked its rising class status by moving from the city to the northwestern suburb of Park Ridge. While it no longer advertised itself as "A Restoring Place of Health & Vigor, The Recreation Place of the Tired & Worn Out," its pitch to businessmen in the 1910s, Park Ridge offered a quick train ride from downtown Chicago to a bucolic "village." Park Ridge came complete with an actual park system, a country club, a thriving economy, and service groups such as Rotary and Kiwanis for men and a range of activities for women.[62]

Taylor become a trustee of the First Methodist Church and characteristically threw himself into congregational life.[63] He and Gloria taught Sunday school in their basement and observed the rest of the Sabbath by visiting family, refusing to shop or enjoy "paid entertainment." The couple also founded a storefront mission and soup kitchen on the Near North Side of Chicago, a once-affluent neighborhood whose steep inequality of wealth the Depression exacerbated.[64] Arranging free donations of bread from a local bakery, the Taylors hired a full-time minister and contributed to the city's intensely ethnographic academic climate by surveying two thousand homes near the mission to find out how many children were going to (Protestant) church, Sunday school, or both. The answer was about half, so they followed up by interviewing parents, the majority of whom were first- or second-generation immigrants.[65] The responses were predictable—lack of interest or, more poignantly, that parents "couldn't afford to buy the kind of clothes their children needed to attend Sunday School"—and exemplified a missionary challenge to urban churches nationwide.

"What we needed," Taylor argued, "were nondenominational organizations that could provide a Christian witness to these children, and their parents, in a way they could understand and accept . . . and eventually, funnel them into the church of their choice."[66] "Nondenominational" was a misnomer. Taylor envisioned an *inter*denominational collaboration of conservative evangelicals: he did not deem Catholics or Protestant modernists to be true Christians. However, even if the goal of the sociological endeavor was to produce more "fundamentalists," a neologism entering its second decade as a synonym for evangelical traditionalists, the methodology showed how much Taylor had imbibed the YMCA's and Rotary's progressivism. Moreover, his solution—doctrinally sound Christians working together to funnel the unsaved into any cooperating church, elevating personal "choice" over sectarian distinctions—drew on evangelical history while riding a twentieth-century ecumenical wave that fundamentalists and modernists shared in common. The notion that Protestantism was a mass market with varied but essentially compatible segments attracted businessmen across the fundamentalist/modernist theological divide.[67]

Once again, Taylor's ecumenical vision hearkened back to the early nineteenth-century "evangelical united front." In the 1920s and 1930s, like their predecessors a hundred years before, white Protestants from different denominations agreed on a common message of salvation that gave them strength in numbers over religious competitors—not the least Protestants with an opposing consensus on the essentials of the faith. The battle lines of biblical inerrancy, the facticity of past or present miracles (an issue that split conservative evangelicals over Pentecostalism), and the relative weight of individual redemption and collective action were specific to their time and place. Taylor's complex loyalties, however, illustrate a common Protestant heritage fixed on the goal of a Christian America, even when Protestants lacked a common definition of "Christian."

CLUB ALUMINUM

Taylor's religious and charitable work in the early 1930s followed a parallel track to his business life. It was clear at the start of the decade that the stock market crash of 1929 had precipitated a familiar plunge in the American economy from boom to bust, though not, at first, to calamity. For much of the year, politicians and businessmen saw soaring bankruptcies, a sinking Gross National Product, and rising unemployment as a temporary downswing no worse than the brief postwar recession of 1921.[68] One of Chicago's looming casualties was Club Aluminum, whose 250 employees would be out of work if it could not stave off its creditors. Networks based partly on business judgment and partly on personal relationships kept the company out of bankruptcy. An official at the Continental National Bank who knew Karker asked the Jewel Tea president to allow Taylor to rescue Club by taking charge of its affairs part time. Taylor's job skills suggested the match: Club Aluminum, like Jewel Tea, produced and sold its products, and he was in charge of both parts of the operation.[69] Karker agreed and let Taylor bring other Jewel Tea staff to help. By the time they finished their report to Club Aluminum's creditors in 1932, however, the economy was in far worse straits than a mere downturn, and the company was $400,000 in debt. As Taylor would stress when telling this story later, the logical decision was to close it down.

Yet echoing Methodism's founder John Wesley, who had "felt [his] heart strangely warmed" on the road to conversion, Taylor sensed that "something strange was going on inside of me" that resisted business logic.[70] Perhaps Club Aluminum offered the position of power that George Perkins, of J. P. Morgan and the YMCA, had urged Taylor to seek so he could devote himself more fully to Christ's kingdom. "It seemed to me that *this* was the company [God had] chosen for me to fulfill the second part of the original plan," Taylor wrote, "where, in the future, I might influence the setting of policies that would enable me to give more and more of my time directly to the Lord's work."[71] Club Aluminum's history gave Taylor faith in its potential. At the beginning of the 1920s, a Methodist seminarian named W. A. Burnette had begun paying his way through school as a door-to-door cookware salesman on contract with an aluminum manufacturing company. His innovative tactics, most famously having female customers invite friends to product demonstration meals in their homes, enabled him to hire a national sales force that pushed everything from pots to vacuum cleaners at generous credit rates. Aluminum was expensive, so its vendors emphasized its durability, hailing the advent of "waterless," burn-free cooking with the metal's even conduction of heat and imperviousness to rust. The metal's high cost and public health concerns in the 1920s devastated the market during the crash, but Taylor was certain that God wanted him to make Club Aluminum profitable again. In 1932, the worst year of the Depression, he left his $33,000 vice presidency at Jewel Tea for the $6,000 presidency of Club Aluminum. Unbeknownst to Gloria, whose father he installed on the Club board, he borrowed his salary from their personal Jewel Tea stock and put up their house as collateral. "I was convinced," he said, "because the Holy Spirit told me so."[72]

Now that he was finally in charge of his own company, Taylor had no boss but God to please and free rein for his managerial ingenuity. He recognized that the female consumer's point of purchase was less the home than the chain store, so he ended the door-to-door product demonstrations and contracted with retail outlets like Gimbel's in New York City. The change in distribution enabled him to slash prices more than 50 percent, generating rapid profits that he put into advertising. In 1935, Club Aluminum contracted with A&P, Kroger, National, Jewel (the grocery chain, not the tea company), and Taylor cooperated with them to refine his product's appeal: a discount for buying a certain number of groceries; a one dollar down, one dollar a week credit system; and free take-home trials.[73] The Roosevelt administration's early experiments with economic reform—bank regulation; the Agricultural Adjustment Administration; and, most importantly to Club Aluminum's manufacturing arm, the short-lived National Industrial Recovery Act, regulating hours and wages while giving workers the right to strike—failed to dent the Depression between 1933 and 1934.[74] Yet due in no small part to Taylor's ingenuity, Club Aluminum was not only climbing out of debt but enlarging its market.

Taylor's papers are scant before the end of the 1930s, so there are only hints as to his political views during the height of the New Deal. But it is clear he cared about partisan combat. In heavily Democratic Chicago, he was a registered Republican who made small but regular donations to local and national candidates.[75] As his and Gloria's surveys of urban children's religious affiliations have already shown, he retained a strong streak of the good government progressivism that dominated the YMCA during his service. Along with other "corporate liberals," a category that included many

Rotarians, he supported strategic cooperation between business and government to bind the New Deal to the survival of private enterprise.[76]

Nevertheless, Taylor remained an evangelical individualist at heart, convinced that a good society came about through right thinking—and by extension, right acting—one person at a time. He attributed Club Aluminum's turnaround chiefly to his composition, in 1932, of what Rotarians call "The Four-Way Test" of business ethics, which by the early twenty-first century, still read: "1. Is it the TRUTH? 2. Is it FAIR to all concerned? 3. Will it build GOODWILL and better friendships? 4. Will it be BENEFICIAL to all concerned?"[77] Taylor's account of its authorship combines the tropes of inspirational literature, hardheaded business advice, and a definition of religious practice that can be read with equal plausibility as nonsectarian or dogmatically evangelical. In his memoir, Taylor describes the Four-Way Test as an answer to prayer as he took charge of Club Aluminum in 1932. "I know [God] didn't want 250 people to lose their jobs and the pay they had coming to them, when they could not get jobs elsewhere," he writes. The first priority, then, "was to set policies for the company that would reflect the high ethics and morals God would want in any business. If the people who worked for Club Aluminum were to *think right*, I knew they would *do right*." Employees could save the company and their jobs if they pleased God in thought and deed, and the burden was on Taylor to show them how. The Sunday school teacher in him saw the solution: "a simple, easily remembered guide to right conduct—a sort of ethical yard stick—which all of us in the company could memorize and apply to what we thought, said and did in our relations with others."[78]

Uniformity was of the essence for two reasons. First, Taylor visualized a successful company as a single-minded organization of many complementary parts, much as the New Testament described "the body of Christ as one . . . [with] many members."[79] Second, Taylor's God inflicted collective punishment for anything less than total allegiance, making it imperative that the Club Aluminum creed win universal consent. Finding that the "right phrase eluded me" in his reading, Taylor bowed at his desk and prayed, then "wrote down the twenty-four words that came to me."[80]

While those twenty-four words, framed in four questions (as quoted above), would indeed become Taylor's and eventually Rotary International's trademark, they were not the first version of the Four-Way Test. His memoir compresses the time line into a tidy conversion narrative that erases his starts and stops amid the crisis facing Club Aluminum. In 1942, ten years after the fact, Taylor gave Rotary International permission to copy the "Test."[81] The *Rotarian* published a profile of Taylor by his friend

William McDermott, the *Chicago Daily News* writer who headed the Family Altar League and served on the Charles Fuller revival committee. Taylor told McDermott that he had been "studying the Sermon on the Mount" over several months as he refined the formula "which he believe[d] more than anything else [was] responsible for the comeback of the Club Aluminum Company." The first two points of the original Four-Way Test, truth and fairness, were the same as in later iterations. Points three and four, as first worded, addressed Club Aluminum's business needs head-on:

> 3. Will it build goodwill for the company and better friendships for our personnel [not just "better friendships"]?
> 4. Will it be profitable [rather than nonspecifically "beneficial"] to all concerned?[82]

The final version amplified "friendships" to general "goodwill" as well as business networking, and stripped out the profit motive in point 4. Pure idealism softened the rough edges of moneymaking pragmatism.

Both the memoir and McDermott describe an interfaith vetting process that shows the tension between Taylor's personally uncompromising evangelicalism and his professional tightrope walk around religious difference. After applying the first Four-Way Test for a two-month experiment—for instance, striking "superlatives" from advertising on the grounds the "best," "finest," and "greatest" violated point 1, "Is it the truth"—Taylor held a meeting with his four department heads, who happened to be a Catholic, a Christian Scientist, an Orthodox Jew, and a Presbyterian. "I asked them if there were anything in The Four-Way Test that was contrary to their religious or moral beliefs." They had no complaints, confirming Taylor's conviction that the test embodied "God's principles, morals, and ethics," which, by definition, were universal.[83] Years after the fact, he found "God's own original version of The Four-Way Test" in Jeremiah 9:23–24: "[L]et not the rich man glory in his riches; But let him that glorieth glory in this . . . that I am the Lord, which exercise loving kindness, and righteousness in the earth." It was this Old Testament passage, which Protestants, Catholics, and Jews held in common, that Taylor quoted in speeches about the Four-Way Test "to groups of business men and professionals."[84] He tactfully minimized the Sermon on the Mount.

By imposing only a behavioral "yardstick," not a theological one, Club Aluminum exemplified Christianity on Taylor's terms without being officially Christian.[85] Taylor was navigating the separate spheres of work and religion that middle-class Americans had mapped out in the nineteenth century by having it both ways: making his executive desk a place for prayer and religious discussion, but not proselytizing. His professional neutrality stood in sharp contrast to R. G. LeTourneau's workplace evangelism, but philosophically, both men were intent on collapsing the separate spheres. In keeping with his emphasis on ethical action and empirical proof, Taylor believed that the Four-Way Test obliterated the line between "religion," vaguely speaking, and business. "The source of character in industry is religious faith," he told McDermott. "We have simply incorporated our religious ideals into a simple working code of four paints." He added, "[W]hat is the use—or fun—of having ideals if you don't back them up with action? I mean really try to live up to them in your business and in your home as well as in church on Sunday."[86]

Even if the Four-Way Test was not doctrinally evangelical, Taylor wanted it to be as life-changing as a revival service, pointing to employees who "have learned ways-of-doing that have changed their own personal lives."[87] Moreover, "evangelism" is not too strong a word for Taylor's methods to make the Four-Way Test ubiquitous. He had it printed on salesmen's calling cards, posters, plaques, and stickers for car windows; required staff to memorize and recite the four principles so that, in one manager's words, "It became a way of life when I was there"; included the test in shareholder reports; and, to the dismay of the merchandising manager, inserted the test into product packaging along with a letter from Taylor inviting complaints.[88]

Tucked into McDermott's account, but not in Taylor's, is an economic calculus of the Four-Way Test's openness to short-term losses to build long-term "goodwill," a trade-off Taylor compared to "a boomerang [that] will return to you tomorrow with a profit."[89] By seeming to level Club Aluminum's power relations with an ethos that made workers moral agents who could call managers to account, Taylor hoped to ward off the threat of unionization. "Most strikes and lockouts can be traced directly to selfishness, insincerity, unfair dealings, or fear and lack of friendship among the men concerned," Taylor told McDermott. "There are many ways to discover the flaw in a given case, but I think one can usually put his finger on it by applying the Four-Way Test."[90] In 1932, a nation accustomed for decades to regular, disruptive, and brutally suppressed industrial strikes elected its first labor-friendly president and Congress. When Roosevelt took office in 1933, a year into Taylor's tenure at Club Aluminum, he signed the National Industrial Recovery Act (NIRA). Although the Supreme Court would declare NIRA unconstitutional in 1935, the pro-unionization clause survived in Congress, and up-and-coming leaders like

John L. Lewis of the Congress of Industrial Organizations (CIO) treated strikes as a tactical bludgeon with which to begin negotiations.[91] Employers such as Taylor and LeTourneau tried to preserve the post–World War I system of welfare capitalism, in which executives sought employee loyalty with good wages and benefits, stock options representing "ownership" of the company, opportunities for promotion, channels for reporting grievances, and company-sponsored socializing, all to create quasi-familial ties that would override ethnic and class identities, preempt labor agitation, and minimize government regulation.[92] Or, as the evangelical magazine *The King's Business* put it, "There would be no capital and labor problem if all men were true believers in and followers of the Lord Jesus Christ."[93]

While Taylor also believed that personal sinfulness, and not political injustice, made labor relations a matter of interpersonal misunderstanding that unions would whip up into mass revolt, he was willing to give parts of the New Deal a chance. In the 1920s, the symbiotic relationship between public service and profit was a truism that reached to the highest echelons of American business, and like the Four-Way Test, it transcended religious identification and political ideology. In 1922, as his newspaper wrapped up a two-year anti-Semitic serial based on the forged *Protocols of the Learned Elders of Zion*, Episcopalian Henry Ford proclaimed that "[s]ervice as a basis for profit-making is coming to be recognized as the true motive for creative industry."[94] General Electric president Gerard Swope, a Jewish alumnus of Jane Addams's settlement house who would become a prominent New Dealer, described "What Big Business Owes to the Public" as the recognition of "[businessmen's] responsibilities as trustees of other people's money, their obligation of service to the public, and their duty to their employees."[95] Roger Babson, an MIT-trained engineer and self-anointed "statistician," and Bruce Barton, an advertiser whose best-selling *The Man Nobody Knows* cast Christ as a virile exemplar of "executive ability," were theologically modernist but politically conservative Congregationalists. "Statistics show that the same qualities which make a man successful in business make him interested in religion . . . faith, vision, courage, sympathy, thrift, and industry," Babson argued.[96] He granted government the duty of "protecting men in freedom of effort and right of ownership; but only religion can energize men unto a maximum of useful service.[97]

For most businessmen after the stock market crash, however, the question was not whether government was a legitimate arena for "service" or its implacable foe. Rather, as in the Progressive Era when Taylor came of age, the question was how to ensure that business was the equal or stronger partner in an unavoidably regulatory state.[98] The spectrum from laissez-faire to corporate liberalism—in the business world, the "left" rarely went closer to socialism than that—was more nuanced than the rhetoric with which purists mobilized their forces. Ford, who devised an all-encompassing infrastructure of welfare capitalism in the 1910s to ward off internal discontent and, by extension, external interference, loathed the New Deal before it started.[99] In the spring of 1932, while Herbert Hoover was desperately attempting to balance free-market principles with limited intervention into the tumbling economy, Michigan workers staged a "Ford Hunger March." Ford's security team killed three marchers, injured fifty, and created a public relations disaster by shooting a *New York Times* reporter in the head. A friendly grand jury blamed the riot on "a few [communist] agitators who go about the nation taking advantage of times of industrial depression."[100] Ford redoubled his efforts to crush labor radicalism with the consent and cooperation of local, state, and federal officials, who already shared the same goal and, in 1932, had reason to fear that hopeless, hungry citizens would turn to revolution.

Yet Ford and other businessmen who tacitly accepted Washington's support when they needed the law on their side insisted publicly on the market's independence from the state. Refusing to comply with the NIRA when Roosevelt came to power in 1933, Ford wrote that government "should stick to the strict functions of governing. That is a big enough job. Let them leave business alone."[101] The enmity was mutual; Roosevelt's deputy Harold Ickes called out Ford by name in accusing "the modern industrial oligarchy which dominates the United States" of holding tight to its wealth until it could replace democracy with a "big-business Fascist America."[102] Gerard Swope, by contrast, helped create the NIRA and other major platforms of the New Deal. His 1931 *The Stabilization of Industry* (quickly dubbed "The Swope Plan") argued that the Federal Trade Commission should supervise controlled cartelization and mandate that companies assume responsibility for employee pensions and life and disability insurance.[103] At the same time, he viewed business self-regulation as the engine of reform, with the state playing a facilitative and supporting role. Just as Ford worked with government when profits or company survival depended on it, Swope intended to protect capitalism from "agitators" with business-initiated, government-backed responses to problems communists identified but couldn't solve.

Taylor was closer to Swope than to Ford in seeing the economic and social value of coordinating business self-interest and government regulation. In July 1932, Hoover signed the Federal Home Loan Bank Act allowing homeowners to tap into frozen assets using mortgage paper as security for loans.[104] The next May, Taylor chaired a group of businessmen that applied under the law to create the Chicago Federal Savings and Loan association; John B. Reynolds, the president of the Chicago Rotary Club, also served on the committee. Far from condemning government entanglement with private enterprise, C. W. Tower, a mortgage broker, told the *Chicago Daily Tribune* that "the advantage of loan associations operating under the federal charter is that they will be under federal supervision," unlike their freewheeling and often fraudulent predecessors.[105] The Chicago bank opened in January 1935, and, under the terms of the charter, offered to refinance up to $20,000 in mortgages on owner-occupied homes with five- to twenty-year loans. The founders hailed their association as "the first institution of its kind . . . to begin operations in Chicago under the new federal savings and loan bank law."[106]

Although Taylor considered himself religiously and politically conservative, his embrace of even one centralizing initiative made his faith and politics suspect in the apocalyptic context of evangelical opposition to the New Deal. So far, growled *The King's Business*, the New Deal was a "most benevolent dictatorship . . . but a dictatorship it is, all the more impressive in that it has been forced upon a great nation, not by the force of arms, but by the force of circumstances."[107] By themselves, *The King's Business* and nonevangelical Roosevelt opponents such as big business's American Liberty League may have been marginal. They were not, however, unrepresentative of more mainstream opinion makers. Sixty-three percent of newspaper endorsements in 1936 went to Roosevelt's opponent Alf Landon, with Colonel Robert McCormick's heavily right-leaning *Chicago Tribune* and Hearst's *New York American* claiming that the Soviet Union had commanded American communists to vote for Roosevelt.[108] The disconnect between anti–New Deal editorialists and American voters, who awarded the 1936 Democratic ticket in every state but Maine and Vermont, meant that moderate Republican businessmen like Taylor (who almost certainly voted for Landon) represented a right-leaning but flexible faction. Retaining their Progressive Era conviction that limited government action could facilitate private-sector solutions to public problems, they had ideological room to maneuver within the New Deal regime.

Despite Taylor's support of certain New Deal initiatives, he viewed Club Aluminum's turnaround under his management as a gift from God, not the government. By 1937 the company was out of debt, empirical proof that with "honesty, fairness, a spirit of goodwill—those fundamental Christian values—[and] calling upon Christ and the Holy Spirit . . . [y]ou will become a thousandfold more productive."[109] At least in hindsight, the Four-Way Test, "good people," and "good products" enabled forty-five-year-old Taylor to embark on the next phase of the life plan he and Henry Sinclair had developed almost twenty years earlier.[110]

CHRISTIAN WORKERS

Now that he controlled a profitable company, he could use it as a base for Christian work in two ways: branding Club Aluminum itself as "Christian," and diverting part of its profits into an organizationally distinct evangelical philanthropy. It is in this framework that he founded the Christian Workers Foundation (CWF). His dual roles as company president and nonprofit "trustee" cemented his reputation as a Christian businessman and drew him into the upper echelons of conservative evangelical activism. The CWF was explicitly fundamentalist, but in the camp that supported interdenominational cooperation, doctrinal minimalism, and revivalist ambition, not religious and cultural separatism. Through its endeavors, Taylor left formidable legacies in evangelical higher education; Sunday school and YMCA-sponsored youth groups; tract modernization and distribution; missionary support; and the National Association of Evangelicals, for which he served as founding treasurer and frequent donor. Taylor's business sense permeated every aspect of the CWF enterprise. Immersed in a top-down advertising culture that believed in its power to manipulate the masses, he had no more tolerance for guesswork and inefficiency in religious projects. Business strategy applied to theology made his career and philanthropy holistic endeavors.

Taylor charted a philanthropic course that demonstrated the utility of the foundation model to businessmen whose empires would not have registered on the Rockefellers' radar. The CWF had a single purpose, supporting national evangelicalism, and its spheres of influence radiated from that center. Although Taylor incorporated the CWF during 1938 and 1939, its first real year of operation was 1940.[111] Its portfolio demonstrates the meticulous yet improvisational nature of the enterprise, guided by Taylor's interests, the need to get the word out in the evangelical community, and the tension between his national ambitions and the local projects that friends and colleagues asked him to support. Many of the organizations that received money were nowhere near the front lines of a world-changing revival, but they played a part in building the local networks that the CWF hoped to unite. For instance, Child Evangelism, Gwendolin Armour's group, received $82.06 for ministry to African American children "on Chicago's northside." Five hundred fifty dollars went to Taylor Missions, run by Taylor's father, Frank, for summer vacation Bible school in Pickford. Two American missionaries in Argentina each earned $22.50 per month, a total of $45 for their "fine job in evangelizing both the peasants and the high government and local city officials."[112]

Earth-shaking investments these were not. They showed the range of Taylor's plans, however, to make the CWF influence the future of conservative evangelicalism as a civic force. But it is crucial in the first place to understand that the CWF's concurrent projects gave Taylor his stature. Whereas LeTourneau outsourced the LeTourneau Evangelistic Foundation to Harold Strathearn, giving its projects a haphazard feel, Taylor personally selected his chief beneficiaries based on their potential to evangelize America over the long term. By 1948, his philanthropic web would embrace Christian publishing; work-study scholarships for students at evangelical colleges and seminaries; the conservative high school ministry Young Life; the YMCA's high school group Hi-Y (focusing on good conduct and citizenship, not religion; Taylor wrote six commissioned pamphlets with titles such as *Time* and *Friends*); Fuller Theological Seminary; support for missionaries worldwide; and a stream of smaller projects such as "rural evangelism" in Kentucky.[113] A close look at Taylor and the CWF's many parachurch legacies, in short, establishes a pattern that would hold from the north side of Chicago throughout evangelical America. Taylor, like his Christian corporate peers, was a check writer not merely for religious enterprises but for active and authoritative participants.

The CWF cannot be studied apart from the context of World War II and the evangelical dreams the early war years evoked. For centuries, white US evangelicals had worked toward a "Christian America" and, by extension, a Christian world. They partnered in domestic and overseas missions with Anglophone allies from Canada, Great Britain, New Zealand, and Australia, advancing an Anglo-Saxon hegemony that imposed "civilized" politics, culture, language, and religion on dark-skinned, Catholic, or heathen aliens. By 1942, Anglophone evangelical leaders saw a geopolitical window opening to invade other lands with the gospel on an unprecedented scale. Allied victory, with America at the forefront, would open the borders of backslidden Europe and unevangelized Asia and Africa. World revival suddenly seemed within reach. As in World War I, conservative evangelicals' triumphalism encouraged a measure of internal unity and politically aligned them with the majority of Americans.[114]

The CWF groomed pious yet worldly men (and a few women) to market the gospel at home and abroad with the efficiency of executives at a multinational corporation. Taylor's top-down philosophy of evangelism, pulling the best and the brightest to deliver the message to the masses, continued to bare financial and spiritual fruit. By middecade, the philanthropy's annual reports called the "phenomenal growth" of its beneficiaries "outgrowths of a wartime society—or at least the Christian's attempt to meet the challenge of a wartime society." Success hinged on "willingness . . . to adapt [organizational] working policy to the needs of the field." It went without saying that rapid, flexible, consumer-oriented adaptation was also the wartime secret to the survival of businesses like Club Aluminum.[115] Meanwhile, two phrases were on evangelical leaders' lips, stationery, and banners: "the evangelization of the world in this generation," which had been the World War I "watchword" of the missionary Student Christian Movement, and, more succinctly, "world vision."[116]

The Inter-Varsity Christian Fellowship (IVCF) began to flourish at this very moment. According to the biographer of C. Stacey Woods, the IVCF's North American leader, "It would be difficult to overestimate the significance of Herbert J. Taylor" in establishing the group in the United States.[117] Taylor's passion for campus Christianity stemmed from his experience with the YMCA at Northwestern in the 1910s. By then, however, many conservative Protestants viewed the Y as a cesspool of modernism and longed for alternatives. In 1924, English medical student Douglas Johnson founded the IVCF as an orthodox challenge to the Oxford Movement in the Church of England, which he felt emphasized personal experience over scripture. Within fifteen years, there was a chapter on almost every campus, and as of 1929, representatives had planted chapters in the United States, Canada, New Zealand, and Australia.[118]

For members, the group's appeal lay in its combination of subcultural defiance and public witness; as in evangelicalism at large, the subculture provided the emotional and intellectual support they needed to speak up to scoffers. IVCF students banded together in prayer, Bible study, and missionary work, relishing their visibility in "secular" colleges and universities. Taylor heard about the group in 1940 from CWF scholarship winner and Young Life worker Ted Benson, a Wheatonite who knew the alumni in charge of the North American effort. C. Stacey Woods, an Australian, had studied at Wheaton and Dallas Theological Seminary in the early 1930s and now ran the Canadian IVCF. Charles "Charlie" Troutman Jr., the American son of a Wheaton trustee, was his closest colleague. Yet despite their recruiting efforts, the IVCF had not caught on in the United States. In Benson's view, it was a perfect test case for the CWF's goal to nurture highly educated, professional-class evangelical leaders.

To say Taylor was "sold" is an understatement. He contacted Woods and asked to sit in on a Canadian IVCF board meeting and meet with students. Convinced that he was witnessing the work of the Holy Spirit, Taylor ordered the CWF to send monthly donations and used the funding as leverage to join the Canadian board. His real goal was to persuade Stacey Woods to try again in the United States. By April 1940, thanks to Woods's CWF-financed recruiting trips back and forth over the border, twenty-two American IVCF chapters had formed, some on prestigious "secular" sites such as Swarthmore, Johns Hopkins, the University of Chicago, and the University of Michigan.[119] The Canadian Executive Committee, unable to stop the juggernaut after Canada entered the war and as the draft decimated its ranks, agreed to a three-year plan to house the skeleton leadership of IVCF-USA in the CWF office, with Woods commuting from Toronto. Like all of the CWF's projects, IVCF-USA could count on substantial but decreasing investments from the philanthropy, giving it time to stand on its own or fail: $5,000 in 1940 (a breathtaking proposition, considering that the 1939 US budget was $6,000), $3,000 in 1941–42, and $2,000 in 1942–43. Chapters sprung up everywhere from Texas to the Ivy League. In September 1941, the Canadian board yielded to Taylor and surrendered Woods full time to IVCF-USA. His family had barely settled in their Wheaton home when Pearl Harbor transformed the evangelistic landscape. Death and hell were no longer abstract, and students flocked both to the IVCF's fundamentalist message and the relationships they could forge with fellow Christians. By 1945, the IVCF covered a broad swath of the United States and sent its first missionaries to colleges in Latin America.[120] In August 1947, another businessman Taylor had recruited to the IVCF board, John Bolten Sr., hosted the Harvard conference that brought into being the International Fellowship of Evangelical Students (IFES). Like the IVCF, the IFES started in Oxford and added Anglophone and European countries. Its world vision matched Taylor's own "to give the utmost possible assistance to evangelical students . . . in the discharge of the divinely appointed task of carrying the Gospel of Christ into all the universities of the world."[121]

Taylor's commitment to the IVCF went well beyond fitting it into the CWF budget. He served as chairman of the United States board from the start and, in his mild yet determined way, exercised the position's power. Stacey Woods later described him as "a close friend, a wise counselor, but never a dictator."[122] Wooing industrialist and lay theologian J. F. Strombeck to the board, he floated the possibility of having the IVCF publish Strombeck's *So Great Salvation* ("excellent and timely . . . I agree with practically everything you said") "to secure wide distribution."[123] Stacey

Woods ran the draft of the IVCF-USA constitution by Taylor before proposing it officially. While Taylor announced that he would be "glad to recommend" the document to the other directors, he offered some businessman's advice. First, every chapter needed to brand itself as affiliated with the IVCF, or "we are losing something in the way of strengthening the national and international unity . . . and also in furthering the bond" between individual members of different chapters. Second, he "suggest[ed]" a candidate for treasurer who happened to be on the committee of the CWF's publishing arm, Best Seller Publicity. He also "hope[d]" that lawyer Donald Flemming "[would] be one of the two Canadian Board members selected to serve on the American Board." Finally, Taylor "would appreciate" it if Woods reviewed the Canadian IVCF's long list of prominent evangelical endorsers and pared it down to the men who were really involved. "As you know, I am not much given to window dressing," he explained, "suggest[ing]" that American references be required to "take an active part in promotion of Inter-Varsity, and to give of their time and influence." Except for the treasurer, who apparently turned the job down, Taylor got his way on every count.[124]

For the no-nonsense Taylor, getting one's way in this context—as in most—was justified. He believed that being God's vessel set him apart as a Christian businessman from other businessmen, and that firm decision making on his part was a sign of his dedication and service to his Lord. This assumption blinded Taylor in ways and made him subservient to the courser side of a transactional theology that privileged the person whose faith and hard work were rewarded for intensity and single-mindedness. But it also bound him to the iron sense of propriety on one hand and evangelical calling on the other that he so deftly integrated in the CWF. The CWF had one clear goal, reflected from Taylor's singular concern: to bring conservative Protestantism into the public sphere and—through support of IVCF chapters and numerous subsidiary ministries—map out a future for the nation in which evangelical leaders cut from the corporate mold could incite widespread revival.

To carry out this task, Taylor recognized the need to enlist other assertive entrepreneurs in his cause, men (and some women) who held as firmly to a transactional gospel as him. This is why the gathering at the Sherman Hotel in early 1942 to celebrate the CWF's past and anticipate its next steps was, in his mind, so pivotal. As much as the energetic CEO saw this meeting as propitious for what was yet to come for American evangelicals during the war years, he also understood that much of the heavy lifting of uniting like-minded Christians as a cultural interest group and a definable if still fragile coalition that could impact politics and the public sphere had already begun. Carrying this burden over the previous decade, during the hard years of the Great Depression, had been a number of Christian businessmen's groups, most notably the Gideons and Christian Business Men's Committee International. Leading members of these groups indeed stood out on the Sherman conference's invitation list of modern evangelicalism's "who's who." Some (such as C. B. Hedstrom and Frank Sheriff) were luminaries in the CBMCI; others (such as Robert C. Van Kampen) were stalwarts in the Gideons. Altogether they came to downtown Chicago in 1942 bolstered by a decade-long history of quieter activism in the boardrooms, classrooms, and pews of middle America and eager to shed some of the quietism for bolder, aggressive influence on the cultural and political mainstream.

CHAPTER THREE

Corporate Christianity's Civil Activism

In May of 1934, as the Depression battered Charlotte, North Carolina, twenty-nine businessmen gathered at Franklin and Morrow Graham's large dairy farm to fast and pray for a citywide revival. These men, like Franklin Graham, belonged to the Charlotte Christian Men's Club (CCMC), part of a predominantly southern movement colloquially known as "the Billy Sunday clubs" and, more officially, the Business Men's Evangelistic Clubs. Sunday, the legendary baseball player turned evangelist, knew that the chief peril of mass revivalism was a community's return to normal after the spiritual excitement faded. He turned to businessmen to sustain the momentum with follow-up evangelism, forming the first BMEC in Atlanta in 1917. White, interdenominational, and comprised of middle-class strivers who were or had connections with local elites, the clubs used social power for evangelical ends. At times, their lay-only membership ran into conflict with clergy. According to salesman Vernon Patterson, a CCMC founder, the local Ministerial Association "completely ignored" the group's first proposal for a large-scale awakening and publicly called the timing "inopportune." Some ministers, however, shared the businessmen's vision of collective repentance for "the spiritual declension" that they too believed had incurred God's wrath on America.[1]

During the months after the dairy farm prayer meeting, the CCMC methodically eliminated obstacles to an interdenominational revival. Getting theologically conservative Presbyterians, Baptists, and Methodists to cooperate with each other was not a problem; ecumenism for the greater good was well established in British and American Protestantism.[2] The co-owner of the Cole Manufacturing Company donated land for a temporary tabernacle after other CCMC members coaxed a reluctant city council into granting a building permit.[3] Meanwhile, the evangelistic team of Mordecai Ham and William J. Ramsay came to the Reid and Spillman insurance firm (Reid and Spillman were CCMC leaders) to discuss headlining the event. Ham, a Baptist salesman turned preacher, ardent Prohibitionist, and florid anti-Semite who had stumped the South for decades, agreed to an arduous schedule of twice-daily meetings for four months, all at his own expense. It went without saying that the CCMC would handle the administrative details of scheduling, advertising, equipment, ushering, and cleanup. Two supportive pastors also attended. Ham attributed continuing clerical opposition to "a real fight . . . between the evangelistic fundamentalist and modernist crowd," with the latter dominating the Ministerial Association.[4]

When the revival began, the CCMC aided Ham with much more than busywork. Patterson galvanized public interest by giving Ham evidence purporting to show that a home across from the high school was a speakeasy and a brothel. Thirty thousand citizens signed a petition to censure the mayor before he knew what had hit him, since Patterson had notified the evangelist and the press first. Standing before thousands at the tabernacle pulpit, Ham accused the mayor and the school board of "lining up with bawdy houses [and] bootleggers." He cast himself as a victim of political persecutors who "want to embarrass this soul-saving campaign." Patterson fueled the excitement by producing a deposition that described *junior* high students buying grain alcohol at the home and going "up to the bedroom for immoral purpose." Ham thundered that Jesus Christ was the only solution to human depravity in general and juvenile delinquency in particular.[5]

The CCMC and Ham were staging a circus of cosmic importance, and one of the sightseers was Franklin Graham's teenage son, whom everyone called "Billy Frank." He went to his first meeting after hearing that high school students were massing at the tabernacle to defend their honor. A dairy farm employee who had been saved during a previous CCMC revival talked him into going, promising to let Billy Frank drive the truck if he answered the challenge "Why don't you come out and hear our fighting preacher?" Graham liked the sound of "fighting," and Ham delivered. The evangelist's voice rang out as he berated the audience for its sins, painted lurid pictures of hell, told stories from the Bible, and, in calmer moments, spun down-home yarns to illustrate subjects ranging from the Second Coming to the liquor trade. Graham was "spellbound" by Ham's authoritative yet accessible masculinity. "[T]he same preacher who warned us so dramatically about the horrible fate of the lost in the everlasting lake of fire and brimstone also had a tremendous sense of humor and could tell stories almost as good as my father's," he marveled. Ham himself boasted, "So far as [Billy Frank] was concerned, nobody ever attended revivals like ours except a lot of old, effeminate men and crazy women and children. Our meeting changed his hero from Babe Ruth to Jesus Christ."[6]

Both men were almost certainly exaggerating after the fact, but for the next two months, Billy Frank came every night and even joined the choir. When he finally walked to the altar, the CCMC was waiting. A tailor he knew embraced him, "explained God's plan for my salvation in a simple way," and prayed with him until he was sure he was ready to "turn myself over to [Christ's] rule in my life." Someone handed him a card to record his name, address, and spiritual status. He checked "Recommitment," feeling that his salvation had begun with his baptism and confirmation. He had been aimless about his immediate future but soon came to believe that God was calling him to a Christian college to train for the ministry. The twentieth century's most consequential revivalist would owe his career not just to Ham's powerful preaching but also to the hard work, example, and ideology of evangelical businessmen.[7]

While Mordecai Ham has earned a footnote in history as the man who set Billy Graham on the road to becoming the next Billy Sunday, the Business Men's Evangelistic Clubs and more local Charlotte Christian Men's Club remain behind the scenes, generally hidden in modern religious history. This is unfortunate, because the BMEC, CCMC, and related groups such as the Christian Business Men's Committee International, the Christian Laymen's Crusade (CLC), and the Gideons did much to institutionalize what historian Joel Carpenter calls "revivalism as cultural politics" during the 1930s and 1940s.[8] Evangelical businessmen's groups formed around a single, specific, and, they believed, timeless purpose, that of winning converts and helping churches to keep them. The groups self-consciously patterned their language, strategies, and hopes after previous generations of proselytizers, minimizing current events to emphasize the eternal need for redemption through Christ. Paradoxically, this focus on saving individual souls contained a totalizing social vision. Adopting a missionary motto from the 1880s, businessmen's groups and their allies would settle for nothing less than "the evangelization of the world in this generation."[9]

This "watchword," as its coiners called it, had foundered on World War I, which forced liberal Protestants to question nationalism and religious and cultural imperialism.[10] Its reclamation by conservative evangelicals as a rallying cry during the Depression and first shadows of World War II frames the story of the businessmen's groups at a critical juncture. What distinguished the BMEC and its ilk from other organizations with the same uncompromising missionary zeal was the conviction that white businessmen were divinely anointed leaders in every sphere of life: home, workplace, church, and civil society. As entrepreneurs, managers, or "white-collared" employees—the winners of the long industrial revolution and the late nineteenth-century triumph of corporate capitalism—they were accustomed to cultural and, to some extent, religious authority.[11] These men were not Rockefellers or Morgans but Babbitts, the small-business men and community leaders that social critic Sinclair Lewis skewered in the 1920s. They owned or worked for enterprises with a few to a few hundred employees, a sector that created nearly two-thirds of America's income.[12] Even in the Depression, the belief that God rewarded faith and virtue with economic success ran deep in American life.[13] So did the corresponding expectation that the successful be generous with their time and money. Businessmen's decisions about where to volunteer or send checks reflected their values and gave them power in public life.[14]

Evangelical businessmen's intertwined assumptions of entitlement and duty put them in complicated yet productive tension with more visible religious leaders—clergymen. For generations, businessmen had served the church by managing congregational finances, endowing buildings, expanding educational programs, organizing revivals, and, in some denominations, playing a decisive role in hiring and firing pastors. In all of these endeavors, corporate and clerical elites negotiated professional turf, with both groups agreeing that a call to the full-time ministry commanded special respect, even when God summoned amateurs to similar tasks. Yet businessmen had a history of doubting ministerial effectiveness. Partly, this had to do with results. Evangelicals tended to identify any given historical moment as an unprecedented spiritual catastrophe, which inevitably called into question the performance of spiritual leaders. In the 1930s, clergy and laymen alike could point to the Depression, the New Deal, the ascendance of theological modernism in the 1920s, and the persistence of perennial vices such as drinking and prostitution as signs of collective failure. More importantly, early to mid-twentieth-century businessmen believed in business almost as fervently as they believed in God, and clergy were not businessmen. Careful not to claim superiority over religious professionals, laymen's groups declared that they were equal and complementary partners in world evangelization.

The ambiguous gender role of the clergy was critical to corporate types' sense of prerogative. Since colonial days, women had outnumbered men in church membership, and their charitable, missionary, and advocacy work gave Christianity a feminine face. Although the imbalance predated the language of separate gendered spheres, elite nineteenth-century discourse placed "religion" in the domestic sphere of home and family, rendering the manliness of clergy and male worshipers suspect.[15] Evangelical businessmen's groups sought to masculinize the church by urging laymen to treat religion as seriously as their careers. As R. G. LeTourneau—who would ultimately preside over the CBMCI, the Gideons, and the CLC—put it, "We are going to sell laymen the idea that they are going to work for Jesus Christ seven days of the week or not call themselves Christians."[16] The groups went on to emphasize Christianity's toughness on one hand and cash value on the other, in terms familiar to their audience. LeTourneau's multimillion-dollar "partnership" with God had a host of antecedents, from Andrew Carnegie's *The Gospel of Wealth* to Bruce Barton's portrait of Jesus as a salesman in *The Man Nobody Knows*.[17] Businessmen circulated a poem, which, by underscoring the link between clergy and women, held them responsible for the survival not only of the church but also of civilization itself:

> Leave it to the ministers,
> and soon the church will die,
> Leave it to the women-folks,
> and the young will pass you by,
> For the church is all that lifts us from the coarse and selfish mob.
> And the church that is to prosper needs the layman on the job.[18]

Echoing the sentiments of this poem, promoting LeTourneau's vision of partnership with God and Taylor's transactional theology, businessmen's groups did their utmost to revive white evangelicalism during the 1930s and early 1940s. They did so by tapping the longings of individual (and individualistic) salesmen, who during the tumultuous years, in a tumultuous marketplace, searched for personal meaning and fulfillment, and grounding, in "The Word"; by uniting these men behind shared causes, organized by and in local and regional collectivities that expanded rapidly over time; and by slowly—albeit with difficult fits and starts—opening the avenues of exchange across regional lines, allowing middle-American Christians in the Midwest and South to envision their interests as one. By the opening salvos of World War II, a once decentralized and diffuse class of Babbitts, toiling on their own in Charlotte, Chicago, and points in between, could begin to imagine themselves as a united front, their endeavor to save America from its sins of complacency and secular, socialist trends as a mandate best carried out with military precession in disciplined unison.[19]

CHRISTIAN "TRAVELING MEN"

The ingredients for an evangelical businessmen's group in an industrial and consumer economy were, first, a common, nondenominational evangelical creed paired with a commitment to save America from sin; second, evangelical practices that alienated would-be members from nonevangelical men, particularly taboos on smoking, drinking, gambling, swearing, and extramarital sex; and, third, exposure to what were, by the late nineteenth century, an array of class-specific clubs formed by white men who worked for a living but did not perform manual labor. The canonical account of the Gideons' founding begins in 1898 at a hotel in Boscobel, Wisconsin, where two traveling salesmen separately longed for Christian companionship. Shoe or paper salesman (sources vary) John H. Nicholson, about forty years old, lived a hundred miles away in the small town where he had been born. He arrived late to the hotel after a long day on the circuit. The only bed available was in the room of paint or grocery dealer (sources vary) Samuel E. Hill, in his early thirties. He was filling out sales orders in the smoke-filled lobby, ignoring the revelers around him. At bedtime, Nicholson opened his Bible. Hill, who was half asleep, shot up and asked him to read aloud, confessing, "I am a Christian too."[20]

Nicholson and Hill agreed to meet again to form an organization of Christian "traveling men." Nicholson invited a pious acquaintance that he had met on a train, salesman William J. Knights. In 1899, the trio formed the Gideons at Nicholson's hometown YMCA. The name came from Judges 7. God orders his servant Gideon to winnow his army to a few fighters, who, because of their faith, scatter Israel's enemy by blowing their trumpets in unison. The reference signaled defiant pride in the minority status of practicing Christians in a male commercial culture that required anonymous, raucous sociability. "God sifted [the Gideonites] down to a few real choice fellows," Knights summarized Judges 7, redefining abstemious Christians as true friends and hearty companions.[21] Rotary (1905), Kiwanis (1915), and the Lions (1917) offered less religious but equally appealing combinations of networking, friendship, and, above all, "service," elevating white-collar work to a calling that transcended dollars and cents while conferring informal or formal civic power.[22] Many men joined more than one club, layering their business, religious, political, and social ties.

The early Gideons adapted the traditions of existing businessmen's groups for evangelism in ways that set a template for like-minded organizations. For decades, they functioned as a near-exclusive professional fraternity like craft unions, medicine, or the bar. In principle, only traveling salesmen could join until 1937, when "businessmen"—excluding doctors, lawyers, and other "professionals"—gained admittance. In practice, the Gideons were more inclusive, befitting a charter that celebrated the very mobility that made them seek each other out as "scattering seeds all along the pathway for Christ."[23] At first, they made man-to-man proselytizing their only goal. To that end, they adopted a typical club accessory: a mandatory lapel pin. It was at once a conversation starter, a brand, a badge of belonging, and a subtle class statement: only men who wore suits to work could wear one all the time. Since magazines were an important method of advertising the club and motivating its members, the *Gideon* debuted in 1900, a year after the group's founding. In 1908, the growing movement launched its signature mission of putting Bibles in hotel rooms for traveling men. By 1910, Gideons were cooperating with clergy, leading revivals and delivering standardized messages to churches that publicized the local "camp" and asked for donations for the hotel Bibles.[24] The next year, a Canadian branch formed. International, yet overwhelmingly midwestern; all male, but with an energetic women's auxiliary; and selling salvation with their other wares, the Gideons paved the way for other northern evangelical businessmen's groups.[25]

In the early 1930s, the Gideons helped create the Christian Business Men's Committee (CBMC) as an informal partner in evangelism. Chicago, now the Gideons' headquarters, was the staging ground. A. H. Leaman, a part-time Mennonite pastor on the faculty of the Moody Bible Institute (MBI), enlisted them and five other laymen's and laywomen's groups to organize a citywide revival in response to the economic downturn.[26] Leaman had two models in mind. One was Billy Sunday's 1914 Chicago crusade, which Leaman remembered as a last show of evangelical unity before white Protestants fractured into "fundamentalist" and "modernist" camps.[27] The second was an on-and-off urban tradition of noonday revival meetings, aimed at professional men on their lunch hours, that dated back to a nationwide "Businessman's Revival" of 1857–58—also inflamed by a market crash.[28] Not atypically of northern and southern Protestants, whose major denominations remained institutionally separate since acrimoniously splitting before the Civil War, there was no indication that Leaman's Chicago group and the southern BMEC knew they were working on parallel tracks. It is likely, however, that Leaman remembered Atlanta's 1911–12 Men and Religion Forward Movement, the goal of which was to repopulate churches with "1,000,000 missing men." It pioneered the modern advertising tactics—billboards, radio and newspaper publicity, and a simple brand-name message—that the CBMC would use to reach the same audience of male strivers.[29] By making noonday meetings the center of his campaign, Leaman ensured that businessmen, not the cooperating women's groups, would be the public face of Chicago's hoped-for redemption.

After Leaman recruited enough evangelical groups to feel confident that God wanted revival, he formed the CBMC to channel the excitement through a central administrative body. The chairman, Swedish immigrant C. B. Hedstrom, was a longtime Gideon who attributed his shoe store's survival to his refusal to work on the Sabbath.[30] Ernest Wadsworth was a lay evangelist with the Great Commission Prayer League. Paul Fischer was a lawyer.[31] The most famous member was Vaughn Shoemaker, the award-winning and outspokenly religious and political conservative editorial cartoonist for the *Chicago Daily News*.[32] The occupations of Executive Secretary Frank W. Sheriff and board member J. S. Lincoln are unknown, but they probably matched the others' vocations as small-business owners, salesmen, or professionals. Leaman and an early booster named Edwin Zorn were ordained clergyman and, as independent evangelists, each had one foot outside the church door. Fischer affectionately called Leaman "the father of the CBMC," testifying to the comity that contained clergy-lay tensions. This was especially true in the CBMC, which, unlike the Gideons and the BMEC, allowed preachers full membership.[33]

Leaman and his team thought the committee would be temporary. They raised $3,000 for a six-week Eastertide extravaganza featuring noon services in Chicago's marketplace, the Loop. When excitement showed no sign of flagging, they kept going: twenty-five more weeks in the Loop, followed by open-air preaching in the summer. In the fall of 1931, they moved from daily meetings in the Loop to Monday-Wednesday-Friday noonday worship in rented downtown theaters. WMBI, the Moody Institute's radio station, broadcasted the services to a wide swath of the Midwest and publicized them in the *Moody Bible Institute Monthly*. By mid-1932, when the Depression was at its worst, the CBMC had raised $25,000 to bring businessmen to Christ. The founders were now working to build a permanent organization of "[c]onsecrated, devoted men whose hearts God has touched with a burden and vision to get the Gospel to a desperately needy generation."[34]

Scholars have often portrayed the 1930s in terms of an "American religious depression," not simply an economic one, yet as recent work by

Alison Collis Greene demonstrates, this very moment of crisis in fact sparked tremendous religious awakening among the poorest inhabitants of the poorest region—the South. "No Depression in Heaven" was both their comforting mantra amid fiscal and familiar hardship and an agenda for building their institutions and advocating for their concerns.[35] There was "no depression in heaven" for evangelical businessmen either, for as the records of the CBMC, Gideons, and especially southern chapters of Business Men's Evangelistic Clubs like the CCMC demonstrate, the Depression was in fact fertile for revival. "Most of us are humble men of very little means . . . and all are carrying their full load in their respective churches," a CCMC member wrote to the newspaper in 1932. Yet they had probably saved more souls "than all the churches of Charlotte combined," while "depression and unemployment have been doing such devastating work upon our poor." He pleaded for donations toward prayer meetings, "three weekly gospel missions," and Sunday schools in "destitute sections" whose residents "for the safety of society need the steadying influence of the gospel of Christ most of all." The editors echoed the call, praising "the robustness, the virility, and the deep, consecrated earnestness" of the CCMC's "emphasis on the evangelistic note in religion . . . that is especially needed in these days."[36]

The editors were prescient. In the 1930s, the Gideons adopted similar methods of evangelism that aimed for mass conversion in addition to "man-to-man" outreach. These included scripture memorization courses, tract publication and distribution, and open-air services with personal testimonies, preaching, and music.[37] Both the CBMC's Leaman and the Gideons had booths at Chicago's centennial "Century of Progress" World's Fair in 1933–34. The informal motto of the business-boosting celebration was "Science Finds, Industry Applies, Man Conforms." It was a perfect setting for evangelical businessmen to challenge the very notion of human progress without God.[38] Chicago's evangelical clergy seized the moment as well. Rev. Paul Rood, a veteran of the 1914 Billy Sunday campaign and president of the World Christian Fundamentals Association, led a revival at Moody Church during the 1933 World's Fair and was active in the CBMC. In 1935, he became the president of the Bible Institute of Los Angeles, the California counterpart to Chicago's MBI. Not coincidentally, CBMCs formed within a year in Seattle and San Francisco, the latter for the express purpose of proselytizing at the 1939 San Francisco World's Fair. Rood recruited investment banker Arnold Grunigen to head to the San Francisco group.[39] CBMC World's Fair organizer Tom Olson, LeTourneau's brother-in-law and in-house author, rented a building to show "Sermons from Science." This one-man act from the MBI entertained audiences with sleight-of-hand demonstrations of lightning and other marvels to argue that God, not evolution, designed the natural world.[40]

The San Francisco CBMC also distributed a pamphlet, *14 Prominent Business Men Look at Life*, that treated capitalist success as grounds for religious authority. Three CBMC-connected "executives," three "manufacturers," two bankers, an "investment dealer," a "steel man," a "wholesaler," a "store manager," and a "merchant" gave brief testimonies. Many were simple statements of faith, but some made a point of tying business conquests to evangelical Christianity. "Christ is as real a companion and Lord in a busy life of everyday living in the heart of the financial district as He is when one is preaching His Word or worshipping Him," asserted a Wall Street executive. The store manager called "Jesus Christ [the] Chairman of the Board . . . [and] the great conciliator in labor troubles." An executive and an industrialist used similar clichés: "No investment yields so sure returns as a life committed to the Lord," and "Eternal assets can never by wiped out." Although the men were uniformly white-collar or upper management, the accompanying text tried to flatten the differences between the pamphlet's subjects and its implicitly male readers. "These men have not dealt in platitudes," Olson (the most likely editor) emphasized. "The truths about which they have spoken are as explicable to the illiterate street hawker as they are to the bank president." With that, he launched into John 3:17–18: "For God sent not His son into the world to condemn the world; but that the world through Him might be saved. He that believeth on Him is not condemned." All fourteen businessmen's narratives built up to an altar call.[41]

As editor of *The King's Business*, BIOLA's monthly magazine, Rood championed the expanding CBMC as "The Ministry of Laymen" and "The Pew Speaking to the Pulpit." Ministers routinely complained that laymen did not do their fair share of church work, and now the CBMC was taking action. Noting that the 1936 annual CBMC rally drew eleven thousand people to Chicago Coliseum, Rood called "this continuous campaign in Chicago . . . one of the most significant and far-reaching evangelistic movements in America today." The new Seattle CBMC was already holding noon meetings and radio broadcasts five days a week in the Metropolitan Theater.[42] In March, the San Francisco CBMC invited Rood to speak at its first week-long revival. *The King's Business* reprinted Arnold Grunigen's closing address to show "what is in the minds of Christian Laymen." Grunigen was not one to hold back. He sneered at businessmen "sitting demurely in a church pew Sunday morning, if the weather is bad, so they can't play golf." He attacked ministers in all denominations for the "excess program machinery and ineffectual whirring of wheels" that "the business world" would not tolerate. His assault on modernism would have done Mordecai Ham proud. Movies, book reviews, "politics, reform, civic betterment, pacifism, prohibition, and cleaning up a sin-sick world had no place in sermons or Sunday Schools." "Put first things first. Preach the Word, convict of sin, present the Saviour; and red-blooded men who read the papers and know the world is bruised, battered, and bewildered will accept Christ, one by one." He ended by echoing Moody's famous statement that God had put him in a lifeboat to save as many as possible from the "wrecked vessel" of the world.[43] If the church did not change, Grunigen informed clergy, "the laymen will run the life boats and you can run the hulk."[44]

NETWORKING FOR JESUS

Publicity in *The King's Business, Moody Bible Institute Monthly,* and other national evangelical publications was one way to build the CBMC movement. Personal connections among businessmen, or businessmen and clergy such as Rood, mattered still more. If Arnold Grunigen sounded remarkably like R. G. LeTourneau—contemptuous of effete do-gooders who alienated "red-blooded me" from the church, exasperated at organized religions lack of business sense, and an electrifying preacher who made a point of identifying with the pew rather than the pulpit—it may have been because they shared the same lay-centered Plymouth Brethren upbringing.

More than that, they once shared a home. The Grunigens were the family with whom nineteen-year-old LeTourneau boarded in San Francisco. LeTourneau and Arnold were about the same age, with the same intelligence, charisma, and hardscrabble ambition. Just as LeTourneau had dropped out of school at thirteen to use his bulk for manual labor, the blond, baby-faced Grunigen dropped out at fifteen to become an investment bank president's protégé. During the 1920s and 1930s, he became a regional manager and transferred to a more prestigious national bank with headquarters in New York as well as San Francisco. Over the same period, Grunigen participated in weekly street evangelism; served as an elder and a deacon at his church, where he also taught the men's Bible study; and was president of the men's club. At the age of thirty-five he became the youngest president of the Mount Hermon Association, a Christian campground where Evelyn LeTourneau taught poor children Sunday school.[45] When R. G. LeTourneau moved to Peoria in 1935, within the Chicago

CBMC's orbit, it was Grunigen who piqued LeTourneau's interest in the group that professed what the industrialist had been saying for years: that religion and business were intertwined.[46]

In 1938, the five CBMCs—Chicago, Seattle, San Francisco, Los Angeles (organized by Rood and Grunigen), and New York—met at the La Salle Hotel in Chicago to from the Christian Business Men's Committee International. The CBMCI would link local CBMCs and coordinate large-scale projects. It would serve as an administrative agency without the centralized authority that conservative evangelical businessmen associated with Catholicism on one hand and the New Deal on the other. The 150 men at the meeting did insist that CBMC members, whatever their denominations, affirm a common set of evangelical beliefs. They approved a nine-point doctrinal statement that a historian distilled to the following: "(1) inspiration of the Scriptures; (2) [belief in the] Trinity; (3) virgin birth; (4) man's sinful nature; (5) death of Christ; (6) His Resurrection; (7) His premillennial return; (8) new birth through faith in Christ, and (9) everlasting punishment of the lost." Only the seventh point, premillennialism, proved controversial. Not all fundamentalists agreed with the eschatological timeline that led to the Rapture, and demanding adherence to a debatable creed ran counter to the CBMCI's lowest common denominator of inclusiveness. In a typical compromise between principle and pragmatism, the convention agreed to welcome nonpremillennialists into almost every aspect of the CBMCI as associate members, though without the right to vote.[47] The conference also reiterated the movement's single-minded focus on evangelism. Prayer, Bible study, and training in "techniques for witnessing" were part of the convention program. Delegates held street meetings throughout downtown Chicago, crowding the radio schedule with live broadcasts.[48]

Finally, the delegates chose the CBMCI's executive committee. A. H. Leaman was now a full-time evangelist, so Chicago chair C. B. Hedstrom became the international chair.[49] LeTourneau was vice chair, Grunigen, secretary, while Dr. N. A. Jepson, a chiropractor who organized the CBMC in Seattle, served as treasurer. The fifth member of the committee, Charles Gremmels, held no official position, but like LeTourneau and Grunigen, he represented national industry and finance. The founder of the New York City CBMC, Gremmels ran a shipping corporation and later established the meaningfully name Providential Realty and Investing Company.[50] Born in a tenement to evangelical parents, he began working at a grocery store when he was twelve. At fifteen, he was saved at the Bowery Mission for the poor. He found his way to the Fulton Street noon prayer meetings, a remnant of the 1857–58 Businessman's Revival, which he would attend for the rest of his life. When his first employer ordered him to work on Sundays, Gremmels quit and found a job at a ship broker's office, where his career began. His religious activities expanded with his success in shipping: fund-raising from missionaries, child evangelism, the Christian Association for the Blind. He joined the Episcopalian Brotherhood of St. Andrew, founded in 1883 to minister to men and boys, and earned a "laymen's license" to preach in the church. He was the president of his county's Gideon camp. His leisure pastimes included golf, fishing, and handing out tracts.[51]

Many scholars have described American religion and capitalism as mutually reinforcing. Each, in its ideal form, rewards competition, innovation, and niche or mass appeal in an ever-changing marketplace. The first CBMCI executive committee comprised a generational cohort that not only embodied this relationship but embraced religious and political conservatism as essential brakes on the forward motion in which they thrived.[52] The "incorporation of America" between the 1870s and 1890s, when all five men were born, encouraged nostalgia for a purportedly simpler and more localized past among protestors and supporters alike. The labor and populist movements pitted the paper riches of corporate shareholders against the producerist virtues of vanishing small farms, family businesses, sole proprietorships, and artisanal trades.[53] William Jennings Bryan, the 1896 Democratic presidential candidate who would represent fundamentalists at the Scopes Trial, spoke for many who objected to the centralization of wealth. "[T]he merchant at the crossroads store" and "the farmer who . . . toils all day," he said, were as much businessmen "as the merchant of New York" and "the man who goes upon the board of trade and bets on the price of grain."[54] In contrast with Bryan's voters, traveling salesmen such as the Gideons belonged to a category of workers with more to gain than to lose from capitalism's new structures. Neither producing the goods they sold nor owning their own labor, the "nation of clerks" faced charges of servility to upper management, functional interchangeability, and physical enervation from a life in offices and trains. Next to rugged farmers and muscular self-starters, which cultural critics sentimentalized more floridly the more anachronistic they became, traveling salesmen bearing Bibles looked emasculated. Nevertheless, by 1938, salesmen, clerks, middle managers, and even hands-on industrialists like LeTourneau—business owners who controlled exponentially smaller units of production than the era's tycoons—formed a middle-class backbone for corporate capitalism.[55]

With no sense of contradiction, these middlemen of the corporate economy shared critics' nostalgia for simpler and more virtuous times, which evangelicals articulated in the familiar language of revivalism. The Gideons, the CBMCI, and their southern counterparts in the BMEC still believed in the producerist ethos, and for good reason. Their leaders came of age during the uneven and unfinished transition from economic localism to economic nationalism. For example, like most young men of their generation, the CBMCI executive committee members—Jepson excluded—went to work without finishing high school. States began trying to raise educational levels with the next age cohort, born around 1900, because reading, writing, and arithmetic were becoming essential middle-class job skills.[56] LeTourneau was acutely aware of the shift in his interactions with younger businessmen. Terrified of public speaking until his debut at the Peoria Chamber of Commerce, he never forgot the critic who proposed that he "hire a graduate of kindergarten to edit his column" in the company magazine *NOW*.[57] The CBMCI men identified with the older economy in other ways. Hedstrom was an immigrant who had made good. LeTourneau's first enterprise was a family farm, and he apprenticed as an ironworker a few years before state and federal governments began linking apprenticeship to educational achievement.[58] Partly because they considered themselves self-taught, and partly because they viewed every human endeavor under the microscope of a personal relationship with a just God, the committeemen were economic individualists. The enemy behind the Depression and the cultural side effects of capitalism—hedonistic consumption, the liquor trade, commodified sexuality—was not incorporation but infidelity. Blaming disaster on personal or collective faithlessness, they poured their hopes for a better society into individual conversions and national revival.

LeTourneau, Grunigen, Hedstrom, Jepson, and Gremmels bridged both the pre- and postcorporate economy and the transition from nineteenth-century evangelical power to twentieth-century evangelical or fundamentalist marginalization. They were children when William Jennings Bryan (who, in their minds, was theologically if not completely politically sound) ran for president on a major party ticket. They were adolescents or young men in 1914, when A. H. Leaman saw Billy Sunday and came to mourn his revivals as a symbol of crumbling consensus. Having lived in both worlds, they missed the Christian America that they believed had nurtured self-made—rather, God-made—men like themselves. In 1938, the CBMCI's leaders were such partisans of corporate capitalism that they defended it against the New Deal. Yet they longed for conservative Protestants to unite around a God who did business the old-fashioned way—one on one with a verbal contract. The nineteenth-century revivalistic tradition taught that Christianity's essential truths, spelled out in the CBMCI's nine-point platform, transcended denominational affiliations. The innovative (and negotiable) doctrine of premillennialism reinforced this ecumenism by arguing that the "true church" was scattered among hypocrites and heretics in all churches.[59] Nor were evangelical businessmen alone in their nostalgia for a white, hegemonic Protestant past. The Ku Klux Klan and many liberal Protestants scapegoated Catholics and immigrants in the same language from a similar sense of loss.[60] Adding the "I" to CBMC confidently forecasted a large market for yet another businessmen's revival.

RALLYING THE SOUTHLAND

Curiously enough, for all of its forecasting of a worldwide surge, the Southland, as Business Men's Evangelistic Club leaders referred to their region, was conspicuously absent from the CBMCI's map.[61] Indeed, the two evangelical businessmen's organizations took little notice of each other until LeTourneau moved to Toccoa Falls later in 1938. In addition to the sectional political and economic differences that LeTourneau was far from the first Yankee transplant to encounter, white American Protestantism divided at the Mason-Dixon line. Baptists, Presbyterians, and (until 1939) Methodists worshiped in separate northern and southern denominations that split in the mid-nineteenth century over slavery and the Civil War. In each case, the South "seceded" from its northern ecclesiastical oppressor, while the North found no compromise that would make slavery compatible with church union.[62] Each denomination had tried at different times to reunite with its sibling, but the Methodists were the first to succeed—in 1939, ninety-five years after the schism.[63] The movie release of *Gone with the Wind* the same year showed how much white northerners and southerners had sentimentally reunited, not least over the necessity of black subjugation.[64]

Still, competing sectional narratives formed a barrier to religious cooperation, and evangelical businessmen's groups were no exception. The CBMCI did not imaginatively inhabit a "Northland," but "America," subdivided into the Midwest, New England, and the West, with the South as something of an afterthought. Conversely, the BMEC tended to think of the Southland as "America" and the North as a spiritual cesspool, notwithstanding northern supporters, crossover southern evangelists, and truly national hubs such as Billy Sunday's base in Winona Lake, Indiana.[65] In October 1936, for example, a relocated BMEC leader from Tennessee organized a chapter in Columbus, Ohio. "This offers a splendid opportunity," BMEC newsletter *Christian Workers* enthused, "as so little work of this nature is being done in this section of the country."[66] The missionary tone overlooked not only the CBMCI but also the Gideons, whom the BMEC knew well.[67] Though predominantly midwestern, the traveling salesmen with hotel Bibles made inroads in the South as early as 1913. There were men active in both groups. Within months of the BMEC's imagined conquest of Columbus, the Gideons would elect their first southern president.[68] Yet they were invisible to the BMEC in Ohio.

The November 1936 issue of *Christian Workers* encapsulated the BMEC's ambivalent interregionalism. "President Hargraves Visits North," the front page announced. Among other appointments, BMEC president Boyd Hargraves met with evangelical lawyer James Bennett; the article failed to note Bennett's leadership in the New York City CBMC, suggesting another missed connection. A New Jersey Sunday school group, "Everyman's Bible Class," went so far as to propose "a nation-wide organization of Christian Laymen's Evangelistic Clubs." Overall, however, Hargraves was "disappointed" with the trip, going home with no firm plans and his regional stereotypes intact, if not exacerbated. "The Christian men and women in our Southland have taken the church for granted," he warned. "We found it when we came here and have indulged in a dangerous assumption that nothing could happen." Evangelical churches with "empty pews," however, proved that "something is happening." Not far from these churches and New York pulpits where modernists questioned the divinity of Christ, the self-anointed Father Divine—black, charismatic, wildly unorthodox—packed in crowds. Hargraves sat through a boisterous six-hour service, "the aisles packed with human beings like sardines in a can," and had to exit by fire escape. The lesson was clear: a short distance separated genteel modernism from racial and political "fanatic[ism]." During the service, Father Divine's "negro lawyer" even reminded the black and white worshipers to register to vote. Hargraves concluded that "no more imperative challenge" faced southern Christians than the "demand for a purely social service program" instead of the gospel.[69]

An editorial in the next issue by a southern Methodist bishop struck a protopopulist note in a markedly shriller key. "United States is a Money Mad Nation" W. A. Chandler seethed in a jumble of timeworn accusations that all pointed North. "The usual raids upon the Federal Treasury, with increased numbers and added zeal, are operating at Washington," he said of the New Deal. "If this money-madness is not checked it will eventually pull down our governmental structure as well as pollute the lives of individuals." Certain individuals were already polluted: "the men who have amassed vast fortunes." They "inflame all the people with the evil malady of greed and self-indulgence. No nation has ever perished on account of its poverty." What really enraged him, though, was the media conspiracy to attack the South, the only part of America that still clung to values higher than money. He meant lynching. Northern "homicides . . . for money and money only" were far more monstrous than southern "vengeance . . . for the most repulsive offenses," and the former outnumbered the latter. Chandler's sectionalized Christians had no need of the social service programs that so alarmed Hargraves. "The greatest peril of the American nation is its continuous and abounding prosperity."[70] As delusional as this tirade might have sounded in 1936, it might also have sounded hopeful. Father Divine promised that material goods "come automatically" in return for "service gratis for the common good of humanity."[71] R. G. LeTourneau had his partnership with God. Neither desperately poor nor plutocrats, subscribers to *Christian Workers* had more reason than most to hope that faith would yield material rewards—and to fear becoming "money mad."

The same issue told readers that an unnamed manufacturer had summoned BMEC national field secretary Willis Haymaker to Peoria "twice in recent weeks for important conferences."[72] Haymaker, the son of Presbyterian missionaries, was born in 1895 and grew up in Winona Lake, Indiana. He became the campaign director and advance man for a star-studded roster of traveling evangelists, including Gipsy Smith, a British preacher who frequently crisscrossed America (the South especially), and Bob Jones Sr., a southern revivalist who commanded a national audience.[73] LeTourneau, it appeared, wanted an advance man of his own. The Peoria plant was a year old, and he may already have been contemplating expansion to Toccoa Falls or somewhere like it.[74] Haymaker obliged with a fulsome and revealing article entitled "Big Business and the Real Gospel."[75]

Haymaker was dazzled by the visibility of conservative evangelical culture in LeTourneau's factory. The soon-to-be standard dedication ceremony for a new building addition featured a well-known midwestern evangelist and netted fifty employee converts. In another preview of future institutional practices, LeTourneau arm-twisted a visiting evangelist at his church into leading a week of noon shop meetings. Tract racks stood beneath every time clock; a man in the accounting department sold Bibles; BIOLA graduates comprised the King's Business Quartet. One singer, a foreman who converted eleven of his twelve subordinates, described LeTourneau, Inc., as "a great opportunity for any young Christian." LeTourneau added that it was a terrible opportunity for any young communist. "In these days of Bolshevism and Red agitation," he said, "our modern industries need young men with a high purpose in life." He was more candid than usual about the role of religion in his hiring practices. Many of the workers were in their early twenties, because young men, in addition to being quick learners, "have a life before them and if won for Christ they can spend a life in service for Him." Many were already evangelical, and LeTourneau culled applicants from their social networks, requiring all potential hires to be "recommended by someone whom we know personally."[76] Haymaker told BMEC readers that proof lay in the profits. "[W]hen you hear that there are 150 agencies in the United States and nearly 200 in foreign countries selling LeTourneau equipment, you come to the only conclusion—this business is being honored by God." Almost in the same breath, he applauded LeTourneau for treating success as a mere "byproduct" of faith. For both men, the line between product and by-product was none too clear.[77]

Haymaker was one of four BMEC leaders whose contact with LeTourneau would catalyze interregional cooperation with the CBMCI after the industrialist moved to Toccoa Falls in 1938. All four had deep roots in businessmen's evangelism. BMEC president Hargraves, a Chattanooga lawyer, was so committed to the organization that he redoubled his efforts to build clubs around the South when the Depression struck.[78] "These troublesome times have caused a great deal of grief to all our clients," he told Charlotte's Vernon Patterson. "My folks sometimes think that I am practicing law as a side issue and [that] I am devoting most of my time to the National Association."[79] The tepid outcome of his 1936 trip north did not shake his commitment to growth. Patterson, for his part, dominated the North Carolina branch of the BMEC and took important administrative roles in the headquarters. He spent his entire career as a salesman for a company that produced business forms, confidently personifying the nation of clerks. "Why should not plans be as systematically laid to cover a given territory with the gospel message as are laid for coverage of a territory in the sale of merchandise?" Patterson asked in a *Christian Workers* essay listing the evangelistic advantages of laymen over clergy. Laymen had "freedom of action in spiritual matters," "access to the masses," and the ability to help "ordinary men in business against the hard knocks of the old world." Any revival they organized would be bigger than "a church membership campaign" and avoid becoming "an extremely emotional series of meetings" or a "bitter religious fight."[80] Finally, there was Rolan

Stoker, the executive secretary of the Georgia BMEC and on LeTourneau's payroll. The ex-dentist was developing a conference center to attract evangelical visitors and dollars to Toccoa Falls.

In August 1940, CBMCI representatives came as guests to the BMEC's annual convention, the inaugural event at LeTourneau and Stoker's deceptively idyllic retreat. The centerpiece was a man-made lake—made by LeTourneau employees—that sheltered visitors from the sights and sounds of the industrial plants only a few miles away. "Motor boating, and swimming and tennis are popular pastimes with the many people who visit this exciting vacation-land," the promotional literature enthused.[81] LeTourneau intended his country club to be a white-collar fundamentalist crossroads, and southerners, significantly, took the first step. The BMEC invited the CBMCI to discuss Vernon Patterson's proposal for a new and jointly administered revivalist organization.[82] To ensure northern attendance, LeTourneau promised local and national CBMCI leaders a free trip, garnering participants from New York to the Pacific coast.[83] The four hundred conferencegoers concurred that the "world crisis"—the encroaching European war, which the CBMCI's Canadians had been fighting for almost a year—was a critical time to rouse unreached laymen and funnel them into their geographically appropriate parent group.[84] "We [in the BMEC] are ready now to throw the weight of our Association back of a great nationwide or world-wide program of vital evangelism," Haymaker said. "[W]e are proud to cooperate in any sound, sane, constructive, Christ-centered and Spirit-led movement that has for its purpose the winning of lost men and women for Christ."[85] The CBMCI anticipated that "these interchanges of counsel . . . will tend to strengthen the work of both organizations."[86] Bringing the inchoate collaboration down to earth, they decided, would require another meeting and intensive prayer for the Holy Spirit's guidance.

Publicity for the "Emergency Called Conference of Business and Professional Men" went out in October. The featured Bible verse, 2 Chronicles 7:14, was the motto of generations of revivalists: "[I]f my people, who are called by my name, will humble themselves and pray and seek my face and turn from their wicked ways, then will I hear from heaven and will forgive their sin and will heal their land."[87] The familiar verse mapped out a familiar revivalist agenda, despite the seeming immediacy of "God's Call to Laymen in the Present Spiritual Emergency." The hundred men who gathered a few weeks later in Chicago prayed "for a great spiritual awakening and the evangelization of the world in the shortest possible time." They hammered out the details of ecumenical cooperation, in this case, the BMEC-CBMCI rapprochement. Both groups' boards were on hand to develop policies and procedures for "how the various laymen's organizations [can] cooperate most effectively . . . and the place and sphere of each."[88] Arnold Grunigen had originally envisioned "a carefully selected list" of invitees representing "the truly evangelical, evangelistic forces" in North America.[89] The self-selected participants, with Grunigen's approval, took his elitism a familiar step further. All evangelical laymen were experts on religious truth. The problem was that too few sold their faith the way they sold their products, and buyers, lacking guidance, were going elsewhere.

In fact, the conference attendees' heightened sense of a world in danger went with, not against, the cultural tide. The impulse that propelled evangelical businessmen to join forces placed them in a broad current of American nationalism in the face of encroaching world war. Evangelicals implicated the usual suspects, such as theological modernism, drinking, and disrespecting the Sabbath, in the "world crisis." Everyday vice, however, was not why *Christian Workers* editorialized at the end of 1940, "Present conditions compel Christian men to think seriously and act quickly."[90] In establishing the Christian Laymen's Crusade as a clearinghouse to support existing evangelical businessmen's groups, the Chicago meeting made the war the subtext of bureaucracy. The CLC's motto, "for the salvation of souls and a stronger fellowship among Christian men," blandly summarized what the BMEC and CBMCI wanted from a dually aligned organization. The logo, on the other hand, depicted "crusade" literally. Three medieval crosses, not standard Protestant fare, surrounded a winged shield, sword, and helmet. These images in turn referenced an instantly recognizable biblical verse describing the "armor of God." Metaphorical weapons of faith could fight against "principalities, against powers, against rulers of the darkness of this world, against spiritual wickedness in high places."[91] In 1940, however, the weapons were real, as LeTourneau, who was manufacturing them, well knew. The British endured relentless air attacks after the Royal Navy had barely escaped at Dunkirk. France signed an armistice with the Nazis. Mussolini's Italy entered the war with Germany and Japan and expanded the battlefield to Africa. Roosevelt was pushing as hard as he could to intervene, and isolationism was losing traction in public opinion.

As much as this context shaped the CLC, it did not change the work at hand. "[T]hese laymen [have] a consciousness of the great spiritual poverty of a world torn by the forces of hate and destruction," another early newsletter read. "It [is] their conviction that the Christian laymen of America [hold] the key to the solution of this great problem" by tackling the existential crisis with sound business methods and frank, businesslike messages.[92] First, the group needed a board of directors. LeTourneau, who headed the CBMCI and the Gideons, agreed to serve as chairman if Patterson, the president, shouldered most of the executive responsibilities.[93] The rest of the hierarchy skewed north, because the headquarters stayed in Chicago. Vice chair Paul Fischer, treasurer Charles Gremmels, and member at large Grunigen came from the CBMCI. William Bond, a realtor from Washington, DC, joined Patterson from the BMEC. Andrew Wyzenbeek, the vice president of the Gideons, came on to represent the traveling salesmen, at last making ties among the three groups official.[94]

Second, the CLC needed a portfolio. The original plan, sponsoring rallies in towns with BMECs or CBMCIs to boost membership in one or the other, seemed too narrow to maximize businessmen's interest in conservative evangelical causes. The board decided that the CLC would advertise other laymen's groups as well. It would act solely as a catalyst for existing efforts, establishing "no local committees or membership" to avoid even the appearance of competition. As with its parent groups, the CLC's militant emphasis on laymen by no means precluded cooperation with clergy, whose support was essential for legitimacy. Rally speakers would stress their desire to "back up their pastors, but also to give a personal testimony of the power of the Gospel in their daily [business] contacts."[95]

Third, the CLC needed a full-time rally director and a list of seasoned speakers to fire up audiences for the testimonies of local businessmen. C. B. Nordland, a Baptist minister from the Chicago suburbs with a history of energizing laymen, accepted the position. Before he could start, Patterson scheduled preliminary events in Raleigh, Charlotte, Asheville, Philadelphia, Pittsburgh, Boston, and Buffalo. For the ebullient Patterson, there was no time to lose. God, he implied, was not waiting for the "evangelization of the world in this generation" but foreshortening the task. "I look forward in faith to a great work leading to a nation-wide spiritual awakening in the coming year," Patterson asserted. If America were God's redeemer nation, as evangelicals had long believed, the other nations would be next, with laymen at the helm. Patterson's North Carolina contacts included the president of Pan-American Bus Lines, the host of the BMEC's daily devotional show ("said to reach 100,000 or more every morning," which was unlikely, but inspiring), and a "[r]ural letter carrier" who "'murders the King's English,' but [is a] great soul winner."[96] This short list, from a major player in the travel industry to a small-town mailman, showed how the common cause of lay evangelism relaxed normal business hierarchies. It also reiterated how much politically and religiously conservative businessmen banded together against a regime that seemed to threaten their liberties on both counts.[97]

REDEEMING THE CLASSROOM, PREPARING FOR WAR

One particularly important field of battle on which these businessmen could easily band together, and around which they could fight in the name of their liberties, in opposition to what they deemed a socialist-leaning, secular-inclined regime, was education. Schoolhouse concerns as much as (and in tandem with) national security issues became their rallying cry.

The reading of a Protestant Bible in public schools, a church-state battleground since the 1830s, greatly concerned the CLC. Historically part of a larger power struggle between Protestants and Catholics, in the twentieth century the King James Version also became a weapon in the evangelical attack on evolution. For example, at the 1925 Scopes Trial, Clarence Darrow unsuccessfully attacked a Tennessee law banning public schools from teaching "any theory that denies the story of the Divine Creation of man as taught in the Bible."[98] Much more was at stake than competing versions of human origins. Antievolutionists such as William Jennings Bryan saw Darwinism as a bomb lobbed not just at God but at the social contract. Many progressives extrapolated the biological inevitability of race and class hierarchies from "the survival of the fittest" (not Darwin's phrase, but at the time, convincingly attributable to his philosophy). Evangelical businessmen also supported white supremacy and all but endorsed "survival of the fittest" economics; survival of the faithful, as preached by the likes of LeTourneau, was very close kin. However, along with a more diverse array of Americans than fellow fundamentalists alone—especially during World War I, when evolution took on unpatriotic, Nietzschean overtones—they saw nihilism in the logic that men and women were animals. Their solution to this new threat was the same one they always offered: Protestant scripture, especially for the young and vulnerable. Between 1913 and 1930, ten northern and southern states bucked a trend toward less specific "moral education" by legislating Bible reading as the highest form of character building.[99]

Z. Park McCallie, who ran a prestigious boys' academy in Chattanooga, Tennessee, was one of these educators. He had been on the CLC committee at Toccoa Falls, and Patterson wanted him to be a rally speaker. In 1922, McCallie designed a clever program to teach the Bible in public schools with private money. The YMCA, PTA, and church members raised the funds, designed the curriculum, and hired the teachers. A Chattanooga school board member described the elective class as a "free gift," and boards throughout the county clamored to implement it. (As of 2009, the "McCallie Plan" is still in effect in Hamilton County, Tennessee.) One selling point was its apparent intra-Protestant neutrality. Although McCallie believed that "let[ting] the Bible speak for itself" would prevent doctrinal disputes, he told instructors to avoid "sectarian or denominational terms." They should refer students with questions about their own traditions to their pastors, on the ecumenical assumption that next to the truth of the Bible and the saving grace of Christ, differences were merely details.[100]

LeTourneau became caught up in the push to sacralize the schools as evangelicals made a case for public veneration of the Bible as a matter of national security. In 1937, the annual conference of the Gideons voted unanimously to "extend [their] ministry to include the placing of a Bible in every [school] room in the United States, the same to be read daily." The association had surveyed schools in the states that required daily Bible reading and discovered low compliance, partly because a large number of classrooms lacked Bibles.[101] Like McCallie, the Gideons saw a public problem with a private solution, albeit less intensive (and expensive) than designing a full-blown course. The campaign for universal access was in full swing when LeTourneau won the presidency of the Gideons in 1940. In his acceptance speech, LeTourneau wove schoolchildren's scriptures into a laymen's call to arms. "Is not the hour overdue for the mobilization of the Christian forces of the world?" he shouted. "Should not the battalions of believers marshall their forces?" He called "put[ting] the Bible in the schools, where it is needed most of all . . . our big task today." The word of God was "the backbone of our civilization," and giving it to the next generation should be every Gideon's top priority. "If each one of us would ask God what He wanted us to do, and if we would do it, we'd get these Bibles into the schools 'in nothing flat.'" In sum, "[t]he need of the nations is a Blitzkrieg of the Bible."[102]

In January 1941, the Gideons made their largest ever one-time donation: twenty thousand Bibles for Georgia public schools. At the Atlanta Civic Center's dedication ceremony, LeTourneau stood in front of an eighteen-foot cross his employees constructed of steel and 1,380 Gideon Bibles, red spines showing. "There's enough power in one page of one of these Bibles to stop Hitler's army," he said.[103] A *Christian Workers* contributor went on to predict that schools without Bibles would teach "pure, unadulterated Bolshevism," training "an army" of youth to "trampl[e] the Stars and Stripes under their feet."[104]

During the year leading up to Pearl Harbor, revival fever accelerated. Conservative evangelicals prayed with equal fervor to stop the war from coming to America and for America to get right with God before it inevitably came. "Sure, we're going to make the world safe for democracy again," a critic of Roosevelt's "war hysteria" scoffed in *Moody Monthly*. "The rights of the individual are to be upheld by uprooting him and placing him in army camps, maiming and killing him, and loading the rest with unbearable taxes." The author advised American Christians to focus on Satan, the real enemy. "Christ has won some into the bomb shelter of His keeping," and the church must rise up "to *offensive* battle for the Lord!"[105] Meanwhile, the journal's editors blasted "modernistic theologians," "Russianized liberals," and "political appeasers" as "a Lilliputian leadership . . . [who] have ignored that Book which makes for character and moral statue." The editors argued that they were "not talking politics," because there were no political solutions. "America and Canada and England need God desperately, and far more than they need men and munitions. . . . Revival is the shortest cut possible to victory and safety."[106]

The BMEC was more optimistic about the state of America's soul. A *Christian Workers* article on "Christian Men in High Office" singled out five governors (four from the South, one from Washington State) whose piety, the writer assumed, spoke well of their voters and must have a trickle-down effect on the rest of the citizenry.[107] At the BMEC's August 1941 annual conference, LeTourneau gave tours of the Toccoa Falls plant, "now helping Uncle Sam's defense program."[108] LeTourneau's new partnership with the government, in the context of what he saw as a religious war for the survival of Christianity and democracy, altered his antistatist political tone. "A friend of mine is president of a 50 million dollar corporation and Washington said, 'We need you.' So he dropped his work and went to Washington for a dollar a year," as was the custom for businessmen who served as ostensibly disinterested government consultants.[109] LeTourneau depicted his friend's decision to move to a different arena of power as self-sacrifice for the greater good, telling the BMEC, "God is calling us . . . to a bigger job than that." Evangelical laymen needed to keep America on God's side in the crusade against atheistic totalitarianism. According to the BMEC national secretary, "America's first line of defense is not the power of the army or navy . . . but it rests upon the Word of God and prayer and personal testimony." Another speaker found a military metaphor for the division of labor between clergy and laymen. "Our preachers preach for years but the laymen must get out and get others to accept Christ. It makes me think of the air force bombing a position for a long time but the privates must go in and take possession."[110] Whether the specialists really outranked the grunts in this image was ambiguous, but the take-home message was clear. Evangelical businessmen must redouble their soul-winning efforts, because God would not let Christian soldiers lose.

When Japan attacked Pearl Harbor on December 7, 1941, a dollar-a-year man in the CBMCI and the Gideons was stationed on the base. Charlie Pietsch, a former missionary to Japan and the son of another prominent CBMCI member, received authorization in the spring to distribute fifty thousand New Testaments with Psalms and Proverbs. The navy chief chaplain also made Pietsch the first-ever layman to conduct officially sanctioned religious services aboard ship. The Gideons were low on money and skeptical of the testament project, so Pietsch, a real estate agent whose job for the administration was chairing the Hawaii Housing Authority, paid for the first ten thousand himself. He passed many of them out while leading Easter services on battle cruisers. The Gideons found a way to subsidize the rest, having adopted a new motto for reaching servicemen and women: "Arm them with the Gospel too." After December 7, the group could not help see Japan's choice of targets as providential. Surely some of the dead at Pearl Harbor had found God through Pietsch's preaching or the inescapable testaments. More importantly, surely so had some of the living.

After the United States entered the war, the government allowed the Gideons to distribute scriptures to the entire armed forces. Pietsch continued to exploit his Washington ties. One unlikely ally was Donald Nelson—president of Sears and Roebuck, dollar-a-year head of the War Production Board, and one of Roosevelt's most prominent corporate supporters during the New Deal. Pietsch helped him open a Sears in Honolulu. Nelson expressed his gratitude by ensuring that the Gideons had a steady supply of printing paper throughout the war, despite the rationing it was his responsibility to enforce. A 1943 photo shows Pietsch ceremonially giving a Gideon testament to Vice President Henry Wallace. Roosevelt and every member of Congress received one as well.[111] For Wallace, it was one of countless photo ops. For Pietsch and his business and religious networks, it was a sign that conservative evangelicals had entered the halls of power.

Pietsch's World War II evangelism would highlight how wartime emotions and government recognition further transformed evangelical businessmen's groups—in concert with other evangelicals and conservatives—from critics to watchful cheerleaders of American politics and culture.[112] The BMEC, whose primary loyalty was about to shift from the "Southland" to the nation, would further exemplify white evangelicalism's patriotic self-righteousness tempered with self-abasement. "President Roosevelt Appreciates Prayers," *Christian Workers* announced with palpable pleasure in 1942. The BMEC was waging a campaign against liquor in the armed forces and had sent the president a resolution to that effect.[113] The president's reply avoided the subject but used the language of spiritual warfare to suggest affinity with its authors. He claimed "to be giving much consideration to things spiritual in this world of madness. It is truly a war for survival and our faith and prayers are a fundamental and essential part of this great conflict."[114]

On the other hand, in a widely circulated tirade called "Christ or Chaos," Rolan Stoker set out a doomsday scenario of ideological invasion and defeat. "The Hydro-headed [*sic*] Octopus of Unamericanism has wrapped its slimy arms around the very heart of America and is pouring into her veins . . . the venom of Atheism, communism, and every other godless, Christless, and hellish poison." Revival was the only cure. America must return to her place as "the watchman on the wall" (Ezekiel 3:17–21), guarding "the freedom of the pulpit, press, courts, and the sanctity of our homes."[115] An early 1940s Armistice Day prayer offered by the BMEC blended ambivalence and ambition: "America must come back to God if we are to win a permanent peace and be a world-leader." Revival was still necessary; America must come *back*. But the prayer struck a new, worldly note in defining God's reward for revival as geopolitical power.[116]

War

CHAPTER FOUR

The Wartime Vision of Laymen's Evangelism

The dominant post–Pearl Harbor impulse in an enlivened orb of Christian businessmen associations was indeed overwhelmingly geared to action—fierce and unwavering—on behalf of God and country. Any chastening by doomsday scenarios and decrying of wartime America's moral drift merely fed the overwhelming confidence among entrepreneurial evangelicals that the global struggle represented their new dispensation in God's unfolding history. Despite all the difficulties and setbacks of war, theirs was now the God-ordained time to marshal all resources—financial and otherwise—and shine a light of spiritual hope and cultural and political transformation on a planet consumed by Satan's destructive intentions.

Herbert Taylor tapped these sensibilities when he assembled allies at the Sherman Hotel in Chicago in February of 1942. Yes, the gathering was to celebrate past victories, and this they did, with hearty, spoken gratitude geared toward Taylor. But it was also to coordinate the Christian Workers Foundation's future agenda and inspire its biggest project yet: a stadium revival starring Los Angeles–based radio evangelist Charles Fuller. Fuller, a third-generation orange grower who had juggled business and the ministry before the agricultural depression pushed him into full-time religious broadcasting, was a star in California's vibrant fundamentalist scene.[1] Converted and later based in Hollywood, he felt God's call to preach, leaving the lucrative directorship of the Mutual Packing Association for intensive study at BIOLA. A year after his 1925 ordination as a Baptist, he established Calvary Church in the fast-growing town of Placentia. His orange groves enabled him to refuse a salary.

Like many evangelicals, Fuller was quick to recognize the potential of radio to create an imagined community of the faithful while using the conventions of the medium—music, crisp production, punchy messages—to lure unbelievers. He did his first religious broadcast in 1927 and resigned from Calvary Church in 1932 to preach from the airwaves full time.[2] Thanks to CWF advertising subsidies since 1940, Fuller had expanded his sunny, sentimental *Old Fashioned Revival Hour* across North America, making him one of the biggest names in radio. Appearing on 456 stations by 1942—almost double the number since the CWF began carrying national advertising in 1940—the *Old Fashioned Revival Hour* eclipsed other programs as America entered World War II.[3] Wright's laudatory 1940 biography, which Fuller sent to listeners and donors, added to Fuller's aura as an evangelical star who had broken through to the wider culture.[4]

Fuller had since proven his ability to pack stadiums, most recently with Wright's support in Boston, and was scheduled to appear in Washington, DC, and St. Louis. At the Sherman Hotel, Taylor proposed an October 1942 date for Chicago to give the assembled groups time to plan. Wright testified that Fuller's appearance at Boston Gardens, sponsored by a thousand churches, drew about twenty-eight thousand people and inspired pastors to bring Fuller's direct message of salvation into their own pulpits. "The typical remark was 'I am not much of a preacher, but I believe I could preach as good as that if I had the same thing to preach about.'" Assuming a trickle-down effect from clergy to congregation, Wright and Taylor proceeded to delegate responsibility. A nominating committee made up of two businessmen and three educators selected a general committee to take charge of the major planning. Chaired by Taylor, who would select the treasurer and finance committee director, with his secretary and right-hand man Bob Walker as secretary, the general committee effectively made the revival a CWF project. (Moody Bible Institute's Will Houghton accepted a symbolic vice chairmanship because, Taylor told him, "some Moody identification" would guarantee "more enthusiastic cooperation.")[5] Taylor's first action would be to write a "circular letter to pastors informing them of their appointment to the General Committee . . . [and] suggesting that each pastor should appoint a contact man." In other words, laymen would lure "fundamental" clergy to rally the faithful by sparing them most of the work.[6]

The nominating committee went on to name chairmen for committees on personal work, ushering, publicity, a volunteer choir, prayer meetings, and the cooperation of youth organizations. Businessmen and professionals led three of the six groups: the CBMCI's Frank Sheriff on personal work, or door-to-door evangelism; the Gideons' Robert Van Kampen on ushering; and newspaperman William McDermott on publicity. Personal work, or one-to-one evangelism, and ushering were such common businessmen's tasks for revivals that Taylor's advance notes assumed that the CBMCI, the Gideons, and the Gospel Fellowship Club would provide all the necessary manpower.[7] The meeting adjourned with a warning about the risk of staging a public spectacle that instead of Christianizing the city would only attract fellow believers. "The [Nominating] Committee further recommended that a strong drive be made to bring the unconverted into the Fuller Meetings to be held on October 4th." Fuller's own statistics showed why this needed to be said. The twenty-eight thousand attendees at Boston Gardens had produced all of one hundred new Christians, about average for urban revivals. The goal should be to bait a trap for the unsaved, not serve comfort food to believers.

Before Taylor and his Chicago team had the chance to bring Fuller to Chicago, World War II intervened. Taylor, Wright, and the committees rallied the ministers, took notes on Fuller's St. Louis and Washington meetings, began an advertising campaign, and even booked Chicago Stadium. Yet by late summer of 1942, gasoline and rubber rationing made Fuller's trip from Los Angeles to Chicago prohibitive. Less than two weeks before the September rally was scheduled, Taylor informed Wheaton College president V. Raymond Edman that Fuller was cancelling the rest of his 1942 commitments "[i]n light of the recommendation by the Government that mass meetings be postponed for the duration." The key word, for Taylor, was "postponed." He suggested that the planning committees should "remain inactive for the present" but be prepared to reconvene for "the great opportunity such a meeting would afford in bringing the Gospel of Jesus Christ to men and women throughout the Chicago area" and in enabling Christ's servants to spread his redemptive message far beyond the metropolis, even to the war front, and make the difficult days upon them "count for the Lord."[8] For Taylor, wartime did not come with the luxury of postponement or pause; on the contrary, it drove home in no uncertain and abstract terms, that the New Testament's Great Commission was an exigent mandate that called true Christians to absolute commitment and sacrifice in the here and now.

Taylor's impatience and determination amid a new age of trials were traits he shared with R. G. LeTourneau and the two men's peers during World War II. Starting in the momentous year of 1942, and with quickening intensity in the months that followed, individuals of Taylor and LeTourneau's ilk took full advantage of their government's mustering of their nation for battle with totalitarian Germany and Japan to acquire new leverage in their own private corporate sectors and mobilize their fellow devotees for what they considered and even more epic, universal battle with the forces of eternal darkness. Each of their professional careers experienced significant war-related boons; each of their ministries expanded accordingly, as did their influence within an emerging "new evangelical" movement. By war's end, and in the months that immediately followed the conflagration, both LeTourneau and Taylor would be widely heralded as God-fearing patriots, philanthropists, and "fundamental" believers of the highest order.

They would also be celebrated for their work in coordinating and inspiring their various overlapping guilds of corporate Christians. With their help, the Christian businessmen's groups that began to flourish in the 1930s spent the war years extending their authority in the pulpits and pews and boardrooms of America. These associations offered three major contributions to white evangelicalism. First, they stepped up efforts to forge a united front out of regional evangelical businessmen's networks—northern, midwestern, and western on one hand and southern on the other—that duplicated each other's work on parallel instead of intersecting tracks. While the northern CBMCI and southern BMEC struggled to work together, their attempts to cross regional lines contributed to evangelical nationalism during World War II. Sneeringly labeled parochial by their critics in the post-Scopes decade, by 1945 few cynics could joke too easily that evangelicals were a provincial bunch; the businessmen driving evangelicalism toward its new national and international potentials ensured this. Second, evangelical businessmen's groups, whose members profited from the defense industry, shifted from blanket antistatism during the New Deal to viewing the military-industrial complex as a godly arm of big government. In doing so, they helped cement what would become evangelicalism's long-term identification with American militarism.

Finally, both despite and because of their fierce Americanism, evangelical businessmen exuberantly promoted what Billy Graham's colleague Bob Pierce called the "world vision" of postwar evangelicalism.[9] For a window of time between World War II and the entrenchment of the Cold War, more countries were open to Americans bearing the gospel than ever before. The evangelization of the world in this generation looked to some like a matter of years, not decades, and businessmen's groups depicted themselves as soldiers on the front lines.[10]

BUILDING AN ARSENAL OF CHRISTIAN DEMOCRACY

Just a few weeks after evangelical businessmen congregated at the Sherman Hotel, newspaper headlines screamed of war and the business of war. In early April 1942, updates rippled from the front, warning of the enemy's productive might and America's need to start wielding its own fiscal muscle. According to one headline, the "Reds," as many Americans still called their Soviet allies, were "Stress[ing] Maximum Action and Production" from their socialized workforce.[11] Fear not, another suggested: Americans could outperform them—and more importantly, the Nazis—provided they start maximizing simple Yankee ingenuity. "U.S. 'Hustle' in Australia Builds Base in 12 Hours," the Associated Press bragged.[12]

Yet for all of their emphases on the business of war, these headlines drew to the surface a fundamental fact: that corporate-minded "Yankee ingenuity" was also a state-sponsored enterprise. Transnational "U.S. 'hustle'" in truth united the Roosevelt administration with previously hostile business sectors.[13] Because national survival depended on the military economy, conservative business interests accepted rationing, price controls, and other temporary regulations in exchange for long-term leverage against the New Deal.[14] Headlines more than hinted at private industry's formidable bargaining power: "Boeing Bombers Get Credit for Army Successes";[15] "[Official] Asks 'Commandos' to Spur Business . . . Stresses Need for Making Every Possible Weapon Now."[16] In this corporation-friendly climate, management was scoring political and public relations victories against labor. Overruling the National Labor Relations Board and foreshadowing bitter conflicts to come, the Supreme Court defined a "Strike Aboard Ship [As] Mutiny Even if It Is in Port," as one *New York Times* headline read.[17]

Striking workers were not the only enemy within, and the war's social transformations spilled beyond the sphere of government and business. Already tenuous lines between "public" and "private" life—politics versus the home, law versus personal liberty, male versus female—blurred almost to invisibility. Four months to the day after Pearl Harbor, the army forced the first Japanese and Japanese Americans from their San Francisco homes to an internment camp.[18] A group after Herbert Taylor's heart, the Golden Rule Foundation selected a heroine for the era of Rosie the Riveter: "American Mother of 42 Has 13 Children and Job."[19] Overseas, soldiers facing death practiced raw religion that no one could dismiss as women's, or womanly, affectation. "[Easter] Services on Bataan Most Impressive," the

New York Times wrote. As Japanese planes strafed the front lines, soldiers with guns at the ready admitted that this truncated outdoor communion was the first time they had attended church in years.[20]

Evangelical entrepreneurs thus found a window of remarkable opportunity in the early 1940s as the context of war, and their willingness to soften their antistatist stand, produced a partnership with Washington that would prove highly lucrative. Middling industrialists—Babbitts—of the evangelical world certainly took part in this networking with the White House and Pentagon, but so too did an emerging high echelon of Christian corporate players. Though much fewer in number, their roles would become increasingly significant as the World War II defense industry morphed into the sprawling Cold War industrial complex.

No one had more to gain from this wartime arrangement, or to offer conservative evangelicalism in the years that followed, than J. Howard Pew. Born into a staunch Presbyterian family, whose long-standing commitment to evangelical causes was strong, raised by a father whose livelihood was tied to the management of the family's independent oil company—Sun Oil Company (Sunoco)—Pew came honestly to his corporate, religious, and political priority. Pew had assumed control of Sunoco in 1912, after his father's retirement. Joining Howard in the head office was his younger brother, Joseph Pew Jr., who would serve as his right hand for the next three and a half decades, the entirety of Howard's presidency. Under Howard, the family-run Sunoco maintained its fiscal and religious conservatism but also became slightly more daring in its outlook. Between the 1910s and late 1940s, Howard, a Cornell-trained engineer, used aggressive international exploration and technological advancements to grow and shape it into a mid-major oil company. By the 1930s, Sunoco's combination of savvy marketing and creative manufacturing, along with its vital production base in Texas and expansive transportation infrastructure, made it a vital player in the industry.[21] By 1947, the year of his retirement, J. Howard Pew along with Sunoco's officials boasted that their boss had grown the business by "40 times" since his installation has CEO thirty-five years earlier.[22]

During this time, Pew also extended his company's reach into politics. Because of his family's deep antipathy toward Standard Oil and large, monopolistic corporations and ingrained suspicions of centralized government, the young Howard had internalized a potent antistatist politics. In the 1930s and 1940s, in a tone that matched his father's in the 1880s and 1890s, he railed against the oil industry's majors that wanted to increase regulations in order to temper fluctuations in pricing that came with overproduction. Fearful that small companies would succumb to large ones, which enjoyed economy of scale and price-setting abilities, Pew set out to democratize petroleum by helping a number of independent oil associations lobby for deregulated markets and local control. In this same vein, he and his brother, Joseph, a powerbroker in the Republican Party, played active roles in opposing the New Deal state. Willing, in this instance, to join hands with monopolistic types they opposed in the oil sector, the Pews helped populate the American Liberty League and stir up anti–New Deal sentiment.[23]

For all of their anti-Washington politicking during the Depression, the Pews' perspective changed during war. Indeed, Sunoco's most dramatic growth came at this very time, thanks to its propitious ties to the nation's capital. The company ledger bore proof of this auspicious bond. Under clouds of war, Sunoco's shipping company emerged as the nation's most prolific producer of oil tankers. Between Pearl Harbor and Japan's surrender, Sunoco built hundreds of freighters, car floats, and destroyers, and with one brush of the pen from Navy Secretary Frank Knox won a government contract for tankers worth $350,000,000. The Pews' refining ventures were just as lucrative. With its innovative cracking units working full blast, Sunoco produced the finest and largest quantity of aviation fuel in the land. By 1945 Pew could boast to secretary of the interior and Roosevelt's "Oil Czar" Harold Ickes that Sunoco's Marcus Hook refinery had blended its billionth gallon of aviation fuel for the armed forces, outpacing any competitor, including archnemesis Jersey Standard. All the while, Sunoco kept pressing for gains in extraction and distribution, privileged access to the "Big Inch" pipeline out of Texas, and political clout that came via the Pews' new proximity to Washington. Sunoco's annual operating income rose accordingly, from $131,500,000 in 1939 to $600,800,000 in 1944, leaving its executives primed for peacetime and a projected burst of corporate expansion.[24]

Meanwhile, thanks to Sunoco's inestimable role in national defense during World War II, Pew gained leverage in Washington, which he wielded on behalf of his corporate and political sectors. Between 1943 and 1952, as US oil companies looked to the Middle East for new supplies, the federal government and US oil's majors tried to iron out an Anglo-American petroleum agreement that would minimize the ability of British oil companies "to exclude American interests" from their territories and bring an "end to the restrictive provisions of the Red Line Agreement of 1928." Through international cooperation, American and British leaders and oil officials hoped to stabilize the process of exploration, extraction, and production in petroleum's hot zones. For smaller companies, the agreement smacked of collusion, something Pew stressed. He let Senate Foreign Relations Committee members know that the Anglo-American agreement was a "first step in . . . [a] plan for a super-state control covering the petroleum industry in all parts of the world." Pew helped kill this agreement—it would flounder in the late 1940s and die in 1952—and essentially ensure that an aggressively nationalist foreign policy, which in his mind best protected the interests of all oil companies, would become ensconced in the American Cold War outlook.[25]

In all of these political endeavors, Pew welcomed the role of watchdog on behalf of the bootstrap, laissez-faire, evangelical-minded entrepreneur, whom he believed embodied American values' purest form. "Nature has been bountiful in the supply of this resource, and we have barely scratched the surface," he charged when speaking out against stricter regulation of petroleum at home and abroad. Why quell individual drive in the present by "preserving supplies of petroleum for the use of generations yet unborn"? Echoing evangelicals' nonconformist pleas, he announced that he "didn't want a nurse for his business, nor did he want anyone else to have one." Pew did not want a "nurse" for his church either. Even as he joined forces with independent oilmen to fight centralizing forces in business and government, Pew also enlisted in conservative Protestantism's fight against the progressive tendencies of their liberal counterparts. He saw these fights in parallel terms: in his eyes, preserving the purity of the Protestant church and the purity of oil's founding spirit were the same, since both sought preservation of the uncompromising individualism that centered American Christianity and capitalism.[26]

Pew's association with the emergent network of entrepreneurial evangelicals would expand in the coming years and place him in direct conversation with men like R. G. LeTourneau, whose wartime experiences with the state's coffers were just as lucrative and impressive. If he entered the war as a Babbitt, LeTourneau exited it hovering around the ranks of J. Howard Pew and the Pews' loftier class, all thanks to his own efforts to arm America with a formidable arsenal. To be sure, LeTourneau's wartime alliances with the military and the state would not go unchallenged, nor would his factories remain strict laissez-faire zones. But there was no denying that the war years marked an instant boon for the Christian businessman and his monetary and ministerial agendas.

The dawning of this potential came in 1939, just as LeTourneau settled into Toccoa Falls; while doing so he saw another challenge and opportunity on the horizon—war. The Nazis seized Czechoslovakia and made pacts with fascist Italy and communist Russia, vindicating evangelicals' and other Americans' conflation of European tyrannies. In September, Britain, France, and Canada declared war when Hitler invaded Poland. Roosevelt assured a nervous public that the United States would remain neutral but was already pushing for higher military spending to help the Allies. The most immediate beneficiary was the manufacturing sector, and in 1940, like J. Howard Pew, LeTourneau again set his anti-Roosevelt politics aside and scored a four-and-a-half-million-dollar War Department contract to manufacture ammunition shells at Toccoa Falls.[27] This meant breaking with antiwar public opinion months before Congress passed the Lend-Lease Act putting America openly on the side of the Allies.[28] Evangelicals were part of the skeptical majority. As early as 1938, an article in *The King's Business* warned of "propaganda aiming to convince Americans that a plunge into war would 'serve the interests of democracy and the stabilization of peace.'" The author told readers to contact their congressional representatives "urging them to oppose" any bills "which would permit war to be used as a pretext for sweeping away the God-given, Constitutional liberties which our fathers died to establish." The "militarists" were New Dealers writ large, "bureaucratic slave-drivers who will tyrannize over once free Americans" by subjecting them to Europe's "war horrors."[29]

More than a dozen evangelicals wrote letters of protest—not "apolitical" complaints that LeTourneau was collaborating with Caesar, but passionate condemnations of the machinery of death. One correspondent cried, "How can you preach so zealously the LOVE OF JESUS CHRIST, and at the same time make SHELLS, that DESTROY those SOULS that Jesus died for??????"[30] Another writer established her evangelical credentials as "a poor woman alone in the world, selling Home made Bread for a living, placing [religious] leaflets in each package of bread." She asked, "Have you ever read where Jesus shouldered a gun to shoot men with?"—adding pointedly that "the Price of Blood" was "thirty pieces of silver."[31] A Congregationalist pastor and *NOW* subscriber in Madison, Wisconsin, more openly insinuated that LeTourneau was behaving like a profit-hungry Judas. "It is true that they sold the Prince of Life for a few pieces of Silver. How can we be making munitions for profit without being charged with doing the same thing!"[32] The brothers of Snyder Brothers Auto Service in Kansas City summed up the disappointment of these fans of "God's business man" and their hope that he would see the light. "We understand that you have dedicated your factories to God, and we pray that you will make them ministries of His service rather than ministers of suffering."[33]

LeTourneau, however, stood firm. In his form-letter reply, he argued that "[t]he aggressor nations of our day . . . are the enemies of God and the Bible." He invoked evangelical respect for high office as a divine appointment, even—or especially—as God chose the officeholder to chastise his people. "The Apostle Paul exhorts us to be subject to the 'powers that be,' not only in the technicalities of the law, but" (LeTourneau could not resist his favorite theme) "in real loyalty."[34] A company memo in July 1941 made the financial considerations plain as well: "With defense business we can stay in business. Without defense business we are out of this business."[35]

Five months later, the Japanese attack on Pearl Harbor made all business defense business, and LeTourneau's dirt movers proved more important than his shells. His cranes were already on the Hawaii base on December 7, and the navy commissioned more to clear the rubble and ride aboard aircraft carriers to move broken planes out of the way for repairs. The army requested, and received, a larger version of the latter design to lift wrecked bombers quickly off the ground. Between March and October of 1942, the Army Corps of Engineers used LeTourneau machines to build the 1,670-mile Alaska Highway as a supply route to Russia and to set up defenses at America's most vulnerable geographic point. LeTourneau's Tournapulls and Carryalls cleared land, built highways, and paved airstrips around the world, from Africa to Britain to Burma. During the lend-lease period, LeTourneau built a factory in Sydney. He recalled that it was soon "carrying both the Gospel and American industrial methods to Australia in gratifying fashion." Sydney's entire output, netting some $3,200,000 during 1941–42, went to the war.[36] And just as LeTourneau products had been present at the beginning at Pearl Harbor, they were indispensable as the end drew near. A correspondent wrote, "I wish Mr. LeTourneau could have watched his equipment working on the beach-head at the time of [D-Day] invasion, doing wonders that one would think impossible." The same equipment helped rebuild London, France, and Holland when peace came.[37]

America's entry into the war transformed cultural critics into nationalists, and conservative evangelicals—who, like ideologues of all stripes, often lived both identities at once—were no exception. George Marsden argues that fundamentalist "ambivalence toward American culture, which is especially apparent in fundamentalist attitudes toward patriotism and social reform," is best understood as a historically rooted "establishment-or-outsider paradox." Until the mid- to late nineteenth century, evangelicalism was the American religious "establishment," and the next generations clung to the memory of hegemony even as they retreated into the loyal opposition of a subculture. While there is ample evidence for this interpretation, Marsden uses it to argue for evangelical distinctiveness rather than evangelical variations on a popular theme—namely, American exceptionalism. Jeremiads and ardent nationalism have been two sides of the same coin since the Puritans. Even Marsden points out that premillennialists were little different, in their rejection of progress, than Mark Twain or Henry Adams, just as "the political attitudes of most fundamentalists were much like those of their non-fundamentalist Republican neighbors." LeTourneau made sure to show that he was a good neighbor.[38]

Not everyone saw LeTourneau as the good neighbor, however; a friend of the state by 1943, some within organized labor considered him an enemy to the workingman and sought to upset his wartime production and profits. In 1943, the same year the American Federation of Labor (AFL) finally triumphed in Peoria, a renegade faction of the CIO attempted to unionize Toccoa Falls. LeTourneau responded with no small edge of hysteria.[39] His primary forum was the LeTourneau Evangelistic Foundation. LEF director Harold Strathearn's *Joyful News* announced, "CIO Out to Communize LeTourneau Company" in an issue largely devoted to the emergency.[40] "The Bible is not silent on the important issues involved and the church should shout out a warning."[41] He claimed that workers had voted not to join the CIO in a National Labor Relations Board–supervised election, but rogue organizers refused to quit. "Remember the government is paying [LeTourneau] for your work," they taunted the workers, calling the plant "A Center of Commercialized Religion."[42] Strathearn defended LeTourneau's shop talks and his Foundation-financed evangelism.[43] He made a spirited case for welfare capitalism in an article entitled "Bible Declares Rights of Capital and Labor," defining employers and employees as spiritually, if not socially, equal; functionally complementary; and possessing reciprocal rights and duties. Scripture, Strathearn wrote, "spares the selfish employer no more than the slothful employee, those who hold back wages no more than those who hold back work."[44]

Outrage drove Strathearn's interpretation of the Bible, above all in his retelling of the New Testament parable of the vineyard. In the gospel accounts, a rich man leases his vineyard to tenants who not only refuse him his harvest but who hurt or kill each servant he sends to collect his due. Finally, he sends his beloved son, whom he is sure they will respect; they kill him too. The rich man represents God; the son, Christ; and the tenants, Christ's crucifiers. With these images very much in mind, Strathearn imagined the hapless servants as "company representatives" and the murderous tenants as "trusted employees" who seized control of the business.

Because the "company representatives were not in sympathy with the new setup," the employees "beat," "stoned," and "killed" them. The rich man and his son remained divine figures in Strathearn's reading. The son's sacrifice, he seethed, showed that "[p]rogressive confiscation will lead inevitably to complete seizure of property. . . . The point in the biblical story is that these wicked men will be miserably destroyed and replaced by those who recognize the rights of the owner."[45] In other words, the battle between LeTourneau and the CIO rebels was only partly about profits. Just as importantly for fundamentalists, the social conflict enacted the eternal war between God and Satan. LeTourneau would never need to retire his speech on "Comm[unist] Hate Christ Love."

Nor would he ever need to curb his enthusiasm for partnering with God and the federal government during global struggle. Rocked by labor unrest, unsettled by criticism within his evangelical camp, LeTourneau nevertheless found myriad opportunities to display and even indulge in his white Christian patriotism. The opening of his new plant in Vicksburg, Mississippi, displayed this in full view.

The ceremonies took place on November 28, 1942, almost a year after America had entered the war. LeTourneau's first political act in the majority-black area was to follow "local tradition" and segregate his employees, although he distributed the "social amenities" of welfare capitalism equally.[46] Yet the regional pride that had characterized the Toccoa Falls dedication gave way to a message of national unity. Visiting clergy, including Richard Forrest, had been building revival fever with morning and evening services all week. The Vicksburg Chamber of Commerce, which organized the factory's consecration to the Lord, called the event "A Tri-State Patriotic Rally."[47] It opened with a war bond and stamp drive, after which the American Legion performed the "Flag-Raising and Pledge of Allegiance." Homer Rodeheaver, a popular evangelical musician who had accompanied Billy Sunday, led the crowd in singing "America" before the invocation. The governors of Mississippi, Arkansas, and Louisiana spoke, as did a visitor from Washington, Admiral John S. McCain. The father of the future presidential candidate thanked LeTourneau for a "grand time."[48] He and the audience enjoyed an exhibition of the LeTourneau, Inc.'s, military-use equipment; a "[p]atriotic display by Army, Navy, and Marine Corps"; a band playing over a top-of-the-line public address system; and, of course, "Free Barbeque for 10,000."[49] No one protested the message that evangelicalism, capitalism, and a militarized state would converge to decimate the enemy.

CLUB TIME

If bolstered by wartime gains in his own manufacturing sector, and indulgent in his own white Christian patriotism, Herbert Taylor expended most of his energy during World War II increasing the range of his philanthropic and ministerial agendas. As witnessed at the Sherman Hotel in spring of 1942, his Christian Workers Foundation was proving to be a success (if not always completely) where networking and planning evangelism were concerned. By the midpoint of the war, his interests began to extend in new directions, triggered in part by the urgency of his day and the need to inspire and propagate—not simply build—an arsenal (in this case metaphorical) of Christian democracy. And so, starting in the later stages of war, he combined religion and advertising in a company-sponsored radio program called *Club Time,* which, through infiltration of America's homes, he believed would collapse the darkness of war by way of the broadcasted good news of Christ's redemption. Starring fundamentalist crooner George Beverly Shea, who would rise to greater fame as Billy Graham's song leader, *Club Time* debuted in 1944 and soared in popularity at the end of World War II. Ads for Club Aluminum products ran between psalms and hymns. Ratings and sales, not just conversions, measured *Club Time*'s impact.

Club Time escalated Taylor's well-established Four-Way Test's challenge to collapse religion and business and code the result as "Christian" in a way evangelicals would recognize and approve, even while playing the Protestant-Catholic-Jew card that he knew from Rotary was both good manners and good salesmanship. If the CWF and its associated projects were Taylor's way of putting Club Aluminum's profits into God's work, his wartime program, *Club Time,* turned God's work into profits. For fifteen minutes a day in Chicago, then weekly nationwide, psalms and hymns would frame an advertisement for Club Aluminum products. Although he would never hitch evangelicalism to his corporate identity with the panache of an R. G. LeTourneau, Taylor aimed for both at the price of one. By contrast with the CWF, which Taylor was simultaneously micromanaging, *Club Time* followed the Four-Way Test, Rotary, and the commercial logic in airbrushing its Christian message to an inoffensive sheen. Yet it also provided a platform for fundamentalist singer George Beverly Shea. Already famous within the subculture when Taylor tapped him for *Club Time,* Shea became an instrumental figure in the Youth for Christ (YFC) movement—all on Club Aluminum's dime. Even when he began to sing at Billy Graham's rallies in the late 1940s and early 1950s, he remained on Taylor's payroll. A former businessman himself, Shea's sojourn with Club Aluminum both Christianized commerce and commercialized Christianity.

When Taylor adopted religious radio as an advertising format in 1944, he was uncharacteristically behind the times. Since the early 1920s, when preachers Aimee Semple McPherson and Paul Rader seized on the new medium's potential to reach thousands of people in their homes, conservative evangelicals had flocked to radio as a tool for mass proselytizing.[50] Likewise, business executives recognized radio's advertising potential, and some incorporated Christianity or generic "faith" into their sales pitch. Whether on local stations with limited range or the coveted national networks, religious shows generally ran fifteen minutes, Monday through Friday, and included a lengthy promotion from the sponsor. From 1936 to 1946, General Electric president Charles B. Wilson personally selected hymns that ended *Hour of Charm*, GE's Sunday broadcast on NBC.[51] In 1940, cereal company General Mills spun off *Hymns of All Churches*, which had also debuted in 1936, and replaced a long-running soap opera with *Light of the World*. A Union Theological Seminary professor, a Jesuit priest, and a rabbi served as consultants to the biblical melodrama.[52]

While Taylor's papers do not indicate why he created *Club Time*, several factors likely came into play. He had divided his time between Chicago and Washington as a "dollar-a-year man" on Maurice Karker's Price Adjustment Board during 1942 and 1943, and his resignation meant he was no longer an absentee CEO. The easing of government restrictions on the production of raw materials revived Club Aluminum's retail business, which the company desperately needed to publicize.[53] Taylor's work with Charles Fuller had impressed on him the widespread appeal of a broadcast combining hymns, Bible verses, uplifting anecdotes, and wartime patriotism. Aware of evangelicalism's conflict with mainline Protestants over radio licensing, he may also have wished to take a stand in the culture war over the airwaves. Whatever the case, the Four-Way Test, the CWF, and Taylor's growing prominence as a layman meant that, at least among evangelicals, Club Aluminum was already "Christian" by association. *Club Time*'s inoffensive, cautiously ecumenical uplift exploited this reputation for sales purposes and tried to serve God selflessly at the same time. It was a difficult and sometimes cynical balancing act, but pairing business and religion benefited both Club Aluminum and the increasingly mobilized white evangelical community.

Club Time began as a local-access program on Chicagoland station WLW, and Taylor ensured a loyal fundamentalist following by making a superb casting choice. Thirty-six-year-old George Beverly Shea, the Canadian-born son of a Methodist minister, shared Taylor's gift for identifying the movements that would shape evangelicalism's future. Indeed, he was already crafting his own legend. Too poor to complete his degree at a Christian college in New York, he joined the Mutual Insurance Company in 1929 and developed a singing career on the side. Craggily handsome with an extraordinary baritone voice, Shea easily attracted the support of evangelical businessmen during the 1930s. Erling C. Olsen, an investment consultant and lay theologian, hired Shea to sing on his New York–area broadcast *Meditations on the Psalms*. In 1939, Moody Bible Institute president Will Houghton offered Shea a full-time administrative job at WMBI. Shea's duties included performing every morning on *Hymns from the Chapel* and on Houghton's weekly dispatch, *Let's Go Back to the Bible*, which gave him a popular fan base. One admirer, freshly minted pastor Billy Graham, hired Shea to anchor *Songs in the Night*, a radio program Graham had inherited from manufacturer William Erny and Erny's pastor, Torrey Johnson.[54] This marked the beginning of Shea's most famous collaboration; by the end of the decade, he and Graham would be lifelong partners in the latter's famous "crusades."[55]

Of course, when Shea met Graham in 1943, neither man knew that they would go on to lead an evangelical empire that would dwarf Moody's, Sunday's, and Finney's. Nor did they work closely together outside of *Songs in the Night*. But they stayed in the same evangelical orbit by focusing on a challenge dear to Herb Taylor's heart: unsaved, delinquent, and otherwise imperiled youth. In 1942, Shea had requested a leave of absence from WMBI to tour with Jack Wyrtzen, another former insurance man. Wyrtzen's Saturday night rallies in Times Square offered a model for reaching servicemen, defense workers, and other wartime migrants to cities filled with temptations. In 1944, Shea was instrumental in pressuring Torrey Johnson to organize YFC in Chicago.[56] Taylor put Johnson in touch with local Christian businessmen and used his radio connections to get the preacher a slot on, of all stations, WFCL, the "Voice of Labor" in Chicago.[57] Shea added the YFC circuit to his lengthening list of appearances.

As a performer, however, Shea served two masters: God and Club Aluminum. Taylor seems to have decided on a two-pronged advertising strategy for *Club Time*. First, he hoped to appeal to as many radio listeners as possible by being as soothing and inclusive as Wyrtzen was harsh and uncompromising. Second, he believed that product placement would be most effective with people who already trusted him or Shea, Chicago's conservative evangelicals. The promotional campaign for *Club Time*, itself a promotional campaign, took place in churches, at YFC gatherings, and virtually anywhere else Beverly Shea's agency booked him. The arrangement was simple. Upon soliciting or receiving an invitation from a church in WLW's area, Shea waived his usual payment, explaining Club Aluminum was his sponsor. He asked that the pastor mention the company in the bulletin, at minimum, and hinted that a word of thanks from the pulpit would be especially welcome. Since a Beverly Shea concert was almost certain to raise church attendance and draw coveted visitors, the pastor was delighted to oblige.[58] These off-the-air concerts were *Club Time*'s bread and butter.

Shea's letters to Taylor reporting *Club Time* engagements illustrate the mutually beneficial arrangement. A January 1945 appearance at the Oak Park Avenue Baptist Church in a Chicago suburb represented a triumph of business and religious networking. Taylor discussed *Club Time* with the pastor, who wrote an invitation to Shea to sing at a Sunday morning service, the prime-time slot for congregational marketing. "[Just] a few empty seats in the back room" kept the two-hundred-strong church from filling to capacity. The preacher "spoke of Club Time on two occasions in the service, making mention of the sponsorship and the appreciation of his people for the daily broadcast." At the end, "it seemed like most of the congregation came forward to greet us."[59] The next week, "there was no alternative [but] to accept [an] evening engagement" at a nearby Presbyterian church. Still, the place was packed: "a 50% increase in attendance," according to the assistant minister, who estimated the crowd at three hundred.[60] YFC's Torrey Johnson pulled out all the stops at a Saturday night rally with thirty-five hundred present and a live broadcast. "Through the goodness of his heart, without a word from me," he "had the song leader, on the air, mention Club Time, 'at 1:15 each day,' etc." Later, "Torrey asked for a show of hands from those who had *never* written to a gospel program. . . . Then he kindly asked that these and others write in a note to Club Time, if they enjoy the program and its being on the air. So, that was a fine little bit of 'promotion.'"[61]

Listener letters were key to Taylor and his team's evaluation of *Club Time*'s cost-effectiveness. Monthly charts, which grew more detailed over time, noted the date a letter was written; the name and address of the writer; to whom the letter was addressed (Shea, Club Aluminum, or, very occasionally, Taylor); "comments"; song requests; and whether the author had included another promotion, such as box tops or prestamped envelopes to the company.[62]

The addressee was important because it indicated whether the writer associated the program with Shea, a known quantity from WMBI, or had absorbed Club Aluminum's branding. "Comments" served the same purpose, showing at a glance which letters only mentioned Shea and which also referred to Club Aluminum or, better yet, specific products. "My prayer is that the program may continue well into the future," wrote Mrs. F. O. Safstrom of Elmhurst, Illinois, to the Club Aluminum Product Company. The stenographer summarized the rest of the letter as: "Likes CAC [a brand-name pan]; works well on aluminum part of burners. Also likes CSP [another company product]. Says she will tell friends about the product and broadcast."[63] Such fans implicitly agreed that a Christian program obliterated any distinction between evangelism and advertising.

The overwhelming majority of writers, like Mrs. Safstrom, were women; housewives were more likely than their husbands both to buy Club products and listen to afternoon radio.[64] Not all, however, felt comfortable intermingling faith and commerce. Mrs. Edith Johnson of Melrose Park angrily summarized a chronic *Club Time* protest: "My favorite hymn singer is on only 15 minutes a day, and seems like ten minutes are wasted in advertising." She signed it "Disgusted." Shea, who had an image as an independent Christian singer to protect, was genuinely horrified to be perceived as Club Aluminum's mouthpiece rather than God's. Once, an overobliging pastor sang the praises of Club Aluminum from the pulpit and asked Shea to elaborate. Shea leaped to his feet and clarified that he had come "'to sing *the grand old hymns*, but not to speak of my sponsor's product.' There was a rather happy burst of smiles and a sort of feeling of relief, perhaps."[65] The awkward moment underscored the skepticism that evangelical businessmen courted in claiming to link God and mammon. Uniting God and Caesar was far less controversial. Robert Walker and Shea infused the daily scripts with wartime patriotism, from the closing song, "God Bless Our Boys," to "human interest" stories about wounded GIs who took comfort in hearing their favorite hymns.[66]

Taylor, Walker, and Shea's audience-building strategies paid off in October of 1945, when the American Broadcasting Company (ABC) bought *Club Time* from WLW and transformed it into a nationwide broadcast. It would air weekly, not daily, showcasing the crisp production and coordinated advertising that only a network could provide. Nevertheless, it retained a certain homegrown charm. Taylor's daughter Beverly joined the staff as a "dramatic reader," and Taylor all but ordered employees to recruit new listeners. In a memo to "All Company Personnel," Taylor framed the rechristened "Club Time—For Thy Good Cheer," as the "best" way to "interpret the 4 Way Test." "[S]urely the greatest service that an individual or a corporation can render its nation is spiritual and moral influence of a constructive nature." He quoted General Douglas MacArthur's statement about the atomic age after Japan's surrender: "'The problem is basically theological. . . . [Peace] must be of the spirit if we are to save the flesh.'"[67] *Club Time*'s ABC debut would be piped through the office. "Meanwhile, of course, we shall all want to tell our friends about the program." Taylor listed all twenty-five cities, stations, and times, and explained that commercials would at first be brief, so as not to alienate new listeners. "Club Aluminum Hammercraft Cookware, Club Glass Cookware, and our household cleaners and polishes" soon would underwrite the corporation's spiritual and moral influence.[68]

Club Time—For Thy Good Cheer hit its stride in 1946, when the promotional team devised a feature called "Favorite Hymns of Famous People." As George F. Drake, the chief advertiser, boasted to the Club Aluminum sales conference, they outsmarted bigger programs that could pay "big-name guest stars" by "writing to famous people, and asking them to let us feature their favorite hymns" for free.[69] In the heightened religious climate following the war, it was a brilliant stroke. Public figures could appear pious and accessible without any work, and *Club Time* could imply support from luminaries outside the conservative evangelical firmament. Fundamentalists already got more than their share of airtime, with Shea's base following him from WLW as it had from WMBI. For example, Olympic runner Gil Dodds and pilot Eddie Rickenbacher lent their fame to YFC, the Inter-Varsity Fellowship, and other Taylor-supported projects. Homer Rodeheaver, hardly a household name, had been evangelist Billy Sunday's accompanist and helped run Sunday's fundamentalist camp and conference center at Winona Lake in Indiana.[70] By including them, *Club Time* not only nodded to fellow believers but also stamped evangelicals as All-American while ratings more than doubled.[71]

Marquee names came from politics and popular culture. Much like Taylor's Four-Way Test, the list gestured toward Protestant-Catholic-Jewish ecumenism while remaining overwhelmingly Protestant. By early 1947, *Club Time* had played the favorite hymns of J. Edgar Hoover, Fiorello LaGuardia, Lionel Barrymore (who chose a Jewish song), Ronald Colman, Catholic actress Irene Dunne ("Mother Dear, O Pray for Me"), General Omar N. Bradley, General John J. Pershing, Supreme Court Chief Justice Fred Vinson, Wendell Willkie, Rotary International president R. C. Hedke (no doubt selected by Taylor), and author Dorothy Dix. Shea told the *Chicago Sunday Times* that only two people had turned *Club Time* down: President Harry Truman, who diplomatically claimed that he "could not single out any one hymn," and United Nations Secretary General Trygve Lie, who demurred that his favorites were Norwegian.[72] ABC affiliates seized the opportunity to solicit listener feedback and cement loyalty to the show, advertising "Maybe You'll Hear *Your* Favorite Hymn!"[73] As before, fans responded, submitting hymn requests, questions about Club Aluminum products, and queries for Club-authored promotions such as "The Beatitudes of the Housewife."[74]

Listeners might have been less enthusiastic if they saw the charts, ratings graphs, and profit-loss analyses that consumed Club Aluminum and ABC in their discussions of the show. In January 1947, Robert Walker wrote to the advertising manager of General Mills about the radio programs *Light of the World* and *Hymns of All Churches.* He asked for "a frank statement evaluating . . . the worth of the show[s] to you as a commercial advertiser" and, more generally, "what you think of 'religion' as a media by which to reach the general public."[75] The response: "The good will created for General Mills . . . is immeasurable," and the audience "particularly loyal" by comparison to higher-rated programs. "The complaints regarding the commercial sponsorship . . . are almost negligible."[76] The same month, the vice president of ABC congratulated Taylor on reaching an audience of close to three million. "I'm sure I don't need to call your attention to the fact that you have now built up and established an equity in 'Club Time' which makes it a highly valuable property."[77]

Taylor, however, never dulled his conviction that his "highly valuable property" served God as well as mammon. Tucked in his files is a clipping from *Printers' Ink,* glued to a page of company stationery. The unnamed author describes the outrage of "the Missus" upon hearing an "oily announcer" tell "'all to go to church—the whole family—if you don't know where a church is, ask your Sunoco dealer.'" He sneers, "On the way to church, stop and get a tankful of Sunoco, the righteous gasoline." Taylor comments, "This is the sort of thing we have studiously avoided on Club Time. We have successfully steered away from: (1) self-righteousness (2) preaching (3) sectarianism (4) commercialism."[78] It was important to Taylor that Club Aluminum not tell people to go to church, not only because he couldn't afford to alienate nonchurchgoers, but because he believed that church was bigger than business. Similarly, church was bigger than "sects," the foes of ecumenical evangelicalism. "Commercialism" did not include dropping the company name in bulletins and from pulpits, as long as he could rationalize that the preacher was Club Aluminum's willing evangelist. Nor did it include interrupting hymns with advertisements or the *Club Time* introduction, which was suspiciously close to the church of Sunoco: "'Club Time' . . . a coast to coast program of best loved hymns . . . presented to you in friendship by the Club Aluminum Products Company of Chicago!"[79]

WARTIME GAINS FOR THE GUILD

As with two of the leading lights in their guilds, Taylor and LeTourneau, war brought challenges as well as opportunities to evangelical entrepreneurialism's primary associations, with gains ultimately outweighing the losses. Curiously, the Christian Laymen's Crusade to unite northern and southern businessmen that had gained steam in the late 1930s foundered during the war, even as the CBMCI and BMEC spoke an identical language of American conquest. Despite the BMEC's subjugation of regionalism to nationalism, the CBMCI fell back in the habit of leaving the South off its map of America.

More prosaically, both the BMEC and the CBMCI—and, by extension, the CLC, their shared spinoff—had trouble doing what businessmen were supposed to do best: raise money. The organizations were too decentralized to have stable finances. The "national" or "international" committees did most of the administrative work while granting locals almost complete autonomy, which mirrored their low-church Protestantism and political objections to big government. They built their budgets on voluntary pledges, not dues, which local groups routinely neglected to pay. While the CBMCI's wealthy board members often made up part of the difference, the BMEC was less well-off.[80] When America entered the war, the BMEC was preoccupied with institutional survival. "Your secretary cannot travel without money," C. P. Pelham dryly informed the readers of *Christian Workers*. "My money is about used up, and I now need some from you." The president of the Virginia BMEC delivered a two-page scolding. "Just how much does this work mean to us anyway? When we gave our hearts to Christ, did we give him our pocketbooks too?"[81] It was in this context that BMEC president Boyd Hargraves first addressed the war at length in June 1942. American men were dying "[f]or victory over a foe, a foe to Christianity, to liberty[,] to our democratic way of life." Yet war "only touches the body," while the BMEC confronted soul-destroying sin. Saving soldiers before they faced satanic enemies in flesh and spirit was not cheap.[82]

In principle, the CLC should have helped the struggling BMEC by holding rallies to found new chapters. By settling in Chicago, however, the CLC became a virtual arm of the CBMCI instead of an interregional booster.[83] Still, the creation had forged durable northern and southern ties, which intersected in the person of LeTourneau. He continued to lead the CBMCI but stayed on the BMEC's executive committee, even as he labored to build his new plant in Vicksburg. He plugged both organizations on his never-ending speaking tour, which covered more southern territory the longer he lived there. He remained in touch with Vernon Patterson and Rolan Stoker, who resigned from LeTourneau, Inc., to devote himself to the BMEC. In what must have been a huge relief to the treasurer, LeTourneau paid Stoker's salary as executive secretary.[84] But LeTourneau was only one man. The early stirrings of the western and southern Sunbelt, built on defense subsidies, independently tugged on America's political, economic, and religious center of gravity.[85] For most of the century, evangelicals in Chicago and California had been more interpersonally and institutionally connected than evangelicals in Chicago and Chattanooga. The CLC, as originally conceived, signaled a larger societal change. As a young, mobile, multiracial population went north and west to follow jobs, southern evangelicals dispersed with them.[86]

One of these migrants was Charlotte's Billy Graham—"Billy Frank," the young man whose exposure to evangelist Mordecai Ham and the Depression-era Christian work of the CCMC, to which his dairy-farmer father was so central, proved life changing. Graham went to Wheaton College in 1940 to supplement his degree from the Florida Bible Institute. He graduated in 1943 at twenty-four and began a suburban Chicago pastorate, intending to qualify for an army chaplaincy. Instead, he got caught up in a businessman's movement to save the young men and women who were flocking to cities for defense work or the armed services. Every Saturday night, starting in 1941, insurance salesman turned evangelist Jack Wyrtzen held a "Times Square Youth Rally" with a radio broadcast that reached as far as Pennsylvania. He gathered enormous crowds through straight-talking charisma, combining distinctively fundamentalist theology with generic jeremiads about American culture. "Every unconverted person in the world has death, judgment, and the Lake of Fire before him," Wyrtzen, the fundamentalist, warned. But it was Wyrtzen the cultural critic who spoke to broader anxieties about too much "commercial excitement, political strife and ambition, money making and pleasure seeking." The wartime context changed the argument about a "money mad nation" that had appeared in *Christian Workers* only five years before. The same gendered (and, in *Christian Workers*, regional) repugnance toward softness, effeminacy, and luxury put a sinful America squarely in God's sights. Yet in early 1940, softness, effeminacy, and luxury were more than sins; they were national security threats that could lose a war.[87] Wyrtzen was in Times Square on Saturday night with the deadly serious intent to provide better entertainment than the myriad temptations on offer.

The rally idea spread to other northern and midwestern urban centers. Organizers attracted nonevangelical attendees, or at least attention, by assuring a delinquency-sensitized public that the meetings were wholesome, patriotic, and above all, fun. No stodgy sermons or dreary hymns would drive the fickle target audience back to bars and dance halls.[88] In St. Louis, servicemen were part of the performance, making free calls onstage to home and families far from Missouri.[89] Minneapolis pioneered the "Singspiration," sacred music with a safely white (but unmistakably syncopated) beat.[90] In early 1944, Graham joined pastor Torrey Johnson, businessman Herbert J. Taylor, and other Chicago-area evangelicals to introduce the phenomenon to the Windy City. They named themselves after one of Wyrtzen's slogans, "Youth for Christ," and chose Johnson—a twinkling-eyed, second-generation Norwegian immigrant with a Wheaton degree—to lead.[91] In May, YFC filled Chicago's Orchestra Hall, with Graham having the honor of the first sermon. In the fall, they drew twenty to thirty thousand to a war-themed "Victory Rally" at Chicago Stadium.[92] The Chicagoans led a temporary national committee from the end of 1944 to mid-1945, when, at Billy Sunday's Winona Lake, they incorporated Youth for Christ International. Graham took a leave of absence from his church to be the field secretary, traveling to get new groups established.[93]

YFC's impressive audiences and tendency to highlight and celebrate conversion narratives of young lives yanked from the pit obscured the fact that the group primarily energized the already born; its revival meetings in this way mirrored the Charlotte services during which a young, convicted Graham "recommitted" himself to Christ.[94] Between the large events and when Orchestra Hall was not available, YFC met at Moody Memorial Church, which was a far cry from Times Square. Similarly, the Minneapolis YFC started at a fundamentalist Bible institute and met weekly at First Baptist Church.[95] In an important sense, though, it did not matter that YFC was reviving evangelicalism from within rather than bringing the tidal wave of new believers its leaders imagined.[96] An energized evangelicalism—a revival in the church—was the prerequisite for the church's revival of the world, and YFC was only one organization among many. Simply by linking conservative evangelical activists who had been acting independently, networks such as YFC's brought them closer to cohesion. YFC made evangelicalism visible to outsiders by emphasizing shared concerns, such as patriotism and juvenile delinquency, and defying fundamentalist stereotypes by exploiting rather than rejecting popular culture. "That the world needs a globe-rocking revival is evident," wrote one booster. "Youth for Christ may bring it!"[97]

Businessmen, especially the CBMCI, recognized YFC's potential early on and were crucial to its growth. In Chicago alone, the advisory council included Herbert Taylor, the CBMCI's Al J. Conn and C. B. Hedstrom, and the Gideons' Robert Van Kampen. Vaughn Shoemaker, Carl A. Gunderson, and Reamer Loomis (all CBMCI) and Andrew Wyzenbeek (Gideons, CLC) appeared on a long list of business supporters.[98] The 1944 "Victory Rally" featured Taylor's personal testimony, a prayer by the manager of Sears and Roebuck, and a corporate vice president on behalf of the New York rally. LeTourneau became a regular YFC speaker.[99] Johnson and his circle of pastors and evangelists, however, were the stars, while businessmen by and large worked behind the scenes. The public image the movement promoted was that of a spontaneous eruption of the spirit in several places at one, a "bonfire . . . completely out of human control."[100] Workaholic Johnson had no illusions about the human labor required to tend the flames, and even coauthored an influential book of YFC "mechanics" for aspiring group leaders.[101] He and his business friends, however, understood that YFC's popularity, like that of any revival, depended on the bonfire. "Spectacles of the Spirit" gained power by cloaking signs of human manufacture, or, as those in the whirlwind understood it, the activity of the spirit's human instruments.

No event better symbolized the quiet significance of the CBMCI to YFC than the second "Victory Rally" at Chicago's Soldier Field, on Memorial Day 1945, three weeks after Germany surrendered. The *Chicago Daily Tribune* estimated a crowd of sixty thousand at the all-day affair. First, the Glenview Naval Station's baseball team "soundly trounced" Wheaton College. Next, "[w]ith a smooth blend of religion and patriotism," a marine color guard and Christian youth group posted American and Christian flags around the arena. A "living cross of nearly 500 white uniformed nurses marched down the field" to a swinging version of "I Shall Not Be Moved." A "missionary pageant" followed "with representatives of China, India, Africa, Russia, and the United States in native costumes." Each of the five countries "formed the points of a vast star." The lights dimmed for a choral performance of "Gospel Lighthouse," during which angelic figures blew trumpets from the colonnades. Charlotte police chief Walter Anderson—a BMEC member soon to be appointed to the Attorney General's Conference on Juvenile Delinquency—addressed the crowd. Torrey Johnson preached "with tonal qualities suggestive of Frank Sinatra." Chicago CBMCI members served as soberly dressed ushers.[102]

Despite appearances, the two organizations were joined at the hip. The CBMCI experienced considerable wartime growth, and by 1945, the first task of many new affiliates was to establish YFC in their communities—at least thirty, by scholar Joel Carpenter's count.[103] A spring issue of *Contact* confirmed the number and noted that other groups were "making plans." Since mid-1944, the CBMCI had welcomed YFC as "God's answer to naturalism, modernism, communism, and materialism, which had invaded our schools and colleges for the past generation." The CBMCIs of Toronto, Milwaukee, Honolulu, Orlando, and Cleveland had taken action around the same time as Chicago's. Detroit, Los Angeles, New York, Philadelphia, Pittsburgh, Louisville, Portland, Fargo, and several other cities in Ontario, Canada, were some of YFC's other CBMCI sponsors by 1945. The head of Milwaukee's CBMCI led YFC as well, and the CBMCI planned prayer meetings, contacted pastors, arranged radio coverage, and hired buses to take Milwaukee youth to the rallies at Soldier Field.[104]

On a smaller scale, the CBMCI of Kenosha-Racine, Wisconsin, not only cosponsored YFC but also hired the personnel director and industrial chaplain of the Quaker Stretcher Company as director. Quaker Stretcher was an evangelical business on the all-encompassing LeTourneau model, and in 1943, the chief executive enlisted Torrey Johnson to help incorporate religion into the routine. "The result: a gospel shop meeting with a radio broadcast so that people listening in could share the novel witness of the gospel being preached in a factory, to men in working clothes."[105] Two years later, the youth of Kenosha-Racine and everywhere else the CBMCI sponsored YFC were in the sometimes-invisible hand of evangelical welfare capitalism and philanthropy. For instance, Torrey Johnson and Billy Graham could promote YFC anywhere, despite rubber rationing and exorbitant airfares. The president of Quaker Stretcher charged their flights to his account.[106]

In addition to YFC, the CBMCI's other priority during the war was establishing servicemen's centers, or "Victory Centers," where soldiers on leave could enjoy food, company, and Christian recreation. The model was the government-initiated United Service Organizations (USO), which brought together "the Salvation Army, Young Men's Christian Association, Young Women's Christian Association, National Catholic Community Services, National Travelers Aid Association and the National Jewish Welfare Board." The practical, comforting, and domesticating goal was to provide "A Home Away from Home," where soldiers could find coffee, companionship, toiletries, a cot, and, most important to many, stamps and paper for letters to their real homes. The extent of public concern about young servicemen's morale and potentially antisocial escapism (drinking, fighting, prostitution) could be measured in charitable donations to the National War Fund. In 1944, the USO received almost half the fund's receipts to support more than three thousand centers around the country.[107]

Why the CBMCI decided to establish its own centers is unclear, but the USO's coalition of Catholics, Jews, the YMCA, and the Young Women's Christian Association inspired the evangelical alternative. Victory Centers provided as many creature comforts as they could afford, but their ultimate purpose was to save servicemen's souls. As with YFC, national networking proved vital, but California stole the lead from Chicago. Well before the war, when sailors on Pacific naval bases mostly stayed aground, an entrepreneurial evangelical named Dawson Trotman and his wife invited as many servicemen as could fit to live and worship with them in their Long Beach home. ("Onward Christian Sailors," *Collier's* would later quip.) Trotman, a BIOLA dropout who did odd jobs to make ends meet, felt called to evangelize naval bases on a larger scale. Descried by his biographer as "cultivat[ing] [a] rugged, he-man image to counter the idea that Christianity was suitable only for women and children," he formed a group called the Navigators base on "man-to-man" discipleship. Leaders of this fledgling organization trained small groups of men in Bible memorization and other evangelistic techniques. The groups dispersed to become leaders and trainers in their own right, ensuring a self-perpetuating organization. In 1938, radio evangelist Charles Fuller began headlining Trotman's annual servicemen's conference. The following year, "Daws" (as Trotman was known) and two businessmen founded the Long Beach CBMCI. A member introduced him to Arnold Grunigen and Harry R. Smith, the vice president of both the Bank of America and the San Francisco CBMCI. In 1942, the team opened a USO-style "Victory Center" in Market Square inspired by, if less intimate than, Daws's house of praying sailors. "Christian Business Men from Land and Sea" was the title of Fuller's dedicatory address.[108] A visual echo appeared in a later Victory Center tract, featuring "a picture of the business man reaching across the globe to shake hands with the sailor."[109]

A 1945 ad for the weekly radio broadcast from "509," the building's address and nickname, laid out what else the Victory Center had to offer. The design resembled a rotary telephone, with different pictures in each circle. At the center, an older businessman shook hands with a serviceman over the CBMCI Service Man's Center logo. "509 Market Street, San Francisco, Where we make 'Man to Man' contact with service personnel—for Christ," the ad read. Counterclockwise next to the serviceman, and directly in line with the "Man to Man" claim, was a picture of older women labeled "With Cookies." Above them, a man read what was likely a Gideon testament to a sailor, above the headline "Only Believe." Next came a premillennialist poster, hanging above a ticking clock, with the verse LeTourneau had chosen a decade earlier for his company magazine *NOW*: "Behold, now is the accepted time: behold, now is the day of salvation." This was "Gospel Time," the prophetic visual announced. Next appeared a picture of Grunigen before a radio microphone, under the heading "The Speaker Today." Then three servicemen relaxing in a well-furbished living room pored over and chatted about the gospel in "Good Reading." An impassioned businessman, hair askew, leaned into two servicemen and pointed at a Bible verse: "Man to Man." Servicemen flanking a piano adorned with flowers represented "Radio Artists," followed by two more crowded pictures, "On the Air," and "After the Broadcast." The last three images were of the 509 entrance; two servicemen and a female volunteer surrounded by middle-class furniture, enjoying "Fellowship" (the headline might as well have been "Women!"), and a sailor asking a staffer, "Any Stamps?"[110] The civilizing furniture, the canteen of Cokes, and the benefit parties attended by women in furs could be found at any USO. The enormous rack of tracts advertising Youth for Christ meetings could not.[111] As with YFC, the Victory Centers were more successful at niche marketing than mass conversion, and few were as strategically located or well-funded as the one in San Francisco.[112] Both YFC and Victory Centers, however, linked business, youth, religion, and patriotism in the hope of uniting conservative Protestants as a force in the postwar world.

REKINDLED ALLIANCES FOR A GLOBAL AGE

Evangelical businessmen's outreach to youth and servicemen reinvigorated North-South hopes to kindle a national—and nationalistic—white evangelicalism. Travel-related rationing and continued financial woes temporarily returned the wartime Business Men's Evangelistic Clubs to fundamentalism's southern ghetto.[113] Local BMECs, however, began initiatives similar to, and sometimes transplanted from, businessmen's evangelism in the North. Birmingham and Macon opened Victory Centers, the latter founded by a couple from Toledo and staffed by a former "hostess" at Chicago's building.[114] BMECs in other cities followed suit. In November 1944, when it was clear that Allied victory was only a matter of time, the BMEC planned to convert the postwar centers into a "program for young people similar to the 'Youth for Christ' movement."[115] The quotation marks around an unfamiliar phrase were telling. The YFC "bonfire" was leaping from the Northeast to the Midwest to the West but not to the South. Even southern adopters, such as the BMEC of Toccoa Falls, were wary of combustion as a metaphor for the spirit. LeTourneau's own businessmen "intended to maintain control over the meetings in a supervisory capacity for a considerable time" before allowing YFC to run free.[116]

One explanation for YFC's weakness in the South is that denominational loyalties overpowered ecumenical revivalism. For instance, the Southern Baptist Convention (SBC), the largest and most insular Protestant community, rolled out a YFC copycat ("Adventurers for Christ") as a way to protect its oversight of southern youth ministry.[117] The SBC, however, did not speak for individual southern Baptists. Prominent churchmen vocally backed the YFC's and businessmen's interdenominationalism.[118] A more plausible argument is that YFC's Chicago-based leadership welcomed southerners but put little effort into building a mass movement. Local YFCs, like local CBMCIs, formed from broad and deep evangelical networks, whether spontaneously or as a result of top-down organizing. Only Billy Graham knew the networks in the South, and his promotional tour with Johnson was a disaster. Rolan Stoker noticed that in major cities, the meetings were "not attended by large crowds but by representative groups interested in 'Youth for Christ'"—more church workers than screaming teenagers. After Atlanta, "Graham broke under the strain of months of hard work and went home [to Charlotte] for a rest." Johnson "took out" after Knoxville.[119]

As a result of the CBMCI's and YFC's wartime regionalism, southern businessmen did their own, less theatrical youth evangelism. There was the Charlotte BMEC branch's (CCMC's) annual Young People's Camp; radio evangelism at Fort Bragg; various campaigns to fill public schools with Bibles; "carrying the message to the factories" in government-approved meetings with the National Youth Administration defense workers; and traditional children's ministries by the Women's Auxiliary, whose hardworking wives lost an audacious bid to become "full-fledged members" of the BMEC in 1944. Although women were doing every kind of evangelism short of public preaching, the executive committee, alert to the appearance of effeminacy, termed their accomplishments "special projects."[120] A former pastor of Moody Memorial Church explicated the gender roles in his anthem "In the CBMCI." Businessmen were "working for Jesus /

In the CBMCI." The "[w]ives of these noble crusaders . . . Gladly self-interests resign; / Urging [men] on in their conquests, / Faithful in prayer standing by."[121]

The war's dragged-out end was the catalyst to reacquaint, if not wholly reunite, northern and southern evangelical businessmen. As it became clear in 1944 that the Allies would win, many conservative Protestants believed that God had given America the long-sought opportunity to "evangelize the world in this generation."[122] The only superpower left standing, the United States could penetrate more nations with Christian and democratic principles than ever before—if it did not fracture from within, as strike waves and racial unrest ominously hinted it might.[123] The BMEC reorganized at Toccoa Falls in 1945, and a joint BMEC/CBMCI committee formed to negotiate "a friendly relationship of fellowship and cooperation." Committee members agreed that if one group already existed in a place the other wanted to evangelize, the second should back down and encourage laymen to join the first. This solution to turf wars treated the BMEC and CBMCI as a single evangelical businessmen's movement, even as regional and institutional identities were maintained.[124] Not that regionalism was at the forefront for the rejuvenated BMEC, which described itself as "On the March, Going Forward . . . An Interdenominational, Pro-Church, Militant, Evangelistic Organization with Worldwide Vision." The BMEC's constituency was still "the Southland," but the group's nationalism did not end with the war. "The Christian forces of America stand on the threshold of the greatest era of opportunity that has ever challenged any generation. Doors are opening . . . calls to *Help us* are being received—the 'Green Light' is ours."[125]

Evangelical triumphalism backed by American military might was neither marginal nor misplaced. Other white Americans expressed the same world vision in different language. Shortly before Pearl Harbor, *Time* publisher Henry Luce christened 1941 the beginning of "the American Century," during which he and fellow Americans would export "our Bill of Rights, our Declaration of Independence, our magnificent industrial products, [and] our technical skills."[126] Columnist Walter Lippmann argued, "What Rome was to the ancient world, what Great Britain has been to the modern world, America is to be to the world of tomorrow."[127] Evangelical businessmen took up these themes, which, once the war began, became popular as well as elite conventional wisdom. In January 1943, *Christian Workers* opined, "The big task of Christianity now is to prepare for the peace that shall follow when the war is over. The world will be wide open for the preaching of the gospel. . . . This is our supreme missionary obligation."[128] It was a government obligation as well. A Thanksgiving prayer looked forward to something like the Marshall Plan, "relief [that] will come to many with the benevolent measures of the Allied Forces benefitting millions who have long endured the horrors of war."[129]

Few commentators, evangelical or otherwise, expected the aftermath to be easy. The Yalta Conference in February 1945, at which Roosevelt and Churchill yielded to some of Stalin's territorial demands, seemed to vindicate fears of Russian treachery.[130] Premillennialists whose theology predicted a one-world government were suspicious of the United Nations charter, although *The King's Business* wondered if "this will be God's method to open doors for another priceless opportunity to preach the gospel to the ends of the earth ere Jesus returns?"[131] No one doubted that the atom bomb could bring about the end of world, and much of the world was already in ruins before Hiroshima. Who would fix it? How? The list went on and on, from the death of Roosevelt to the unfolding revelations of the Holocaust, about which evangelical "Hebrew missions" had sounded an early warning.[132] "Surely God has set before us an open door," a doctor wrote in *Contact*, "and enormous responsibilities have been placed on us."[133]

Evangelical businessmen's overwhelming responsibility was funding, and in some cases founding, foreign missions in the spirit of *Pax Americana*.[134] "When our boys in uniform won the victories, they didn't stop at the borders, they went in and possessed," said one CBMCI board member. "So it should be with us . . . more than conquerors through [Christ] who loved us."[135] The missionary imperative coincided with economic expansion and the resurgent global conflict between capitalism and communism. The CBMCI began living up to its "International" name in 1946, when inquiries about forming affiliates came from "China, Korea, Jamaica, Australia, South Africa, England, Scotland, and Holland." Seattle chairman N. A. Jepson was headed to China. Washington, DC's, Glenn Wagner had already gone.[136] Wagner met with the fledgling CBMCI-China, whose members included Andrew Gih, formerly a singer for CBMCI-Chicago. To complete the convergence of evangelical business networks, Wagner, who was representing the New Testament Pocket League, came loaded with six hundred Bibles from the Cleveland Gideons for China's CBMCI.[137] In 1947–48, the Gideons budgeted an unprecedented $21,300 for their own International Extension Program. They sent a representative to Japan at General Douglas MacArthur's request for Christian missionaries to start, in his words, "a revolution of spirit . . . which will more favorably alter the course of civilization than has any economic or political revolution in the history of the world."[138]

As close as Asia was to the hearts of some evangelical businessmen, others agreed with CBMCI secretary Paul Fischer that missionary work was "most important . . . in Europe."[139] Although it was a shock to think of Protestant Europe as a mission field, evangelical theology dictated that suffering nations must have sinned in the eyes of God. "[F]or a century or more England has been sending Bible teachers and evangelists to America," Wheaton president V. R. Edman wrote to LeTourneau of the conference establishing Britain's Youth for Christ. "[B]ut now, conditions, spiritual and material, have reversed the process."[140] LeTourneau hoped to improve England's spiritual and material conditions and to move from producing earthmoving equipment *for* other countries to producing it *in* other countries, by opening a factory in Stockton-on-Tees.[141] The revivalistic dedication ceremony was as elaborate as any of his had ever been, and he tacked on a month-long preaching tour.[142] The British press was fascinated by the All-American industrial invasion of what one columnist called "some 200 lbs. of dynamic, restless hustle."[143] LeTourneau himself quipped, "I have not figured out yet whether I am over here to start a factory or to run an evangelistic campaign. But I know that if I let evangelism take first place the Lord will take care of the factory."[144] He was wrong—the Stockton-on-Tees plant never got enough traction to make a profit—but his publicity machine captured the exuberance of American business and American evangelicalism immediately after the war. "God's Business Man, R. G. LeTourneau, Goes Global," one *Joyful News* headline read.[145]

So did Billy Graham, who compared his itinerancy on behalf of YFC to the time he spent before college selling Fuller brushes. "I was a traveling salesman again—not displaying a case of brushes this time, just brandishing my Bible."[146] Between 1945 and 1947, American servicemen started Youth for Christ chapters in Germany, Okinawa, Guam, the Philippines, Portugal, Sweden, Ireland, and France.[147] In 1946, Torrey Johnson, Graham, and two other men who had never left North American soil spent six weeks promoting YFC in Great Britain and Scandinavia. The following year, Graham spearheaded a well-publicized but not well-financed follow-up tour saved by a last-minute $7,000 check from LeTourneau.[148] Graham suggested to British and Irish YFC organizers that they create "a Christian Business Men's Committee such as we have in America."[149] Torrey Johnson made the same point in a meeting with CBMCI leaders, stressing businessmen's ability to "follow-up for the YFC rallies . . . to effectively maintain the interest, testimony, and to lend personal assistance and counsel to those won to the Lord." Without coordinated evangelism, Johnson warned, "other 'Hitlers'" would rise in Europe.[150]

Johnson's fear was rooted in political reality. By Harry Truman's election in 1948, doors were closing to Americans. Stalin's iron curtain was taking concrete form in Eastern Europe. More heartbreakingly for evangelicals, Mao Tse-Tung's imminent victory in China's two-decade civil war meant the downfall of Chiang Kai-Shek and his outspokenly Christian wife in one of American Protestantism's oldest mission fields.[151] The standoff with the Soviet Union and Mao both heightened evangelical anticommunism and underscored its place in the mainstream of American politics. Liberals and conservatives, religious and nonreligious, all equated communism with totalitarianism, though they disagreed about the centrality of atheism and the economic implications for the post–New Deal state.[152] Evangelical businessmen, however, could never think negatively for long. As business interests tamed elements of the New Deal, the members of the CBMCI, Gideons, and BMEC remained confident in their ability to sway potential consumers and converts.

Billy Graham, self-described "salesman" for God, expressed the excitement, anxiety, and continued fractures of early Cold War evangelicalism. Still famous as one of Torrey Johnson's YFC lieutenants, not yet as an independent evangelist, he addressed the BMEC's 1947 annual conference and led a revival in Charlotte a few months later at Vernon Patterson's invitation.[153] The second event, in which LeTourneau participated, brought Graham's "recommitment" full circle. The motto was "Christ for Crisis."[154] A slew of form letters signed "Your Pal, Billy Graham" marveled, "Boy, this is SOMETHING for the South!"[155] Within weeks, Graham was at the CBMCI conference, reminding northern evangelical businessmen why they needed to sell their brand of Christianity to Europe. "Everyone is talking about the third world war. Not if, but when," he said. There was only one response, and like the men around him, it was defiantly hopeful. "May we dedicate ourselves to getting the gospel around the world within the next two or three years."[156]

Graham and his business friends were too impatient to imagine waiting a generation to evangelize the world. This is why they busied themselves on another front. Even as the CBMCI and its many subsidiaries and partners in wartime evangelism pursued their gains among young people and servicemen, across north-south-west divides, and industrialists like J. Howard Pew, R. G. LeTourneau, and Herbert Taylor forwarded their own agendas in a moment of unprecedented economic and political energy, enterprising evangelicals as a whole started to create an organization, a movement, that could solidify their interests. Individualists still, highly protective of their local churches and decentralized associations, they nevertheless inched toward yet another compromise: ecumenism. As they had demonstrated in their dealings with the wartime state, evangelicals were principled but also pragmatic. Beginning in 1942, and with accelerating momentum during the late stages of war, they proved this point yet again by downplaying some of their denominational particularities to construct an umbrella entity that could wage a different type of battle against liberalism, secularism, and an enlarged state. Businessmen, as was usual by then, led the charge.

CHAPTER FIVE

The Wartime Consolidation of Laymen's Evangelism

While newspaper headlines in April 1942 screamed of the business of war, they also announced the latest deadly violence from the field. Daily updates, offered in bold print, kept readers abreast of Allied and Axis maneuvers in Europe and Asia and all points of bloody conflict in between. "Paris District Bombed Again,"[1] "Nazis over Malta in Big-Scale Air Raid,"[2] and "MacArthur Hailed as Symbol of Spirit That'll Beat Japs"[3] were among the headlines. It was in this context that on April 7, 1942, readers of the *St. Louis Post-Dispatch* came across the front-page headline "Church Group Warns U.S. against Totalitarianism," continued inside with "Fears Radicals in Government."[4]

The story that followed described the first convention of a new group, the Temporary Committee for United Action Among Evangelicals (hereafter "United Action"). Boston preacher Harold J. Ockenga, in an otherwise revivalistic speech, condemned Roosevelt's "managerial revolution" as one cause of the "break-up of the moral fiber of the nation."[5] William Ward Ayer, pastor of a leading fundamentalist church in New York City, told the assembly of three hundred that Americans were "directed and governed by members of bureaus which were not part of our original democratic system," in which "men, not elected by people, are assuming dictatorship of the people." He warned, "We are living in an age of regimentation. Everyone is being counted, labeled, signed, classified. We may be sure religion will not escape," especially given communist advances within the American government. Because "[t]he state is demanding that every force, educational, social and economic, shall be governmentally controlled," evangelicals must fight back. "If we unite, we might be able to save the American democracy of our forefathers."[6] Only evangelicals resisted absorption into

Roosevelt's mechanistic, anonymous state. A faithful remnant in a fallen land, they must guard the covenant.

"If we unite" brought Ayer to the purpose of the conference, the political salience of which was subtler than the *Post-Dispatch* headlines implied. In the fall of 1941, competing factions within conservative evangelicalism announced their intention to organize a national force for spiritual revival. One of them, United Action, was meeting in St. Louis to publicize its goals and begin setting up a formal structure; its leaders included Herbert Taylor. It denounced what it perceived as an unholy alliance between the federal government and the Federal Council of Churches (FCC), a modernist body representing most mainline denominations that claimed to lobby on behalf of all American Protestants. United Action wanted evangelicals to enjoy the same benefits that the Roosevelt bureaucracy gave the FCC: network radio time, on which modernists held a monopoly, and expedited passports instead of months of hassle for missionaries unaffiliated with the FCC.[7] Both issues cut to the core of the evangelical mission to spread the gospel as widely as possible and highlighted the entanglement of the New Deal in noneconomic aspects of American life. Also in St. Louis was United Action's evangelical antagonist, the American Council of Christian Churches (ACCC), which agreed with the platform but held stricter membership standards. United Action made a point of including as many evangelicals as possible, including those languishing in conservative denominations or churches that belonged to the FCC. The ACCC, by contrast, required its adherents to sever all FCC ties. The standoff was a classic fundamentalist confrontation between ecumenists and purists, and it did not bode well for the unity all professed to want.[8]

In part, the *Post-Dispatch*'s coverage emphasized wartime politics because few nonevangelicals could read between the lines of the internecine battle over how to revive America. That said, they accurately reflected the anti–New Deal politics imbedded in evangelical fears of "totalitarianism," which flowed into and complicated the wartime politics of "unity." After all, Ayer's paeans to democracy and collective responsibility could have come from a presidential fireside chat. United Action's purpose, according to founder J. Elwin Wright, was "to find common ground upon which we may stand in our fight against evil forces, to provide protective measures against the dictatorships of either government or ecclesiastical combinations," and "to seek ways and means of carrying on for Christ unitedly and actively, but with freedom of action" for constituents.[9] Translated, "we" meant evangelicals of Wright's ecumenical stripe, not the ACCC's separatists. "Government or ecclesiastical combinations" alluded to the New Deal state, the Catholic Church, and the FCC. "Freedom of action" signaled Wright's fealty to conservative Protestant federalism. Evangelicalism's voluntary association of diverse faith communities, each accountable only to God and conscience, rebuked the alleged dictatorships of Catholicism and the FCC. By implication, the ACCC was arrogantly blocking a "spiritual union" of Christians on narrow-minded technical grounds.[10] Wright and his colleagues devoted most of the conference to arguing that "united action" on their expansive terms was not only doctrinally sound but also pragmatically necessary, if evangelicals were serious about strength in numbers.

For all its disparagement of the ACCC's elitism, United Action viewed the nonevangelicals it eventually hoped to reach with the alarmist condescension of "mass society" theorists. Wright's "we" relegated not just the ACCC but most of America to the democracy-threatening ranks of the tyrannical or malleable. In 1939, leftist commentator Dwight Macdonald accused Stalin of "conditioning" the "masses" to appreciate superficial and soul-degrading art.[11] Austrian conservative Friedrich Hayek countered that socialists like Macdonald were dragging the masses down "the road to serfdom" with planned economies like the New Deal.[12] Businessmen pursuing mass markets had a sunnier view of mass manipulation, with Depression-era advertisers "want[ing] to exercise moral leadership" over fickle consumers.[13] These strange bedfellows shared one conviction with each other and United Action: they, the enlightened, must protect democracy from the *demos*.

Shortly after St. Louis, United Action one-upped the American Council of Christian Churches by renaming itself the National Association of Evangelicals.[14] The clerical leaders wanted a businessman to be treasurer, but their first choice bowed out. Wright called Herb Taylor, whom he and radio evangelist Charles Fuller had visited at home to recruit to United Action. Taylor accepted the position and instantly became the most powerful layman in the overwhelmingly clerical NAE.[15] For his six years as treasurer and many more on the board, he and a growing cadre of businessmen would play key roles in making the NAE a "clearing house for evangelical activities . . . with a front in relation to government."[16] In 1942, however, it was by no means obvious that the NAE would survive its infancy, let alone become an influential public voice for some forty denominations representing forty-five thousand churches by 2009.[17] Flush with the nationalizing and internationalizing impulses of wartime, J. Elwin Wright dreamed big. He imagined a conservative evangelical counterpart to the Federal Council of Churches—a vast network to advocate for "Bible-believing Christians" unrepresented by "representatives of Protestant Christianity [who] have departed from the faith of Jesus Christ."[18] It was a recipe for a great awakening.

Building such a network among historically decentralized fundamentalists would be no small feat. Local, state, and federal governing authorities recognized the FCC as the voice of American Protestantism, a political equivalent to the Roman Catholic hierarchy. The specter of a papist super church made the sheer scale of Wright's proposal hard for some evangelicals to swallow.[19] Fundamentalist federalism, as the Christian Business Men's Committee International and Business Men's Evangelistic Clubs were also learning, valued independence of action over consensus of thought. Meanwhile, the ACCC continued to lump the NAE with FCC apostates and compete for members.[20] The same regional differences that thwarted a CBMCI-BMEC alliance made the NAE's first initial stand for "Northern" more than "National." As with the nearly bankrupt Club Aluminum in 1930, Taylor was taking on an enormous project with a minimal budget and every possibility of failure.

Once again, Taylor's instincts about the project's potential were sound. Businessmen midwifed the NAE in two ways. The first was operational. Without businessmen's loans, donations, and tireless fund-raising, the NAE would have folded in its first five years. The mercurial Wright boasted an entrepreneurial streak, but his faith in God's provision encouraged an unbusinesslike appetite for risk. Before he initiated United Action, he inherited and developed his father's ministry and the real estate investments that sustained it.[21] However, he was reckless with the NAE's money when he was following the spirit and lost at least one close financial counselor as a result. The more even-tempered Taylor, who already had Wright's trust as an adviser, was able to influence the NAE's long-term direction.

This influence was Taylor's second, more visionary contribution to the NAE. Wright's ecumenical, civic-minded, and large-scale evangelicalism was what businessmen had been doing for years. The NAE's ecumenism, with a lowest-common-denominator statement of faith and a preference for collective action over theological wrangling, echoed that of the CBMCI, Gideons, and BMEC. Its motto, "Cooperation without Compromise," came from the Navy Chaplain Corps.[22] Taylor's belief that evangelicals should participate in public life echoed the "service" ethos of Rotary and other business clubs. His desire for the NAE to make a truly national impact paralleled his philanthropic Christian Workers Foundation, which generally snubbed local or regional evangelism. By contrast, the ACCC's decision to purge all traces of the FCC exemplified what many evangelical businessmen scorned as self-defeating fussiness. They modeled evangelism on the mass market, while the ACCC was an island of the elect. Finally, as the speeches in St. Louis showed, the NAE was business friendly. In a time of war, the founders of the NAE, like millions of other Americans, linked capitalism, Christianity, and democracy as causes to fight and die for.

The NAE's first several years of existence must, then, be accounted for from the perspective of businessmen. Their traditional strengths—networking, behind-the-scenes organizing, and, of course, managing money—complemented the efforts of clergy, theologians, and full-time evangelists to convince churches, denominations, and independent ministries that "cooperation without compromise" was essential to evangelicalism's public witness.[23] Just as significantly, businessmen made their interest part of NAE programs. "Industrial chaplaincy," or the placement of chaplains as a bridge from management to labor to prevent worker unrest, was a high priority at the start. Although the initiative would fail in the short term, its spirit would resurface in a Cold War guise.[24] Other scholars have told the story of the NAE's entanglement with conservative business interests during the Cold War, but the alliance began at the association's birth.[25]

J. ELWIN WRIGHT'S CALL FOR "UNITED ACTION"

Before the NAE, there was the NEF. J. Elwin Wright's New England Fellowship had been an outpost of fundamentalism since 1931, when Wright renamed and restructured the Pentecostal ministry his father passed down to him in the mid-1920s. Rumney, New Hampshire, was not an obvious evangelical mecca. Yet Wright made it a scaled-down version of Billy Sunday's Winona Lake with help from fundamentalist contacts from his real estate ventures in Florida.[26] In addition to conferences and camps at Rumney, the NEF supervised dozens of evangelistic teams, Bible study teachers, rural outreach, a radio show, and "gospel teams" of businessmen.[27] Wright invoked his real estate experience to explain what he thought evangelical churches needed to do: "cut the red tape of precedent and explore new fields."[28] He moved the NEF headquarters from out-of-the-way Rumney to Boston, whose evangelicals had a history of interdenominational cooperation in the face of an insurmountable Catholic majority. The NEF found offices next to Park Street Church, a conservative Congregational redoubt. Its incoming pastor in 1936, Harold J. Ockenga, admired the NEF and would become one of the most powerful intellectual and administrative leaders in the NAE.[29]

In 1937, Wright traveled across the country, preaching with the Fellowship Radio Ensemble and making more connections: Charles Fuller, Moody Bible Institute president Will Houghton, and the Africa Inland Mission's Ralph T. Davis. It was Davis who suggested, in late 1940, that evangelicals represent themselves in Washington. His immediate concern was to protect missionaries from the draft, but he also feared the loss of religious liberty to a growing federal state in combination with the monopolistic Federal Council of Churches.[30] So did the separatist founders of the American Council of Christian Churches, with whom Wright and Davis skirmished before forming the Temporary Committee for United Action Among Evangelicals in the winter of 1941.

War was the catalyst for the two fundamentalist factions to put the rhetoric of evangelical unity into action. As in World War I, conservative evangelicals rose to a fever pitch of patriotism against what they saw as an existential threat to America, God's second Israel.[31] With "unity" as a watchword for the entire country, evangelicals felt a cultural warrant to join together and advocate their hopes for the nation.[32] The competition between the ACCC and Wright's United Action demonstrated how difficult it would be to muster every denomination, church, and individual identifying as "evangelical" under one roof. Yet both organizations responded to the centralizing circumstances of World War II by reimagining the perennial hope for revival as an immediate and collective challenge. Like Allied victory against the Axis powers, revival could only be thwarted by internal divisiveness (United Action's primary concern) or conspiratorial subversion (the ACCC's).

The push for evangelical unity stoked nostalgia for Protestant "united action" before theological modernism ostensibly corrupted a once-Christian America.[33] Moody, Sunday, Finney, Whitefield—the hallowed names of interdenominational empire builders in the past—legitimized the ecumenists of the present. The strategic fight between the ACCC and United Action masked the common ground they shared with other evangelicals who, by the early 1940s, longed to restore their lost cultural power. In 1936, *The King's Business* complained, "We are too narrow, too provincial, too circumscribed. God wants to lift us out of our provincialism and to give us a world vision."[34] In mid-1940, *Moody Monthly* was so preoccupied with American unity that the prerequisite of evangelical unity was a given. While the editors continued to bash "the totalitarians now in control in Washington," they followed their gibes with a plea to exercise evangelical custodianship over the nation through the ballot. Voting was "the self-conscription of patriots in an army set to save the American idea" from Nazism, communism, and fascism.[35]

The King's Business was under the editorial control of Paul W. Rood, the president of BIOLA and, since 1929, of the World's Christian Fundamentals Association (WCFA).[36] Founded shortly after World War I to coordinate revolts against German higher criticism within established denominations and eliminate evolution from public schools, the WCFA was a prototype for both the ACCC and the NAE.[37] Under Rood, the WCFA became one of several meeting grounds in the 1930s for clergy and laymen who wanted fundamentalism to invite people in rather than shutting them out. His recruitment of Arnold Grunigen to organize California CBMCIs paid off in attendance at the 1937 WCFA conference. Grunigen, C. B. Hedstrom, Jepson, and William Pietsch—father of Pearl Harbor missionary Charlie Pietsch, and president of the quasi-denominational Independent Fundamentalist Churches of America—were featured speakers, along with LeTourneau and tract writer Tom Olson. There was a motley crew of pastors from Swedish Tabernacles (Rood's background) and assorted Baptist, Presbyterian, and independent "Bible" churches. Missionaries to Russia, Belgium, and Syria gave presentations. Premillennialist Bible study alternated with working sessions such as the CBMCI-dominated "Laymen's Day" and " Stewardship Day." Participants could also learn "How to Have a Perennial Revival."[38] An early supporter of the NAE, Rood saw it not as a competitor but as part of a web of evangelical networks that grew stronger with each strand.

Taylor seems not to have participated in the WCFA, but he was among the first laymen to join United Action in 1941. Wright wasted no time in asking him to recruit business support for the spring conference in St. Louis. "It is not thought desirable to send out any general call for funds," Wright said, "but rather to find out if there may be several of the Lord's steward's [*sic*] who might like to join in underwriting the movement during this formative period." A Woolworth executive and a New York stockbroker were already on board, and Wright hoped for one or two "such men [who] should more or less equally divide the expense" of $2,500.[39] No large benefactors materialized, so in January 1942, Wright took a page from the CBMCI and made a promotional and fund-raising trip to the South. In Chattanooga, BMEC president Boyd Hargraves presided over a lively debate between Wright, whom a newspaper identified as a "Boston executive," and evangelical clergymen with varied views on the need for a counterweight to the FCC. A Methodist bloc voted no, led by two pastors who "said they believed in all the fundamentals and did not believe the [FCC] was deserting them as charged." Another opponent thought that conservative evangelicals should make their case within the FCC, instead of diluting Protestant strength through division. This was a sticky point for a group calling itself *United Action*; Wright resolved it by arguing that the FCC's apostasy had divided Protestants already.[40] Likewise, he would blame the American Council of Christian Churches for discord within evangelicalism, in each case positioning United Action as rock of orthodoxy in someone else's storm.

No one mentioned the ACCC in Chattanooga, however, and despite the dissenting Methodists, Hargraves stacked the deck in United Action's favor. Perceived or actual government intrusion into religious liberty topped audience reasons to look favorably on the new movement. Grievances included government-distributed materials for possible inclusion in sermons; censorship of religious radio scripts; and, according to an army chaplain, documentary proof that "the [FCC] leadership was saturated with Communism." Wright also red-baited the FCC, asserting that Roosevelt had a cabinet-level "minister of religion" in the works "to end independent religious action."[41] At a Hargraves-hosted dinner of eighty-five men, Wright's proposal to institutionalize an alternative to the FCC won by a vote of 81–4.[42] It was symbolic, but it was a start.

The central problem galvanizing United Action and the ACCC, fundamentalist access to radio, had business as well as religious and civic dimensions. Starting with the printing press, evangelicals had exploited technologies of mass media for mass evangelism.[43] In the early 1920s, when radio was in its infancy, star preacher Aimee Semple McPherson wired her Angelus Temple for sound and received the third radio license in Los Angeles.[44] While most subsequent evangelical programs were cheaply produced and local or regional in scope, national broadcast networks enabled a lucky few entertainers and advertisers—or both, such as George Beverly Shea on *Club Time*—to gain a wide audience. By 1941, thanks in large measure to Taylor's absorption of his advertising budget, Charles Fuller's coast-to-coast *Old Fashioned Revival Hour* was one of the most popular programs on the air.[45]

After Europe went to war, however, industry and federal regulations imperiled evangelical radio in two ways. First, in 1939, radio networks began giving free time to Protestant, Catholic, and Jewish religious programs "to promote the spiritual harmony and understanding of mankind." Because the FCC represented "Protestantism," evangelicals could not take advantage of this perk even if they were willing to abandon hellfire-and-damnation sermons.[46] More alarmingly, mainline religious leaders proposed to ban paid programming, the only way evangelicals could get on the air.[47] Carl McIntire paid to preach on the air, and he founded the ACCC to fight back. "The very nature of radio," he said, "calls for a central body representing the historic faith," lest the din silence of Christian truth.[48]

J. Elwin Wright's close ally Charles Fuller, with no hope that his network would subsidize the *Old Fashioned Revival Hour*, had another reason to fear for his ministry and livelihood.[49] In August 1942, the American Federation of Musicians, a branch of the AFL, called a strike. The strike's primary target was recording technology such as the phonograph, which, the union contended, jeopardized the jobs of live studio musicians.[50] Fuller's music was always live, but his players were not unionized, engulfing him and them in a labor conflict that would drag on for years. One of United Action's first projects after St. Louis was to enlist the antilabor National Association of Broadcasters to defend Fuller and other evangelical radio hosts from union pressure. "Racketeering" was Wright's word for the American Federation of Musicians' national organizing campaign. "[T]he voice of united church must be raised against all interference on the part of the union with religious broadcasts."[51] While endorsing the evangelical logic that converting opponents was the only long-term solution, Wright was adamant that hope lay in lobbying the Federal Communications Commission. As untrustworthy as the other FCC (the Federal Council of Churches), but more accountable to the public, the Federal Communications Commission might respond to aggrieved and organized evangelicals.[52]

Between the St. Louis meeting in April 1942 and the constitutional convention thirteen months later, Herbert Taylor was uniquely placed to advise the newly christened National Association of Evangelicals on government and radio matters. Maurice Karker, the World War I naval commander who had brought him in to rescue the Jewel Tea Company, became chair of the navy's War Contract Price Adjustment Board. Its congressional mandate was to prevent the three million companies supplying the war effort from making "excessive profits," according to the vague language of the statute. "The game is extremely profitable to the government," *Time* grumbled. After a thorough audit, with "gimlet-eyed price-board agents hang[ing] around to make sure no penny is mislaid," a manufacturer could expect "a proposal to slash profits 25%, 50%, or maybe more." With little room to haggle for fear of losing the contract, "voluntary kickbacks" put millions of dollars in federal coffers.[53]

Taylor's vice chairmanship of such flagrant state intrusion into free enterprise revealed more than his loyalty to Karker. Again, Taylor was willing to judge Roosevelt's initiatives on a case-by-case basis instead of condemning the New Deal wholesale, using his Four-Way Test as a guide. Taylor would not have taken the unpaid post, which siphoned time and energy from Club Aluminum and the CWF, without running it through his rubric of honesty, fairness, promoting "goodwill," and "benefit[ing] . . . all concerned."[54] Although *Time* viewed price adjustment as highway robbery, he (and the administration) saw it as thwarting profiteering and financing a just war while enabling substantial post-Depression growth. Not long before, the same companies had no profits at all. Wartime imperatives of "unity" and "service"—the latter, again, a talisman for a dedicated Rotarian like Taylor—also justified keeping big business and big government intertwined.[55] Finally, the Price Adjustment Board made Taylor even more valuable to the NAE. He had an office in the Pentagon, experience testifying before Congress, and familiarity with Washington's esoteric ways.[56]

As for radio, *Club Time* and Charles Fuller had acquainted Taylor with the business side of broadcasting, including the self-regulating industry bodies whose decisions were as binding as those of the Federal Communications Commission. Taylor and Robert Walker—who was writing war propaganda for the Office of Civilian Defense and running the CWF during his employer's long absences—gave Wright a crucial piece of advice in April 1943: attend the annual meeting of the Institution of Education by Radio (IER).[57] Founded at the Ohio State University in 1930, IER promoted radio as a progressive educational tool in schools, colleges, and for the general public.[58] The IER disapproved of paid religious broadcasting, ostensibly because it was partisan advocacy, but more because of the membership's liberal politics and taste. The IER agreed with *Christian Century*'s denunciation of "independent peddlers of spiritual nostrums who have no more 'church' behind them than a microphone . . . and a post office box in which to receive their proceeds," which tarred every hand-to-mouth evangelist as a gold-digging Elmer Gantry.[59] Asking listeners to give money for spiritual programming crossed a liberal line between religion and business, the sacred and the profane, that conservative evangelicals did not draw when preaching the gospel was at stake. The government's favoritism toward the FCC, bolstered by the IER, left them no other choice.

The first IER annual meeting after Pearl Harbor, held in 1942, brought liberal concerns about "independent" religious programming to a head. America could not afford another Father Coughlin, the unpredictable and eventually protofascist "radio priest" who had aroused a huge over-the-air following in the mid-1930s.[60] Nor, IER participants believed, could democracy survive religious division. This was the same rationale that the NAE and the ACCC gave for reviving America and rejecting each other, but where evangelicals wanted to recruit, the IER celebrated diversity to the point of denying religious differences. It recommended that the Federal Communications Commission end paid time and require "that religious radio programs . . . be addressed to a cross-section of the public—to Protestants, Catholics, Jews, and nonbelievers—and not to members of any one faith."[61] Either proposal would endanger evangelical radio, but as the IER's 1943 gathering approached, Taylor and Walker saw a chance to intervene. The Federal Communications Commission had not made any changes yet.

Wright and another NAE representative went to the IER conclave.[62] Wright understood that the radio crisis was a dry run for the NAE's largely untested claim to be able to achieve for "evangelicals," as a group, the goals that eluded them when scattered. The IER marked his debut as the NAE's emissary to liberal outsiders instead of other fundamentalists. As Taylor and Walker had hoped, his presence gave evangelicals visibility and a voice. The same rules of liberal pluralism by which the IER threatened to silence them gave them a place at the negotiating table. Wright earned his nascent organization its first victory, leading a successful charge against the directive to encompass all faiths and none. The IER, however, preserved the restrictions on paid programming, which the Federal Communications Commission soon adopted.[63]

Wright's small triumph and larger loss not only vindicated the need for the NAE at its constitutional convention a few weeks later but also validated the elitist identity overlaying its grassroots structure. Speaker after speaker imagined the NAE in much the way the IER imagined itself: as a cadre of leaders responsible for educating and inspiring the confused and easily swayed masses. In the NAE's case, the masses were the American people in general and disorganized evangelicals in particular. "[W]e had better frankly admit that fundamentalists have not always been wisely led," Wright said, in a dig at separatists such as those affiliated with the ACCC. The premise of "a new strategy under competent leaders" would be that "not all modernists are hopeless apostates" but are misguided by "apostate leaders." The NAE would rescue "the masses of the common people," which Wright believed were "not hostile to the gospel," from the FCC, "those blind leaders of the blind who have brought the church to its present low state spiritually."[64] Macdonald and Hayek would have appreciated the biblical reference. They too saw themselves as prophets contending with Pharisees who held the masses in their thrall.[65]

EVANGELICAL REVOLUTION

Harold Ockenga, the Boston preacher, made the political resonance of Wright's language explicit. Whether *Moody Monthly* was decrying the hordes that voted for Roosevelt or the *New York Times* was condemning Germany's "blind obedience" to Nazi propaganda, the solution was the same: America must embrace its destiny as the scourge of tyrants.[66] Conservative evangelicals began by convicting everyone, especially Christians, of rebellion against God. "The heart of western civilization today is heathen rather than Christian," Ockenga argued, and the result was "authoritative rule from above." Yet expert authority, freely granted from below, was at the heart of Ockenga's vision for the NAE. A "chastened" postwar America would be "ready for an advance under the proper type of leadership"—evangelical. "It is up to us to make sure that the Christian church will return to a new leadership, producing statesmen for our governmental circles, influencing education, and rebuilding the foundations of society."[67] This was an aggressive version of the standard evangelical riposte to the social gospel, the New Deal, Marxism, and other ideologies of human progress. A revived church would "produce" the Christians who would, by God's grace, change the culture.

NAE clergy's emphasis on "leadership," in addition to locating evangelicals within mainstream political discourse, paralleled the advertising philosophy of every businessman in the room. Wright welcomed lay participants effusively. "[T]heir counsel and participation is essential. They will meet at various times . . . to prayerfully consider how they may be most helpful in a great advance movement for the church," and the "report of their deliberations will be received with great interest."[68] The report did not surface in Taylor's papers, but Wright had good reason to be solicitous of businessmen's opinions, having raised a $24,000 budget from churches, denominations, and individual pledgers whom Taylor discreetly harassed into fulfilling their commitments.[69] "We have had a rather close time of it financially," Wright admitted in January 1943, "but fortunately I have been able to get along without drawing salary." He remained an unshakable devotee of the contractual theology to which R. G. LeTourneau, among others, attributed earthly wealth: God always rewarded obedient servants. "I feel sure," Wright continued, "that we will reach the required amount if we continue [to be] faithful."[70] So they did, but the act of God required human agency. Taylor, for example, promised the NAE $1,250 from the CWF and later added a $1,000 loan that he was willing to write off as a gift. The CWF also transferred its funds for Fuller's radio broadcast to pay Wright's salary and arranged the accommodations for the convention.[71]

Whether other NAE leaders valued laymen's ideas as much as their checks was an open question. Ockenga singled out the BMEC and Gideons as examples of "organizations of business men . . . which should be closely identified" with the NAE. Yet he went on to name only practicing clergy and the ordained Fuller as the "strongest [Christian] leaders in this nation," ignoring the same groups' fervor to drag what they considered a moribund church into a lay-led Christian America.[72] In fact, none of the first businessmen in the upper echelons of the NAE had close ties to the CBMCI, BMEC, or Gideons. John Bolten, a German immigrant who manufactured plastics in Massachusetts, served on the boards of Wright's New England Fellowship and Taylor's Inter-Varsity Christian Fellowship. After the war he traveled to Germany on a mission trip to youth cosponsored by the IVCF, NAE, and Youth for Christ. Around the same time, he sold his company to buy an evangelical publishing house in Cincinnati.[73] Tacoma timber baron and philanthropist C. Davis Weyerhaeuser paid to distribute IVCF literature at Yale, his alma mater, when Taylor and Stacey Woods were getting the American IVCF off the ground. He had been the NAE leadership's first choice as treasurer.[74] NAE secretary and legal counsel J. Willison Smith Jr. was similarly pedigreed. Born to Philadelphia's high society, he became a lawyer after graduating from the Wharton School of Business at the University of Pennsylvania. He lent his time to the Bible Institute of Pennsylvania, the Brotherhood Mission, and the Williamson Free School of Mechanical Trades. Keenly interested in evangelistic publishing, as were Taylor and Weyerhaeuser, Smith was the vice president of Bible Magazine, Inc.[75]

All four men's biographies, especially their commitment to college evangelism, suggest a higher-caste demographic than the hardscrabble ambition and man-to-man bluntness of R. G. LeTourneau. (LeTourneau's plant magazine, *NOW*, placed the chronically overbooked industrialist elsewhere for both the St. Louis meeting and the NAE's constitutional convention.)[76] For the NAE, having three Ivy Leaguers—John Bolten sent his son to Dartmouth—and Taylor's Northwestern degree sent the message that fundamentalists were qualified to lead the country.[77] "We know that the evangelical faith is not incompatible with the highest culture and the most effective education," one speaker argued at the constitutional convention.[78] To groom establishment-credentialed clergy and theologians, Ockenga was mentoring evangelical students at Harvard Divinity School.

Charles Fuller was making plans to endow a rigorous seminary that he hoped would demolish the not entirely undeserved stereotype of fundamentalists as close-minded absentees from American intellectual life.[79]

The constitutional convention and Taylor's CWF connections brought a familiar roster of businessmen (and patroness Gwendolin Armour) into the NAE's expanding bureaucracy. The Business and Professional Men's Committee consisted of the BMEC's William Bond, a real estate agent in Washington, DC; from the CBMCI Arnold Grunigen, New York banker Philip Benson, Seattle's Jepson, and Chicago's Frank Sheriff and Carl Gunderson; and Erling Olsen, president of the Fitch Investors Service in New York and IVCF board member.[80] Armour served on the large national advisory committee with Weyerhaeuser and multimillionaire James L. Kraft of cheese-selling fame, her colleague in Taylor's aborted effort to host a Fuller revival in Chicago.[81] Texas manufacturer and cattle rancher John Mitchell, an important backer of one of Taylor's other projects, Young Life, was also on the national advisory committee.[82]

The star businessman of the NAE's first year was finance committee chairman Kenneth Keyes, who owned one of the largest real estate companies in Florida and the nation. A Presbyterian elder who, like Taylor, was a dollar-a-year man in Washington during the war, Keyes took very personal charge of a $50,000 fund-raising campaign.[83] In September, he declared his intention to join Wright on a tour of the Midwest "for the purpose of interesting business men in the movement," in Wright's words. "He has a burden on his heart . . . that the business men of this country shall realize their responsibility as stewards." In New York, Philip Benson was doing just that, arranging a small, exclusive meeting for Wright to pitch the NAE to "men who are going to be able to make contributions not only of money but service in other ways . . . the executive type who are in positions of some responsibility."[84] Not to be outdone, Taylor began his treasurer's report with an introduction to the Four-Way Test, followed by a Four-Way Plan: "1. Get the facts 2. Use the facts for a basis of plans 3. Sell the plan 4. Follow up and see the plan go through." It was Business 101 for clergy, and perhaps especially for the spontaneous Wright, who enthused of his tour with Keyes that "[w]e are expecting under the blessing of God that this will be very beneficial in a financial way." Anticipation was not a plan.[85]

Businessmen such as Keyes and Benson worked hard for the NAE during the alternately promising and frustrating year of 1943–44, but Taylor and the CWF played a special role. Taylor was the leading lay representative in Chicago, NAE's headquarters and the evangelical and business capital of middle America. He was as much the NAE's salesman as Wright, who regularly consulted him and Robert Walker on how to present the new organization to the evangelical and general public. Marketing "united action" was proving even more difficult than the founders expected. The continuing agitation of the ACCC, combined with doctrinal differences among evangelicals and unshakable fears of surrendering institutional autonomy, presented setbacks. Wheaton College, MBI, and Dallas Theological Seminary, all initially supportive, retreated from the ACCC-NAE crossfire by adopting stances of studied neutrality.[86] Although individual southern Baptists served on NAE boards, the Southern Baptist Convention, representing five million evangelicals from outside the Midwest, Northeast, and West Coast, chose its usual insular course.[87] These losses shrunk the budget for goals that the NAE had to show potential members it could achieve: widespread mass evangelism; a mission board to bypass modernist creedal requirements and send evangelicals into the field; a "Department of War Services" for chaplaincies and servicemen's evangelism along the lines of the CBMCI's Victory Centers; strengthening evangelical education; keeping evangelicals on the radio; and opening a Washington office.[88]

Inspired by Philip Benson's plan for a businessmen's banquet in New York, Wright asked Taylor to organize a copycat event in Chicago under the auspices of the Midwestern Regional Committee, let by pastors Torrey Johnson and Dr. Harry Hager.[89] (In the fall of 1943, Youth for Christ, which Johnson would lead, was barely on the horizon.) Since Taylor, the CBMCI's Carl Gunderson, and their secretaries took responsibility for every time-consuming detail, Taylor peppered Wright with questions to narrow down the goals of the event and the message with which to maximize participation. "How do you announce the purpose of your meeting in your invitation to those you want to attend?" Who, exactly, did Wright want to attend? "Are you limiting your invitation to known conservatives? Or are you inviting some liberals? . . . Do you limit your invitation to those you feel can make a sizeable contribution to the work?" Wright reiterated his belief that only "business executives, or [men] in the higher brackets of income" should be on the guest list. The presence of liberals "would probably be embarrassing." The "announcement" should be brief, advertising an informational meeting about the NAE with "an opportunity to discuss the movement intimately around the table." Finally, although the NAE had just brought in much of the national CBMCI leadership, Wright suggested inviting "men who are in many cases not active in organizations such as the Gideons and the Christian Business Men's Committees. Such men are usually snowed under with their work in connection with these organizations."[90]

Wright's concern about overwhelming the businessmen's groups was curious, because as the final list of about eighty prospects showed, to be an active evangelical layman was to be overcommitted. Taylor included only a few CBMCI officials and the indispensable Andrew Wyzenbeek, national vice president of the Gideons and member of the Christian Laymen's Crusade. To coax the remaining multiply affiliated men into giving the NAE a hearing, however, Taylor and Walker dispensed with Wright's demure invitation and took aim at the invitees' profound sense of duty. One draft to go out under Hager's name flattered each recipient as one of "Chicago's and the midwest's responsible evangelical lay leaders," appealing to laymen's service ethos as a source of religious and social power. In language that could have come from any CBMCI or BMEC publication, the letter continued, "Now it is *our* turn and our time as business men" to back an "undertaking that calls our churches and our nation back to basic fundamentals—back to the Bible, back to 'born-again' religion, back to Calvary, back to the empty tomb . . . and then onward with God."[91] A personalized letter from Taylor elicited a pitch-perfect RSVP from an NAE finance committee member who could not attend: "I shall be glad to do anything I can to help with this work and would like to know just what is expected of me so I can fulfill my obligation."[92] Another sympathetic no-show left a message: "up to neck in church drive busy very much interested."[93] If Wright was still hoping to find a few businessmen who would drop everything to make the NAE their primary cause, as he had in 1942, he was disappointed. Like everyone else, the NAE would have to coax limited amounts from a large donor pool.

The Chicago dinner invitees with easily identifiable names and occupations fit the same demographic as the CBMCI and the Gideons (none of these northerners would have joined the BMEC). They were small, often family, business owners; manufacturers several notches below Taylor or the still-absent LeTourneau; executives; lawyers; journalists; bankers. Letters went to Martin H. Chapman of Chapman Laundry, Hammond, Indiana; Ralph Ullman of Chicago's River Copper & Brass; Frank McConnell of the Illinois Bell Telephone Company; Albert C. Bass of the I. B. William Leather Company; banker Frank Taylor (no relation); and Arnold Torsell of the *Chicago Daily News*. Taylor did not neglect evangelical business stalwarts who, like he, had far too much to do but would at least give a hearing to a plan for national revival. There was Torrey Johnson's industrial chaplaincy client, Walter Black of the Quaker Stretcher Company in

Wisconsin. There was a trio of early recruits to the IVCF administration: D. Cameron Peck, famed for his collection of hundreds of vintage cars; Paul Westburg, the district manager of West Electric Instrument Corps; and J. F. Strombeck, a toy manufacturer from Moline, Illinois, who had just recently opened an office in New York.[94] Publisher Robert Van Kampen, president of the Chicago Gideons, served on the boards of Young Life and IVCF. Although no one took much notice at the time, he hired Billy Graham out of Wheaton College to pastor the church where he chaired the board of trustees.[95] Fifty men accepted the invitation, "over three-fourths" in Taylor's estimation "business and professional men."[96] There is no detailed record of the outcome, but of the names listed above—Frank Taylor, Walter Black, and all of Herb Taylor's IVCF colleagues—either became or already were associated with the NAE.

Not only did Taylor supply the NAE with businessmen from his other CWF organizations—the IVCF's mission to college campuses dovetailed with the NAE's quest for elite evangelical "leadership"—he used his role at the NAE for the CWF's profit. For instance, Wright often asked Robert Walker, whose writing and editing portfolio had earned him a journalism lectureship at Wheaton, to approve NAE publications before they went to print. Walker scolded him for the quality of the brochures the NAE planned to send out after the constitutional convention. "[I]n presenting any project to the public," Walker explained, as from an expert to a pupil, a promoter must use "proven techniques of gaining attention and the desired action from those you are attempting to reach." Visually, the pamphlets did not reach the bar. The NAE needed to follow "modern advertising procedure" and "be more colorful and attractive to the eye." After all, "in the Lord's work especially, we should use every means to make [our materials] as attractive as any product the world has to offer."[97] "Better Printing of Christian Literature" happened to be the motto of Good News Publishing, founded by the CWF. Wright also gave manager Clyde Dennis carte blanche "to print a new issue of 25,000 for us at once, dressing it up as you think best."[98] Afterward, the NAE became a regular Good News client.[99] Wright asked Walker to write the *Flash Sheet*, a newsletter keeping national and regional administrators up to date. "We need a catchy heading for it," Wright worried, but *Flash Sheet* it remained.[100]

Being "modern" in the tactical, not theological, sense of packaging the same old gospel in contemporary wrapping was central to the NAE's identity. The twin foils were the FCC's theological modernism (a new gospel) and the American Council of Christian Church's separatism (obsolete and ugly wrapping). To distinguish itself from the ACCC, the more immediate threat to large-scale fundamentalist organizing, the NAE defined its goal as "positive" evangelical unity based in common ground instead of "negative" unity obsessed with common enemies. "It is the firm belief of the brethren that the purpose of any new association . . . should not be inaugurated on a negative, but a positive basis; not to attack" the FCC, but to "represent an alternative Protestantism," Wright stressed to a leadership council after St. Louis.[101] However, the distinction was strained for two reasons. First, the NAE regularly assaulted the FCC, both from genuine enmity and to disprove the ACCC's insinuations that the two groups were in league. For example, "positive" could hardly have been the word that came to readers' minds when the *Chattanooga News–Free Press* paraphrased Wright's accusation that the FCC "[c]irculat[ed] sex literature so vile as to be unfit for decent people to read."[102] Second, and related, the interdenominational hospitality that the NAE cherished as its improvement on nitpicking fundamentalism stopped at a statement of faith that was "inclusive" only on evangelical terms. The fundamentals were all there, from the necessity of new birth to biblical literalism, artfully worded to include almost anyone already in the fold. From within evangelicalism, Wright's orchestration of an NAE creed without a premillennial plank and "acceptable to extreme Calvinists on the one hand and . . . and Pentecostal and holiness groups on the other was nothing short of a miracle."[103] From without, the NAE gave "sectarianism [a] new lease on life," in *Christian Century*'s judgment.[104]

An early episode in which Wright sought out Taylor's advice suggests that businessmen and evangelists or preachers differed about how to brand the NAE as "positive" by contrast with the ACCC. For a businessman such as Taylor, "positive" and "negative" were advertising terms. They stood for tactical choices about how much to bathe the consumer in good feelings about buying a product or prey on anxieties about not having the product.[105] After instituting the Four-Way Test at Club Aluminum, Taylor banned advertising that implicitly denigrated the competition, which he considered neither "true" nor "fair to all concerned." He told the marketing department to eliminate "superlatives" from ad copy. "No more would we be using words like 'best' or 'finest' or 'greatest,' nor even phrases such as 'better than another brand,'" he wrote in his autobiography. "From now on . . . we [would] only tell the facts as we knew them about our product."[106]

This emphasis on "facts" was a mantra of the "scientific" advertising that Taylor would have absorbed as a young businessman in the 1920s. Marketers believed that national consumer choice among "products offered . . . impersonally through the marketplace" would keep quality high and prices low, enabling winning manufacturers to increase and diversify production for an ever-growing percentage of the buying public.[107] The shift by the 1940s to emotional manipulation through color, tone, and popular psychology—that is, the changes Walker wanted in NAE pamphlets, fewer words and better visuals—presumed a less rational consumer but did not necessarily dethrone "facts." For someone who believed as wholeheartedly in his product as Taylor, the challenge was to present the "facts" in the most alluring possible light, informed by "scientific" analysis of the emotions that swayed consumer judgment.[108]

For a preacher like Wright, superlatives and comparisons told the "facts" of religion. Christianity was not pots and pans; it was a narrow road to salvation surrounded by malevolent forces on all sides. The ACCC's obstructionism was a case in point. Souls were at stake. The nation was at stake. Christendom itself was at stake, and founder Carl McIntire seemed only to want loyalty oaths. Of course, McIntire believed that Wright was taunting God by associating, however indirectly, with the FCC. Wright was not content to go the positive advertising route, puffing the NAE and ignoring the ACCC. The stakes were too high. Rather, he wanted to go to the mat with McIntire and show the world whose side God was on. In the advertising parlance of a later age, he wanted to go negative.

The opportunity arose when the *Sunday School Times*, a popular evangelical newspaper out of Philadelphia, aligned itself with the ACCC after St. Louis. "There is no question that the National Association of Evangelicals is holding firmly to the fundamentals of the faith," the editor, a member of one of the ACCC's founding denominations, was careful to say. However, the fight against the FCC bore clear parallels to World War II, as a pastor in McIntire's camp had recently written: "The basic issue may be stated in two words: Exclusivism vs. Inclusivism." The latter was "a policy of appeasement" toward the FCC, bound to end in "some kind of ignominious 'peace in our time.'" The *Sunday School Times* carried the pastor's analogy further, to the European war "and finally Pearl Harbor." Then, at last, "the American people were fused into one . . . against their common enemy, the Axis powers; but it was almost too late." In short, St. Louis was Munich. The NAE's "inclusivism" toward FCC-affiliated evangelicals was as naïve as Neville Chamberlain's pact with Hitler. Almost parodying the NAE's exhortations for conservative Protestants to set aside "inessential" differences, the *Sunday School Times* decreed, "[A]ll the Fundamentalists of the country should be willing to submerge their own personal interests and prejudices, and unite not only in a proclamation of the pure Gospel and the great doctrines of Scripture, but also in open opposition to a common enemy."[109] The NAE, it seemed, was fundamentalism's Vichy France.

Wright drafted a scathing reply and sent it to Taylor for approval. He addressed the war analogies immediately, calling the ACCC "ill-advised and presumptuous" for creating an organization by one man's fiat without "bringing [evangelical] leaders together and letting them build the movement from its very foundation." In other words, the ACCC was totalitarian, while the NAE functioned "in a most democratic way." Wright repeated the *Sunday School Times'* acknowledgment that the two groups were theologically united. Instead of arguing, as he usually did, that their strategic differences could be overcome, he refused to separate the council's mission from its methods. "They evidently sincerely believe that the emphasis should be on attack," Wright fumed. "We have witnessed this strategy for a generation and seen it fail. . . . The net result has been to make the word 'fundamentalist' synonymous with 'bitterness,' 'strife,' 'ranting,' and 'division' in the minds of a great section of the public." The NAE intended to change that image instead of indulging the ACCC's bid for attention. "[W]e do not propose to answer in kind the attacks to which we have been subjected since the St. Louis Convention," Wright concluded. "We prefer to 'saw wood' and let the results speak for themselves."[110]

In Taylor's world, Wright's letter was the equivalent of taking out a full-page ad against a competitor instead of promoting one's own brand. Taylor retorted that "[y]ou are surely answering in kind" and recommended an alternative to brawling with the ACCC that combined the Four-Way Test with Rotarian civility among competitors. The NAE, barely born, needed to manage first impressions, not least with the evangelical press that could give it free publicity and influential endorsements. "It seems to me that it would be better strategy" to meet with the editor in person and lay down "the facts which you have presented in your proposed letter," Taylor said. A polite conversation, he believed, would inspire a follow-up piece that "would contribute to the prestige of the National Association of Evangelicals." Taylor argued further that the NAE should be positive in its dealings with the ACCC. "I have always found that when you have a controversy on your hands it is better to walk into the other fellow's camp, find out where he is vulnerable and attempt to sell him on your point of view, rather than"—pointedly—"to write a letter to him which might just 'put oil on the fire.'"[111] Wright listened. The next month, the *Sunday School Times* published excerpts from a much milder letter that stuck to factual clarifications. The editor apologized profusely for any "misunderstandings."[112] Modern marketing principles had earned favorable coverage for the NAE from a prominent ACCC supporter.

ANTICIPATING A NEW WORLD ORDER

Such collaboration between NAE's clergy and businessmen grew in importance through 1944 and 1945 as an Allied triumph seemed inevitable. "The time has come for the NAE to render constructive service as its major business, allowing organizational promotion to take second place," President Leslie Marston, a Free Methodist bishop, wrote to Taylor in May 1944. His priorities were the creation of "a handbook of proven evangelistic procedures and principles" for revivalists; the "critical field" of Christian education; and mobilizing evangelicals around laws in most states that allowed students time out for religious instruction. "If the liberals capture this field"—that is, if only FCC churches offered programs for which children were allowed instructional leave time—"the tragedy would be great." At the top of the letter, Taylor scribbled another mission: "Program for returning service men."[113] A July *Flash Sheet* noted a postwar relief meeting that had taken place at the Bankers' Club in New York. Attendees included Wright, several clergy and businessmen, and a Chinese-born YMCA worker who was a veteran lobbyist for humanitarian aid. "THERE IS MUCH THAT IS BEING DONE THAT WE CANNOT RELEASE TO THE PRESS AS YET," the *Flash Sheet* warned in capital letters.[114]

So many projects made businessmen and some NAE clergy nervous. Leslie Marston copied Taylor on a letter to Wright observing that "[s]ome fear we may spread into new fields before consolidating our earlier gains toward our initial goals," a sentence Taylor marked. In particular, war relief was shaping up to be a larger, more complicated, and more expensive proposition than anyone in the NAE had realized. Wright had rushed into it without "reasonable certainty as to procedure and governmental authority" or "whether missionary or welfare organizations of experience are actually functioning in this area." The "persistent refusal of passports by our own state department" to missionaries did not bode well (and, Marston did not add, was one of the problems that the NAE had originally formed to fix).[115] The government information that Wright finally received gave the NAE two bad options: to "operate as a religious or mission board" with no financial or diplomatic help or to "register as a War Relief agency." The price of official recognition was $25,000, which Wright cheerfully assumed that NAE member churches would cover.[116]

One problem with this plan was that the NAE was already trying to raise $30,000 for its 1945 convention, and it was counting on businessmen, not churches. While some congregations were active in the movement, most had been grandfathered in by their denomination, and the affiliation was meaningless to most parishioners. Wright perpetuated the fiction that the NAE's "grass-roots" might be counting denominational censuses, enabling him to claim to represent millions of evangelicals who, in reality, had little interest in the cause.[117] Only a month earlier, at the end of 1944, President Marston had written to Taylor and other large donors that "during these initial years of foundation laying most of the financial burden must be borne by a comparatively few churches, organizations and individuals who have caught the vision of the immense importance of this work." A postage-free return envelope accompanied the hint.[118] In February, Wright asked Taylor and "several [other] people from whom contributions of a rather sizeable amount are to be expected" to turn in their midyear pledges early in order to avert a "financial crisis."[119] Wright's secretary, who faced going without salary, thanked Taylor effusively for a $500 check. "It is a real source of anxiety that we do not have the necessary funds to carry on efficiently," she confessed.[120]

Another problem was that Wright, exhausted, wanted to be relieved of his position as executive secretary, but nobody wanted the job. Perhaps trying to broaden the NAE's geographic appeal, the executive committee deputized Taylor to interview two Californians. Bank of America's Harry R. Smith demurred, saying that he wanted to focus on the San Francisco CBMCI.[121] Next, Taylor wooed an assistant to a prominent Los Angeles evangelist, disregarding not one but two "nos" before reluctantly admitting defeat.[122] After the rejections, Wright soldiered on, and Taylor stayed loyal to him amid palace intrigue. He told another NAE administrator how much he had been praying about the executive secretary position since the second man turned it down. "I recognize Dr. Wright's limitations and realize that he has many times moved ahead on important matters before securing proper authorization," Taylor said. Yet Wright was "sincere," "under great pressure," and "most anxious to make a great showing to our constituency as quickly as possible." It was true that "many of us have wondered whether . . . the work is progressing under his leadership as much as if we had another man." But the NAE owed its very existence to Wright's creativity and drive. "[Dr.] Wright is an excellent pioneer. He is not thin skinned, [and] he takes constructive criticism in a splendid manner. . . . I lean toward keeping Dr. Wright on as a top man in the administration of NAE until the Lord provides us a better man for the job."[123]

In the NAE as in his other philanthropic interests, Taylor was a power broker because he negotiated personality conflicts and philosophical disputes as deftly as he handled money. When the *Protestant Voice* asked President Marston to select three NAE leaders to profile, he picked himself, Taylor, and Harold Ockenga. Taylor declined the honor, explaining that "publicity . . . tends to hinder me in the Lord's work."[124] He probably anticipated a deluge of funding requests after the story, but the real danger was to his reputation as a diplomat. Evangelicalism was full of men who craved a spotlight. Not being one of them gave Taylor the credibility to influence events behind the scenes, which is not to say that he was popular there. At least once, his determination to pay outstanding bills before salaries caused the NAE secretary to erupt. "I have been giving toward the support of my widowed mother and younger brothers and sisters since I began working in high school, and we are dependent on my salary," she told an executive committee member.[125] Taylor brought his impersonal treatment of Club Aluminum employees into the NAE, with unsympathetic and undiplomatic results.

As the war drew to an end, more businessmen came to the foreground, including a new crop of hired hands rather than volunteers. Banker and CBMCI powerhouse Philip Benson set up war relief warehouses in New York and Philadelphia without compensation. His paid assistant and soon-to-be successor, Philadelphia insurance executive Frank D. Lombar, introduced himself to Taylor with the unctuous observation that "our business back-ground gives us much in common."[126] Robert Kelly, a former corporate treasurer with "a great deal of experience in sales promotion work," charged fifty dollars a week to plan "NAE Week," a publicity and fund-raising blitz akin to the CWF's "Tract Week."[127] Taylor, Keyes (who also sent $500 in response to Wright's "financial crisis" plea), and Chicago's Dr. Harry Hager formed a committee to tighten the bonds between headquarters and regional affiliates, a centralizing step they felt was long overdue.[128]

The NAE's federalism had always been a fiction. Unlike the bottom-up growth of the CBMCI and BMEC, the NAE started like a modern corporation, with a small group of innovators perceiving a vast consumer need. Yet it operated as if it were a popular movement instead of an elite-led experiment that could not even compel member groups to pay dues. Marston's presidential successor, R. L. Decker, signaled a shift in the title of his inaugural speech at the 1946 convention, "An Evangelical 'Over-All Strategic Concept.'" He meant the phrase, stolen from Winston Churchill, in two senses. One was evangelical stewardship of the postwar world.

"Why do we not train our young people to take their places in the state department, in the diplomatic service, yes, in politics? Others do." The other was the democratization and centralization of the NAE. He recommended that a UN-style general assembly elect a board of administration to implement NAE initiatives as it saw best, with a budget to which everyone contributed.[129]

In this climate of missionary exhilaration, but internal professionalization, J. Elwin Wright's less-than-businesslike leadership style finally led to his resignation. At the beginning of 1946, Taylor had to mediate between Wright and a furious Kenneth Keyes, whose bond from stumping together for the NAE was unraveling. The immediate issue was Wright's creative money management, which Taylor also reproached. Keyes saw the episode, which involved poaching money from the War Relief Commission for the critically low general coffers, as a symptom of Wright's overemphasis on program expansion and neglect of basic solvency.[130] "Frankly I am not at all pleased with the financial showing for last year," Keyes, still chairing the finance committee, grumbled to Taylor in April. Only two-thirds of expected contributions had come in.[131] After another war relief brouhaha, Wright, smarting, threatened to resign. "I am conscious of my unfortunate tendency to run ahead of explicit orders," he said. "This tendency is one of the principal reasons why I have always felt that I was not competent to carry out the duties of the Executive Secretary of the NAE."[132] President Decker asked Taylor to attend a meeting of all the parties. The entire War Relief Commission wanted to quit "because Dr. Wright is making commitments and giving press releases out which they feel are so dangerous and disruptive . . . that they can not go on."[133] The meeting ended with everyone still in their jobs, but tempers still on edge.

When Wright decided to investigate the spiritual condition of postwar Europe and left at the beginning of October, Keyes was apoplectic and Taylor deeply disturbed. Keyes wrote a long letter to Decker after being notified that he had been reelected finance committee chairman against his will. "I am certain that in a business organization . . . the top man would not have made plans for a 5 to 6 week trip to Europe"—even, as in Wright's case, at his own expense—"at a time when the employees of the organization were having to wait for their salaries and the organization was not able to pay its current bills." He added that he "came to know and love J. Elwin on our western trip in the early days of the NAE, but as a businessman I just cannot see his policy of going seren[e]ly on his way with the expansion programs without laying the proper financial foundation as he goes along."[134] Taylor informed Wright that he was considering resigning as NAE treasurer. "I do not believe that when funds have not been provided for projects which have been approved, that we should go ahead and commit ourselves" to new ventures. "As you know, we have continually done that in NAE, and it has definitely placed us in hot water time after time." To say the least, Wright was burdening his staff and abusing Taylor's generosity. "I was a little surprised that . . . you wrote to me asking for an extra contribution from [CWF] of $1500, at a time when you were leaving a bad financial situation to go to Europe." Unlike Keyes, however, Taylor gave the European tour the benefit of the doubt. "Now, Dr. Wright, you may have definitely had the guidance of the Holy Spirit. . . . I am therefore not going to reach any definite conclusion until I have had a chance to discuss the matter with you."[135] He was satisfied enough with Wright's explanation to stay on as treasurer.

The uproar added to mounting administrative concern that Wright, who had poured superhuman effort into the NAE from the beginning, was "really worn to a frazzle."[136] In May 1947, Wright's NAE title changed to "assistant to the President." He held "no executive responsibility" but resumed the role in which he had done so much to get the NAE started: that of salesman. "His chief function for us will be to continue to cultivate the individuals with whom he is already in contact, for larger gifts . . . [and] add to this list," Decker told Taylor.[137] Another line the NAE threw out to businessmen was the creation of the Laymans' [*sic*] Advisory Committee. The group hired its own fund-raiser in the hope of getting a thousand men to commit to the NAE.[138] Scaling back Wright's financial role—he remained NAE's visionary in chief for years to come—removed a wild card but did not change the fundamental problem: the NAE's need to energize the millions it claimed as members. "After traveling among the churches four or five months I am convinced that the 'educational' phase . . . is going to take much longer than most of us first supposed," Decker told the CBMCI's Carl Gunderson, slipping into advertising language. "The top executives of the denominations and the more alert, better informed pastors of the larger local churches were easy to sell on cooperation among conservative Christians" but then grew "discouraged over our financial difficulties. The remaining denominations . . . are going to be more favorably impressed when our financial condition is better." The vicious circle of needing members to give money to get members highlighted the real challenge. "Cooperation per se does not appeal to conservative Christians by and large. They want to know, 'What is it doing for my church? How is it helping to win souls and advance the Gospel?' We have to prove it does."[139]

EVANGELICALISM'S VANGUARD

Ultimately, the NAE needed to prove itself to nonevangelicals if it wanted to revive America. Many of its businessmen combined missionary work and self-interest through the Commission on Industrial Chaplaincies, formed in 1944.[140] Just as army and navy chaplains embedded in fighting units boosted infantry morale, the commission promised, pastors on the shop floor would boost worker morale. Members were "studying plans to reach organized labor with the gospel," in the hope, as Wright put it, of "greatly reducing industrial unrest in the days of reconversion ahead."[141] Chairman Irwin McLean came to the NAE through the Cleveland CBMCI. He was now a full-time NAE staffer in Detroit, where he had ample opportunity to witness industrial unrest firsthand.[142] Because other NAE projects kept McLean busy, the commission's driving force was A. H. Armerding, "consulting engineer" of a Newark company that produced automatic stokers for furnaces.[143]

All but one of the ten members of the commission (the other was a cleric) owned or held powerful positions in small manufacturing outfits, like Armerding. They were concentrated in the Northeast and Midwest, like most of the NAE, and their other religious networks left few degrees of separation. Walter Block of Quaker Stretcher, IVCF benefactor J. F. Strombeck, and Young Life supporter John Mitchell were on the masthead.[144] So was C. F. Agerstrand, a native Swede who founded a one-room steel treatment plant in Muskegon, Michigan, in 1937 with $300. He made enough money to build a $10,000 addition in late 1940, possibly with the help of a government contract similar to LeTourneau's. R. F. Nelson was the vice president of Brooklyn's Arma Corporation, which originated with a navy contract in World War I. Rollin M. Severance, of Severance Tool Industries, established the Assemblies of God church in his Saginaw, Michigan, headquarters and volunteered for the Prohibition Party.[145] Samual A. Fulton, who had served two terms as president of the Gideons since he joined the organization in 1903, manufactured automobile parts in Milwaukee.[146] Torrey Mosvold, the president of Neptune Shipping, Inc., was from a prominent and philanthropic Norwegian family. Based in New York during the war, he had spent the late thirties in Chicago, where his sisters were in Bible school. Cementing his ties to midwestern evangelicalism and eventually the NAE, he attended the ethnic church in which Torrey Johnson had grown up.[147]

Herbert Taylor was supportive but wary. "[F]rom the start," he wrote later, "I felt the program was faced with tremendous handicaps and questioned whether or not the time, money, and effort . . . could not be used to a better advantage in the Lord's service."[148] Although more post hoc than he admitted, his judgment was right in the short term. The argument that evangelical religion protected business interests had little traction outside the fundamentalist subculture, for two reasons. First, psychologists had already claimed the field of "human relations" for science.[149] Second, the religious diversity of the workplace forced the NAE Commission on Industrial Chaplaincies to choose between a forceful evangelical witness and a vague ecumenism that appealed more to employers. Over four years, the commission went from being "one of the major projects of the N.A.E." to folding, at least temporarily.[150] The popularity of more sophisticated versions in subsequent decades, however, vindicated the commission's instincts in the long term.[151]

Putting pastors in factories to tend to the spiritual and emotional needs of employees, alleviating grievances that could lead to union organizing, was not a new idea. The YMCA had offered such services to manufacturers during the heyday of welfare capitalism before World War I. Volunteers led shop-floor Bible studies at lunch break that mirrored noontime revival meetings for white-collar men—except, of course, white-collar men were free to leave their workplaces for worship. During the 1920s, however, the YMCA folded into the social gospel movement, whose radical edge was growing. Leftist urban preachers such as Reinhold Niebuhr in Detroit supported unions, went toe to toe with welfare capitalist barons (in Niebuhr's case, Henry Ford), and demanded fundamental changes to what they saw as an unjust and unstable industrial order. Employers saw diminishing returns to industrial chaplaincies as workers enlisted chaplains to make bread-and-butter demands or treated them as a hostile arm of management and went on strike despite their counsel. Trapped between a shrinking pool of business backers and a swelling chorus of angry workers who had chaplains' support, the YMCA closed its underfunded Industrial Department shortly before the Wall Street crash.[152]

R. G. LeTourneau brought the industrial chaplaincy back to life at his Peoria plant in 1941, motivated by the army chaplains he dealt with as president of the Gideons and CBMCI.[153] It was easy to transfer the chaplaincy's spiritual, therapeutic, and advisory roles from the hierarchical setting of the military to the hierarchical setting of the workplace. In both places, the chaplain stood outside the hierarchy as a sympathetic ally, someone who paid attention to men as individuals and reassured them that their superiors did not see them as interchangeable units. However, the paid onsite minister had little immediate effect on LeTourneau, Inc.'s, robust religious routine. Visiting evangelists still came to preach at "shop talks," one of whom, Toccoa Falls radio host Elliott Linblad, became LeTourneau's industrial chaplain in Georgia.[154] Evangelical employees continued to practice their own forms of witness. "The Word by Workers," for instance, combined music and "testimony" in the company chapel at noon and midnight each Wednesday.[155] *NOW* chronicled the achievements of individual workers and encouraged employees to take collective pride in the company's contribution to the war effort. "When we buy Defense stamps & bonds & when we pay taxes we're helping to buy the materials we work with & to pay our own wages, because LeTourneau is practically 100% on war work," a feature on the global market proclaimed. "Wherever our armed forces & our allies go, picture LeTourneau equipment. . . . Because it's wartime around the world it's wartime around the clock & the calendar at LeTourneau's."[156]

LeTourneau's was, in truth, a cautionary example for would-be practitioners of evangelical welfare capitalism. Neither patriotic calls to sacrifice nor the chaplain prevented the rogue CIO organizing effort at Toccoa Falls in 1943. Two years later, the Supreme Court ruled that LeTourneau had broken labor laws by using threats and intimidation to quash a union formed by Peoria workers.[157] These inconvenient facts notwithstanding, the midcentury industrial chaplaincy movement counted on spiritual enlightenment and interpersonal empathy to mend the breach between management and labor. Even before the war ended, advocates were nostalgic for the self-denying patriotism they claimed had brought brief peace to industry. Resolutely ignoring countless wartime strikes, they argued that religion was the only force powerful enough to replace nationalism as a bond between labor and management.

Industrial chaplaincy took different forms across the spectrum of Protestant theology and politics. In 1943, the year of a devastating race riot, the War Emergency Commission of the Detroit Presbytery hired an "industrial chaplain" for the entire city. He steered clear of shop floors and founded the People's Institute of Applied Religion. Loudly pro-union and antisegregation, the People's Institute deployed an integrated "brotherhood squadron" to poor, black churches. The same year, the Federal Council of Churches arranged with the AFL and CIO to pay for a chaplain-cum-social worker in several Massachusetts factories. The FCC hoped that he could earn workers' trust as a church employee and not the company's.[158] In an important sense, however, these theologically and politically liberal industrial chaplaincies had the same goal as LeTourneau: to calm the explosive social forces beneath a fragile, if not fictitious, wartime unity.

By 1944, the NAE needed to revise its founding analogy between America, united in war, and evangelicals, united in faith. The Commission on Industrial Chaplaincies offered a layman's narrative of the NAE's relevance to the postwar world. "Prior to the war, clashes between labor and management were prevalent," a sleek promotional report informed attendees at the 1945 convention, which took place the week before V-E Day. Pearl Harbor had tempered "selfish interests" but had not destroyed them. "[T]he fires of industrial unrest are still smoldering and ready to burst into flame as soon as wartime restraints are removed." Thankfully, "moral and spiritual forces are equal, if not superior, to any patriotic motive" for comity.[159] The cover of the brochure showed a Bible beaming rays over a factory with workers pouring in and out. In the foreground were representations of three core constituencies: a woman, hair coiffed like a secretary; a man in a business suit and tie; and a bulkier man with his sleeves rolled up under his apron. He was carrying a tool and rubbing shoulders with the businessman, who listened closely as he talked.[160]

Other pages elaborated on the illustration's industrial paradise of reciprocity between employer and employee. "The underlying principle of the Industrial Chaplaincy program is to bring to bear upon the industrial worker, and upon management as well, the challenge of spiritual and moral considerations."[161] According to a piece reprinted from the *Army-Navy Chaplain*, "G.I. Joe will hardly settle for less than a chaplain on the job with him who will talk his language and who has the same staff status that his Service Chaplain enjoyed." The author imagined G. I. Joe deciding that "home missions had better begin at my work bench when I get back."[162] A. H. Armerding diagnosed "voluntary absenteeism," a common form of worker protest, as "evidence of a sinister disease which is gnawing at the very heart of employee-management relations." The cure was "mixing religion with business."[163] Walter Block of the Quaker Stretcher Company, who owed his minister for hire to Youth for Christ's Torrey Johnson, took "mixing" literally by combining the jobs of chaplain and personnel and public relations director. "[The chaplain's] function . . . includes the direction of Chapel services, personnel counseling, sick visitation and the editing of our Company's publication."[164] From beyond the NAE, the Ford News Bureau sent pictures of five thousand white and black employees worshiping together on Good Friday. The accompanying article did not note that Ford's wartime strikes outnumbered the weekly "devotional services" institutionalized in 1940.[165]

As Armerding's references to nonspecific "moral and spiritual forces" and categorization of industrial strife as a "disease" showed, he was familiar with his chief competitor: industrial psychology. Like chaplaincy, the "science" of human relations located labor-management problems in the emotional lives of individuals, not the structure of the workplace. But psychology was thoroughly humanistic. By attributing agency to "forces" rather than "God" or "Satan," Armerding gestured toward the language of human potential without ruling out the supernatural. Nowhere was the balancing act more apparent than in his foreword, which clearly addressed a nonevangelical reader. "In every well managed manufacturing plant, the machinery employed is given regular inspection and service in order to maintain the highest productive efficiency." Workers deserved "just as much, if not more, consideration," but not in "cold-blooded" performance reviews. Armerding rejected "[a]ny program based on the premise that the worker is merely a cog in the great industrial machine." Industrial chaplaincy "recognizes the personality of the worker." It was not "mercenary." In addition to "promot[ing] happier relations between management and labor," its "benefits will be projected into the homes and family life of all concerned."[166] By positing personal, familial, and social happiness as industrial chaplaincy's ultimate aims, Armerding airbrushed its theological moorings. The *Industrial Chaplaincy*'s cover Bible and testimonials about communal "devotion[s]" and prayer, however, brought evangelical Christianity to the fore.[167] The warring messages plagued the commission throughout its tenure.

After the convention, the commission formed an independent, nonprofit corporation called "Chaplain Counselors in Industry" and introduced a certification course at Wheaton College. New commission director Ernest L. Chase, another engineer, explained that being linked to the NAE (or "any one organization") limited their outreach. The new word "counselor," he added, was another concession to the norms of nonevangelical industries they had canvassed. These businesses had rejected "the shop-meeting approach" of LeTourneau, Walter Block, and John Mitchell for a more therapeutic role. "[I]f we trained [our] men to act as personnel counselors, we would be acceptable to management, and have equal or greater privilege of presenting the Gospel in a personal way to laboring men and women." Yet Chase was uncomfortable using the vocabulary of "atheistic psychologists." He asked Taylor "not [to] mistake the scientific phraseology to mean we are forsaking the old Gospel"; they were simply smuggling God's word into the enemy camp.[168] Whatever Taylor thought about the language, he was invested in the outcome. Having bailed the commission out of a financial scrape once already, he made it a line item in the CWF budget for 1945–46.[169] Not only that, he developed a strategy for approaching Chicago-area industries and promised to pay for the first chaplain in return for having a say in the hire. Chicago, like the rest of the nation, was enduring a record strike wave for the first half of 1946, and Taylor was in the mood to "experiment."[170]

The Wheaton curriculum, for which Taylor earmarked $525, further muddied the mission of industrial chaplaincy by restoring Christian proselytizing to the job description. Military chaplains and seasoned clergy were eligible for the first six-week summer program in 1945, and five enrolled. College faculty and evangelical businessmen traded teaching duties. They started with "Personal Evangelism," a "review of the need of the individual sinner for the knowledge of the Gospel . . . the responsibility of the Industrial Chaplain to meet the need and the most effective ways of dealing with the individual." Next came an introduction to "Factory Organization and Administration," succeeded by "Personnel Administration and Industrial Relations," a "survey of relations between management and labor, and the techniques most successfully used to promote efficiency and harmony." A week on "Organized Labor Problems" followed, covering the history and, intriguingly, "rights and privileges of organized labor in the average industrial plant." Would chaplains try to hold employers to the standards of the National Labor Relations Board? After a primer on health and safety, students investigated "Community Resources" for referrals. There was more than a hint of the social gospel in the safety net "dealing with crime, the handicapped, family welfare, housing conditions and child care . . . local government, public safety, health care, educational and recreational resources, and considerations for foreign born and racial groups."[171] At the same time, it was in management's best interest to outsource social problems to agencies that would help workers for free.

Last came the task of persuading employers that the salary of a Wheaton-certified chaplain counselor would pay for itself many times over in employee contentment. It became very clear, very quickly, that the commission had high-octane marketing to do. At the 1946 convention, Armerding put the best face on the situation. Only two of the five men in the first Wheaton class found chaplaincy jobs. "The accomplishments in the shop are still not sensational, and yet personnel problems are under control," one characterized his encouraging, if not electrifying, opening months. Still, these were early days. Thanks to Japan's surrender and the commission's publicity campaign in the conservative Protestant press, Wheaton had thirty-five applicants for the 1946 summer program, a majority of them former military chaplains. Chaplain Counselors for Industry, Inc., now with the CBMCI's Benson and Grunigen on the masthead, met a $10,000 budget without help from NAE headquarters. Armerding conceded, however, that fund-raising was a problem. "The early experimental stages of this work were not of such a character as to provide incentive for contributions from Christians generally," he said. "A few of the trustees carried the entire financial load."[172] To an extent, the commission found itself in the top-down plight that plagued the NAE as a whole. Unless a member church was in an industrial battle zone, it had no reason to care about an initiative by and for the NAE's businessmen. But the commission's shifting identities and inability to communicate a clear purpose in crisp words were its own problems, no matter whom it was asking for money.

Armerding was far less upbeat in a fund-raising letter a few months later, which he titled "Prayer for Industrial Evangelism." Abandoning psychological terminology, he reflected on the commission's two-year anniversary of "deep concern for the millions of men and women in American industrial plants who are not being reached by any evangelical testimony." The story, as he told it, was of unwary adventurers groping through an untrodden path surrounded by saboteurs. "From a religious standpoint, Rome was . . . drawing the working classes into her fold. From a political standpoint, the Communists were making great strides." Such opposition was to be expected, but they knew they were "venturing into the Devil's territory" when even "the Lord's people" abandoned them. "[T]o our amazement, the large majority of Christians have shown utter indifference to the need and to the vast possibilities of this work. It is our hope and prayer that this apathetic condition will be dissolved." He asked readers for "prayer," meaning "prayer and money," and signed off. At the bottom of the stationery ran the Chaplain Counselors for Industry, Inc.'s, innocuous and, in context, incongruous motto: "A Nonprofit Association for the Development of New Techniques in Industrial Relations." Perhaps the Devil was not solely responsible for evangelical lack of interest.[173] If Taylor responded to Armerding's letter, it is not recorded. He did donate five hundred shares of Club Aluminum stock to inaugurate a business program for Wheaton students, dwarfing his contributions to industrial chaplaincy.[174]

In 1947, still dissatisfied with the commission's progress, Armerding switched discourses again. He steeped himself in the literature of industrial psychology and regurgitated his findings in a ten-page, single-spaced, pseudoacademic paper for employers. "'Chaplain Counselors' for Industry: A Scientific Development in Counseling for Industrial Workers" was a brief for evangelical Christianity as the key to a happy labor force. Armerding got to the point on page 8, after discussing, among other topics, "self-values and other(s) values," "basic urges (drives or needs)," "libido fixation," "whole personality," "human adjustment," and "non-directive Rogerian styled psychotherapy." Chaplain counseling, he said, helped hypothetical workers "Bill" and "Mary" "incorporate in their own life spiritual resources from beyond themselves. These resources lie in the essentials of Christianity as found in the Bible. These become permanent values and new goals for an increasing maturity of life and efficiency on the job." Any other therapeutic regime encouraged "neuroses and general unrest . . . mak[ing] the ground fertile for the seed of Communistic or other agitators," and preventing "Bill" and "Mary" from "learn[ing] to adjust happily within industry's limiting frameworks of authority."[175]

According to Armerding, who was by no means coherent, "Biblical Christianity" was a technology, not a theology. It was "the most powerful force known in the field of adjustment of human personality when used in a scientific therapeutic relationship." It was a "personal function of the individual" that lacked any "denominational, organizational, or church function" or "outward forms and ceremonies." Because "Christian spiritual means . . . answer man's basic drives," they could be applied inoffensively to "men of all faiths." Science had spoken, and Chaplain Counselors for Industry, Inc., was ready to serve.[176] Ernest L. Chase, the nonprofit's director, had already contacted Union Carbide and Carbon, Marshall Field, National Cash Register, and other big businesses.[177] The commission's financial plan for 1947–48 was to solicit fifteen evangelical businessmen to pay expenses until one of the corporate behemoths signed a contract, enabling the nonprofit to become self-sufficient. Taylor at least considered, and probably joined, the group of fifteen. It topped out at ten, or two-thirds of the budget.[178] Union Carbide never called.

In 1949, the NAE's Commission on Industrial Chaplaincies dissolved. "It is obvious that religious work as such is unacceptable to industry," Armerding said. However, "[t]he larger industries seem to be very interested in securing the services of capable counselors, and we believe that evangelical Christians should seize the opportunity to secure such positions."[179] The 1948 convention report struck a rueful, but hopeful, note. Ernest L. Chase suggested a new iteration of the program, Insight Counseling "(the technical name for Chaplain Counseling)," to "125 of the largest, most progressive employers in America." He asked forty to allow a demonstration, and quoted some negative responses. They ranged from time, cost, and redundancy to "you lack statistical scientific proof from previous experiments"; "wait for the next year—then we shall be needing new plans badly"; and "this would raise the religious issue with Catholics no matter how skillfully you handled it." Chase concluded that "years of patient planning" lay ahead, unless indeed there was another war. "In such a case, we believe that many concerns will be tolerating our Christianity in order to reach the benefits of our program." In the meantime, Insight Counseling would plod along, reaching out to new manufacturers and working to establish its scientific credentials.[180]

By the 1940s' end, another war was, of course, already simmering, with nuclear annihilation and the obliteration of the entire human race entering the mix. The Red Scare was, once again—though with unprecedented acuteness—descending on America, infiltrating the hearts, minds, and homes of a new postwar suburban middle class. Corporate leaders, bolstered by the postwar economic boom, fearful of communist threats, emboldened by closer proximity to Washington, were becoming anxious that their World War II gains would reverse. And evangelical citizens—steeped as they were in an apocalyptic reading of time—were starting to clutch at their Bibles and the book of Revelation more firmly, as preparation for the worst. As this new global struggle intensified and assumed epic proportion, the NAE's chaplaincy program would indeed—as Chase predicted—find favor again in America's factories. So too would the evangelical clearinghouse's many other programs, offices, and initiatives. Carved out of the difficult but rousing exigencies of World War II, the NAE entered the Cold War more than equipped and ready to deliver its message—Herbert Taylor's, R. G. LeTourneau's, and CBMCI's message—to a wide, anxious, mainstream market.

Conclusion

In 1966, *Popular Mechanics* published a long article about R. G. LeTourneau, his earthmoving equipment, his faith, and his future. "At age 77, R. G. LeTourneau is in a class with the buffalo and the quilting bee, a slice of Americana disappearing from the scene," the author wrote half admiringly. "In an era when corporations are run by 'teams' and committees," there was little room for a "self-taught engineer who rose from garage mechanic to president" of a business that he "controls with the dictatorial rule of a benevolent despot."[1] LeTourneau's talent and stubbornness had kept him in the director's chair. In 1953, he sold LeTourneau, Inc., to Westinghouse for $31 million and a promise to stay out of the earthmoving business for five years. Now based in Longview, Texas, the site of his last plants, he used the time to develop oil rigs. His first client was future president George H. W. Bush. "Our feeling was that anyone who had that much confidence in himself was worth the gamble," Bush later said.[2] To Westinghouse's litigious chagrin, LeTourneau returned to his beloved machines the day the contract expired. He obsessed for years over an electric wheel, almost sliding into bankruptcy in 1962 before emerging with a design that transformed the field. "The Lord chooses the weak to confound the mighty," he crowed.[3]

The culture of LeTourneau, Inc., did not change much after World War II. God was still LeTourneau's partner and co-despot. An engineer grumbled off the record, "[I]f you argue, he'll start spouting the Bible. I mean, how can you disagree with God?" LeTourneau remained a staunch welfare capitalist. In Longview, as in Toccoa Falls, he built a training school to funnel "country boys" into his factories. "I realize we don't always pay the highest wages, but we make it a rule that a man can have all the overtime he wants," he informed the stunned reporter, who called him "an anachronism in the age of fringe benefits."[4] Somewhat less anachronistically, LeTourneau, Inc., was a family business at the highest levels. Each of LeTourneau's four sons had begun working in the plant on Saturdays and in the summer at age ten, for ten cents an hour. In one case, the molding backfired: the patriarch clashed with and fired his son Roy, who forgave him and got his BA at thirty-six. The reporter observed that LeTourneau seemed bemused that anyone would want so much education but thrilled to be the parent of a college graduate.[5]

Although LeTourneau liked to say, "I'll retire in a pine box," his son Richard took over the company a month after the article's publication. For the next two years, LeTourneau devoted himself full time to evangelistic activities, some old, some new. He continued to fly around the country and preach. *NOW* went to 600,000 addresses every month, subsidized by the LeTourneau Foundation.[6] He favored the NAE over the American Council of Christian Churches and was a loyal trustee of his home denomination, the Christian and Missionary Alliance. In the 1950s, the foundation took a page from Henry Ford and went into "industrial-missionary enterprises" overseas.[7] The Liberian government leased half a million acres of jungle. LeTourneau's agents cleared enough of it to open a village, Tournata, to local inhabitants and adventurous North American evangelicals. In Peru, LeTourneau and a corps of Mennonite missionaries destroyed acres of rainforest on the Amazon River to build Tournavista. "The objective was to open up the area, develop it, and colonize it," a mid-1950s brochure states. Accompanying photos showed Amazon natives in school and church.[8] Tournavista never mustered a profitable industry and became solely a missionary town in 1966.[9] Tournavista lives on as the name of a district in Peru and in a Facebook group created by former missionaries and their children.[10] On June 1, 1969, LeTourneau died from complications of an earlier stroke.[11]

LeTourneau's legacy continues to thrive in Longview, Texas. LeTourneau Technologies, Inc., a subsidiary of Rowan Companies, Inc., produces earthmoving equipment, oil rigs, electrical power systems, and steel.[12] LeTourneau University's central campus is down the road, with satellites in five Texas cities and online. Its mission is to nourish both spirituality and scholarship, "encourage[ing] . . . the qualities of ingenuity and entrepreneurship that contribute to free enterprise and the democratic process."[13] "Serving as an ambassador of Christ, you are a Christian leader," the school tells some thirty-five hundred students. Graduates should leave with "an attitude of leadership, a desire to make a difference, a commitment to change the world for the glory of God."[14]

Herbert Taylor did not have LeTourneau's luxury of ignoring changing business trends as the economy roared into prosperity after World War II. As chief executive and majority stockholder of Club Aluminum, he essentially had free rein, and other stockholders rebelled. The company saw profits from 1947 to 1955, peaking at $13 million sales volume in 1948. In the same years, however, the Korean War once again diverted aluminum to the armed forces, and the invention of lightweight, cheaper stainless steel revolutionized the cookware market.[15] The *Club Time* radio program, still starring George Beverly Shea, fell to budget cuts in 1954. In 1958, a commissioned survey of the staff and sales force found a growing mismatch between Taylor's management style and industry trends. As manufacturing and sales business merged into larger and more stable units, the strong-arm, high-volume advertising on which Taylor had cut his teeth was going out of date. Because Club Aluminum relied on an outside supplier, it could not respond rapidly to production problems that tarnished the brand name. Even the Four-Way Test and Taylor's other ostensibly nonsectarian truisms came under attack. Workers longed for a more complex approach to problem solving than slogans such as "Right Mental Attitude," Taylor's secular shorthand for "believing that what God wants done can be done." In 1961, the American Stock Exchange delisted Club Aluminum for the low volume and value of its shares. Taylor retired and handed the business over to the son-in-law he had groomed as his successor.[16]

The transition was smooth, because Taylor's philanthropic and service commitments had made him all but an absentee president for years. As early as 1946, two major stockholders protested the number of shares held by the Christian Workers Foundation, and the toll the CWF took on his time. In 1954, Taylor rose to the presidency of Rotary International. His biographer called the honor "the end of [his] productive years in the cookware business."[17] Taylor and wife Gloria spent months on a world tour of thirty-eight nations, and *Newsweek* put him on its cover to honor Rotary's fiftieth anniversary.[18] When Taylor returned to Park Ridge, he became a more public evangelist than ever before, preaching "a blend of the Four-Way Test, the virtues of prayer and Bible memorization, the need in American society for higher moral standards, and folksy advice, especially to teen-agers, on being successful in life."[19] He told the lessons of his life on television. He wrote for *Guideposts*, Norman Vincent Peale's magazine of Christian and capitalist inspiration; its multimillionaire bankrollers included retailer Stanley Kresge, newspaperman Frank Gannett, and oilman J. Howard Pew.[20] He spoke in high schools and anywhere else he could get an audience of youth.[21]

Taylor spent years organizing Billy Graham's 1962 comeback crusade in Chicago, an event that marked the mainstreaming of conservative evangelicalism during the Cold War. Graham, once Youth for Christ's second in command, was now giving Richard Nixon political advice. He was close to Pew, who, in 1956, had given Graham and his NAE circle $25,000 to establish the magazine *Christianity Today*.[22] Moreover, in the wake of Catholic John F. Kennedy's election, a group of fundamentalists wanted Graham to run for president in 1964. The businessman behind the draft, John Bolten, was a longtime Inter-Varsity Christian Fellowship and NAE patron. Fittingly, Taylor chose Bolten to buy out Club Aluminum and disperse its assets in 1967.[23]

Taylor, the Rotarian evangelical, managed to grow simultaneously more liberal and more conservative in his last active years. In 1967, he angered many conservative Protestants by endorsing the Good News translation of the Bible, which simplified the text in contemporary English. His flexibility about biblical literalism did not mean he had relaxed his doctrinal standards, however, especially those he held tight to in his home denomination, the Methodist Church. He withheld money from congregations that he accused of straying from "a real gospel message."[24] He turned his back on Northwestern University, his Methodist alma mater, when the president asked him to be a trustee. He refused to give to the scholarship fund of a denominational seminary until he investigated the orthodoxy of the student body. In 1970, Taylor formed the Good News Movement for conservative Methodists with Stanley Kresge, the *Guideposts* financer. Optimistic that "the fires of evangelism are again starting to sweep through this great church," he helped to sustain a conservative voice in the denomination that he loved.[25]

Herbert Taylor was almost eighty when a stroke incapacitated him in 1975. He lived for three more years, unable to speak, but continued taking daily walks, going to church, and listening to recordings of Bible readings. He died on May 1, 1978, and Shea sang at his funeral.[26] The Christian Workers Foundation reverted to the Taylor family as a private philanthropy. Rotary International continues to trumpet the Four-Way Test.[27] Robert Walker, Taylor's right-hand man, was an evangelical journalist and publisher until he died on March 1, 2008. Among Walker's legacies are a nonprofit foundation to support missionaries and the trade publication *Christian Retailing*.[28]

The corporate community of influence that entrepreneurial evangelicals like Taylor and LeTourneau helped bring to fruition in the World War II years certainly created legacies of its own in the Cold War period. Granted, these legacies were also shaped—profoundly—by forces of change far outside the control of the Christian business sector.

Consider, for instance, the geopolitical shifts sparked by the wartime conflagration. The public-private World War II defense industry that wrested the United States out of the Depression changed the nation's political and religious geography in several permanent ways. When the CBMCI and BMEC launched the ill-fated Christian Laymen's Crusade in the early 1940s, the Sunbelt was only beginning to challenge the North and Midwest for industrial and demographic dominance.[29] A warning flare went up in 1951, when Demos Shakarian, a dairy farmer and officer in the CBMCI of Downey, California, started the Full Gospel Business Men's Fellowship for Pentecostals. In 1960, the BMEC (now operating under the label "Fishers of Men") dissolved into the CBMCI.[30] Seemingly another instance of northern evangelicalism swallowing the South, the merger proved to be the other way around. Resistance to the civil rights movement, anti-unionism, foreign policy hawkishness, and cultural traditionalism lifted evangelical businessmen below the Mason-Dixon line from subcultural obscurity into Richard Nixon's "silent majority."[31] Chicago, the capital of fundamentalism for fifty years, and other northern cities faced crumbling infrastructures, a white exodus to the suburbs, and soaring rates of poverty and crime. Meanwhile, the southern and western growth spurt that began in World War II steadily progressed.[32] In Palm Springs, California, in 1969, the CBMCI smashed attendance records for its annual convention. Half of the twenty-five hundred were walk-ins, a sign of the Sunbelt's evangelical and entrepreneurial energy. In 1977, the CBMCI moved its offices to Chattanooga, Tennessee, where Boyd Hargraves had led the Depression-era BMEC.[33] Located just a two-hour drive northwest were the CBMCI's old neighbors, the Gideons. In 1964, the organization had changed headquarters from Chicago to Nashville.[34]

Geographical moves of this kind produced slight theological and methodological ones as well. Today, personal evangelism is still the CBMCI's primary emphasis, although the first generation's street theater has given way to self-help books such as *The Complete Christian Businessman* (1991) and *Eternal Impact: Investing in the Lives of Men* (1997). The current CBMCI permits women to be members, and its leadership spans the globe from Ecuador to India. Workplace ministries such as Operation Timothy, "leveraging the natural connections that form in the trenches of day-to-day life," show the lineage of industrial chaplaincies.[35] Local CBMCIs hold prayer breakfasts, drawing mayors and city councils. The seventy-fifth anniversary in 2006 issued the same challenge as the first: "We will never lose sight of the Holy Spirit changing the hearts and lives of businessmen, one life at a time!"[36]

As witnessed in the postwar trajectories of the CBMCI, within the changing geopolitical realities of the Cold War era entrepreneurial evangelicalism still enjoyed plenty of leverage—indeed, an increasing amount of it—as well as the ability to gear new conditions to its benefit and dictate wider discourses about faith and labor, faith and politics, according to its prescriptions and whims. Within this climate of rising cultural clout, the NAE enjoyed its own advances in the public sphere. Still clergy-dominated at the highest levels, the NAE spent the Cold War period continuing to wrestle with fundamental theological challenges that stemmed from evangelicals' new confidence in political and social engagement. The questions that NAE luminaries consistently entertained were, to a degree (especially to the eager, bottom-line business types among them), paralyzing: "How does one define 'evangelical'?" "What does it mean to be 'evangelical'?" Carl Henry and a host of new evangelical theologians based at Fuller Seminary in California helped keep these questions front and center in the NAE orb and in the NAE intellectual makeup.[37]

Yet not at the cost of "united action." Even as the NAE found itself surrounded by other enlivened civic religions in the age of Eisenhower, it remained determined to express its wishes in Washington on matters, for instance, pertaining to America's formal diplomatic ties to the Vatican, and especially in relation to radio and television and evangelicalism's access to broadcasting privileges. As one historian notes, "Long before the privatization push of the 1970s by neoliberal economists and politicians, evangelical activists wanted radio and television programming—then defined as 'public goods' for the 'public interests'—turned over to the market."[38] During the 1950s and 1960s, the indefatigable NAE lobby continued to wage this battle in policy circles, while also promoting—successfully—the expansion of media outreach on a broader telecommunications plane. In this endeavor NAE proponents exemplified the growing willingness of evangelicals over the second half of the twentieth century to forge coalitions with religious "others." Politics was not church; allies in worldly battles, they began to see, need not share the same fate in the afterlife. In fact, as businessmen already believed, the most effective place to witness—and promote market principles—was on neutral ground. If answering God's summons to preserve American strength and virtue meant mingling even with Catholics, perhaps God was taking another route toward the evangelization of the world. It was in this mind-set that J. Elwin

Wright, ever the visionary, returned to Europe on the NAE's behalf to organize the World Evangelical Fellowship, a remarkably global (boasting representatives from twenty-one different countries) and ecumenical (though not nearly to the degree of its counterpart, the World Council of Churches) venture that held its first meeting in the Netherlands in 1951. This fellowship was merely further proof that the NAE brand of postwar evangelicalism was gaining ground by way of institutional flexibility and its drive for innovation and larger market shares of a nation and a world in the midst of upheaval.[39]

The NAE, one could say, enjoyed other, less visible successes during the Cold War era as well; some were more profoundly culture shifting than the campaigns the NAE took on in conspicuous political fashion. One of the most significant legacies, in this regard, was the continuation of the ideology of "welfare capitalism" first espoused by LeTourneau and company in the 1930s, and coordinated during World War II by the NAE's Commission for Industrial Chaplaincies.

The Commission for Industrial Chaplaincies formally disbanded in 1949, yet its spirit lived on in other emerging programs, including Chaplain Counselors for Industry, Inc. A. H. Armerding may have grieved the end of the NAE's industrial chaplaincy initiative at the time, but his was a short-lived lament. Two examples from a small but potent religious boom in industry, already in progress when the NAE commission collapsed, vindicated Armerding's somewhat clumsy attempts to integrate faith and the psychology of human relations in workplace ministry. In 1949, Winston-Salem's R. J. Reynolds started the movement's shift toward the South by hiring a former air force chaplain as "pastor-counselor." The company's wartime union troubles were legendary, and it had only recently struck back by severing its labor contract. Now it was in the middle of a bruising National Labor Relations Board–supervised election. The chaplain, like the company's free subscriptions to self-help preacher Norman Vincent Peale's *Guideposts*, was part of its renewed interest in welfare capitalism as a solution to labor-management strife. He called his job "applied Christianity in the human relationships of industry and at the workaday level of personal problems." Keeping at arm's length from management and giving a sympathetic ear to workers, he received the lion's share of the credit for rising employee retention and falling absenteeism. An R. J. Reynolds board member declared that he would not only "recommend" but "crusade for" "religious counseling in other companies."[40] On the other, liberal ecumenical side of the religiopolitical fence, the United Church Men of the National Council of Churches formed a Religion in Industry Committee in 1953. It identified low worker self-esteem as the preeminent industrial problem and an industrial chaplain capable of "building spiritual values into work relationships" as the answer.[41]

Fifty years after its first incarnation, the industrial chaplaincy still crossed white, middle-class Protestant party lines by appealing to fears of social disorder. Anticommunism, with its tendency to root class conflict in individual pathology, could still be either liberal or conservative. In 1948, the CIO and the Congress of Racial Equality purged communists from their ranks, and former state department official Alger Hiss fought charges of treason. In August 1949, the Soviet Union dropped its first atomic bomb, and two months later, Mao Tse-Tung took China. Over a dozen states instituted loyalty oaths for public employment. In February 1950, Senator Joseph McCarthy made himself a sensation by inviting news cameras to watch him wave a piece of paper, on which he malevolently fabricated and named two hundred more communists in the State Department. It was the NAE commission's misfortune to run out of money and energy just as the cultural climate for industrial chaplaincy was heating up. "[M]ixing religion with business," to quote Armerding and LeTourneau, was shedding its stigma in a divided world facing nuclear annihilation.[42]

For political and economic conservatives, a fight against communism was a fight against the New Deal. The National Association of Manufacturers (NAM), which housed some of Roosevelt's most ardent and wealthy opponents, embraced workplace religion and industrial chaplaincies to both ends. J. Howard Pew and the American Liberty League; his close ally Jasper Crane of Du Pont, where the Liberty League originated; and leaders from the likes of General Motors and the National Steel Corporation fought taxes, regulations, and unions in the political system, the courts, and public relations campaigns. Government-industry collaboration during the war began to turn the tide in favor of the NAM, the Chamber of Commerce, and the Council for Economic Development, NAM's more ideologically diverse siblings and sometime rivals.[43] The 1947 Taft-Hartley Act, which restricted the right to strike and forbade "closed shops" that hired union workers only, was a NAM-led victory for the entire business community. Christian anticommunism was both a rhetorical strategy and, by the early 1950s, a workplace practice. "Christian freedom will give way to atheistic slavery . . . and the dead hand of bureaucracy will close the throttle on progress," prophesied an NAM spokesman during the Taft-Hartley debate.[44] The church-industry relations group encouraged companies to supply workers with *Guideposts* and other religious literature and took note of a spike in industrial chaplaincies in the early 1950s.[45]

One of the first acts of the NAE's Commission on Industrial Chaplaincies in 1944 was to appoint a liaison to the NAM, which indicates that some or all of the industrialists on the board were members. The goal was to lead a panel on industrial chaplaincies at the next NAM annual convention. "By attendance at the meetings of the American Management Association and the National Association of Manufacturers, we have made many worthwhile personal contacts," Armerding commented later. "We have also learned the current language of industrial leaders, and we are putting this to use in our literature and promotional work." The replacement of "chaplain" with "counselor" was a direct result.[46] Like the NAE's founders, NAM members wanted their faith to transform the world. Over time, throughout the 1950s and into the 1960s, they carved out a minority but influential management style that began to infiltrate and define the workplace. From Chick-fil-A to Walmart and Hobby Lobby and countless shop floors and strip malls throughout the Sunbelt and nation, midcentury entrepreneurial evangelicalism's ideology, combining therapeutic individualism, family values emphases, and notions of Christian service and stewardship in the aid of industrial relations, manufacturing and affective labor, and, broadly, welfare capitalism, quickly made its way into the heart of America's corporate establishment. The NAE—directly through its cross-fertilization of leadership and influence, indirectly through its sacralization and rigorous promotion of these values—was there to help inspire and enable this philosophy's advance.[47]

Even as the NAM and NAE forged this future for evangelicalism's welfare capitalism, another entity burst on to the scene in the Cold War period and stole some influence away from the older evangelical organization. During the 1950s, evangelist Billy Graham and his supporting cast in the Billy Graham Evangelistic Association (BGEA) became modern American evangelicalism's public face. Graham and the BGEA's effect on postwar evangelicalism and evangelical entrepreneurialism were weighty, measured on a couple of levels.

The first of these was theological. Along with intellectuals connected to Fuller Theological Seminary, of which Herbert Taylor was a generous trustee, Graham helped precipitate a thorough and traumatic breach with the American Council of Christian Churches and other separatists. During the 1950s the combatants severed "evangelical" and "fundamentalist" identities in clear, decisive ways, fracturing their common religious subculture along theological and ecumenical lines. Billy Graham and the BGEA (and NAE), self-described "new evangelicals," asserted that the Bible addressed social issues as well as individual sinners, and the issues they picked amounted to a left turn. The defining text of the movement, Carl Henry's *The Uneasy Conscience of Modern Fundamentalism* (1947), argued that conservative evangelicals had allowed "pagan idealist[s]" to control public debate over "aggressive warfare, political statism, racial intolerance, the liquor traffic, [and] labor-management exploitation."[48] Although statism, "labor-managerial exploitation," and the liquor trade were hardly absent from fundamentalist discourse, Henry's opponents accused his circles of succumbing to modernism and the social gospel.[49] Graham's decision to work with the Federal Council of Churches for a New York City revival in 1957 symbolically sealed the rift.[50] LeTourneau, Taylor, and the businessmen's groups sided with the new evangelicals, but it might just as easily be said that the new evangelicals sided with them. "While the evangelical will resist the non-evangelical formulas for solution[s]," Henry wrote, "he assuredly ought not on that account to desist from battle against world evils," but rather "give them a proper leadership."[51] Businessmen had practiced this philosophy all along.

Indeed, the Graham camp's role in further solidifying ties between business and evangelism was one conspicuous effect of its Cold War crusading, while a related outcome was the BGEA's melding of corporate sectors within evangelicalism's own ranks. During World War II, thanks in measure to the defense industry's generous funding of Christian corporate and industrial firms of all sizes, the gap between evangelicalism's middling business ranks and the more elusive realm of big business began to shrink, slightly but significantly. LeTourneau and J. Howard Pew's parallel and intersecting economic paths during war—with both benefiting from substantial government contracts and proximity to Washington—were but one clear example of this. In the 1950s, the gap narrowed even more, allowing evangelical entrepreneurialism to be imagined and active on a larger stage. Harboring increasingly larger ambitions and ministerial range, as well as more demanding pressures for cash, postwar evangelicalism looked to big business for assistance. In the process, it itself became big business.

Pew's relationship with the BGEA was at the center of this metamorphosis. Transitions in his personal and professional status made this possible. In 1947 he retired from his post as CEO of Sunoco. Retirement allowed him to focus on a task he would take seriously over the course of the next two decades: funding a conservative religious and political revolution. Pew's ability to do so came via his formation in 1948 of the J. Howard Pew Freedom Trust. His goal, articulated in his trust's constitution, was transparent:

> To acquaint the American people with the evils of bureaucracy and the vital need to preserve a limited form of government . . . to expose the insidious influences which have infiltrated channels of publicity . . . to acquaint the American people with the values of a free market, the dangers of inflation, the paralyzing effects of government controls on the lives and activities of people . . . and to promote the recognition of the interdependence of Christianity and freedom.[52]

Pulling no punches where politics was concerned, Pew also held nothing back when bankrolling allies for his cause. He was as business-minded about giving his money away as he had been about making it, and in the wake of his retirement he fashioned a routine of giving that was relentless in every regard. For the remaining years of his life he devoted his greatest energy to financing a vast network of schools, churches, social agencies, and media outlets that could help him roll back Roosevelt liberalism.[53]

None would benefit more from this benevolence than the growing body of ministries associated with Billy Graham, the BGEA, and their brand of new evangelicalism. Besides sending checks to the intellectual flagship of this constituency and its founder—Charles Fuller and Fuller Seminary in Pasadena, California—Pew most notably donated to Graham's rapidly expanding ministry. Several of Graham's projects, from evangelistic crusades to radio programming, received Pew's blessing, and money, and throughout the early Cold War years Graham's team could count on hearing ideas and requests from the oilman (some welcomed, others merely endured) pertaining to next possible steps in conservatism's quest for cultural (and political) supremacy. In 1956 Pew's funds helped Graham and Graham's father-in-law, L. Nelson Bell, undertake the momentous task of founding *Christianity Today*, a magazine that evangelicals could read as the conservative alternative to liberal Protestantism's *Christian Century*. Though they differed on finer points—for instance, the degree to which *Christianity Today* should be explicitly hard-hitting, right-wing, and vocal in its political reporting and advocacy—Pew, Graham, and Bell nevertheless saw eye to eye in their promotion of a magazine that could advance a "new form of socially engaged, conservative Christianity," geared to the political questions (and largely Republican solutions) of the day. For this reason, Pew kept supporting Graham and his team right until the Sunoco magnate's death in 1971.[54]

For his part, Graham honored Pew—and Taylor, LeTourneau, and their illustrious corporate brethren—by adopting their economic and political discourse and explicitly framing his gospel in the language and logic of evangelical entrepreneurialism. In 1954 the evangelist scribed a telling essay for *Nation's Business*, a mouthpiece of the US Chamber of Commerce, in which he celebrated the message and the decades-long labor of Christian businessmen and their various guilds. He wrote:

> We have the suggestion from the Scripture itself that faith and business, properly blended, can be a happy, wholesome and even profitable mixture. . . . Too long have many helped the idea that religion should be detached from life, something aloof and apart. . . . Thousands of businessmen have discovered the satisfaction of having God as a working partner. It puts integrity into their organizations, sincerity into their sales, and spiritual and monetary profits into their hearts and pockets.[55]

So many great men in business—so many of his dear friends, he underscored—had successfully "corroborated the fact that religion and business can be mixed for the spiritual and material profit of all concerned." Right belief in God, right understandings of governance, and right notions of America itself, the evangelist intimated, were thus part and parcel of right thinking about mammon; each essential element of this multifaceted New Testament doctrine was, according to the famous preacher, evidenced aplenty in the boardrooms of the country's evangelical corporate sector. With this flourish of laissez-faire proselytization Graham legitimated a class and a generation of Babbitts that had for decades worked diligently, determinedly, in their industries and on their factory floors to make fellow citizens see and accept this truth.[56]

LeTourneau. Hedstrom. Grunigen. Patterson. Taylor. Pew. These are not marquee names in the historiography of twentieth-century evangelicalism, but brought to the fore, they reframe the story. Between their shoe leather and their pocketbooks, they and other businessmen made revivalism happen, from Billy Graham to lesser luminaries. As much as they preferred action to rumination, they thought a great deal about policies that helped or harmed business. The New Deal pushed them to the right wings of the Republican or Democratic parties. Their conviction that God was sovereign over the "sacred" and the "secular" without distinction made regulations, taxes, and unions religious issues. A new and fractious conservative movement gave some of them ballast, while almost all took up the cause of a united and conquering revivalism. Evangelical businessmen in the 1930s and 1940s tried not to be of the world, but their faith firmly planted them in it.

NOTES

INTRODUCTION

1. Sinclair Lewis, *Babbitt* (New York: P. F. Collier and Son, 1922), 13.

2. Ibid., 312.

3. Ibid., 313.

4. Ibid.

5. Ibid., 314.

6. Ibid.

7. Ibid., 315.

8. Ibid., 316.

9. Ibid., 230.

10. Carl McIntire, *The Rise of the Tyrant: Controlled Economy vs. Private Enterprise* (Collingwood, NJ: Christian Beacon, 1945), xi.

11. "Evangelical" and "fundamentalist" were interchangeable identities during the 1930s and 1940s, which is why they are used interchangeably in this book. Granted, specialists will recognize many of the subjects herein as "new evangelical"—those who distanced themselves from "fundamentalists" midcentury, a transition that will be touched upon in the last sections of the book. George Marsden, *Reforming Fundamentalism: Fuller Seminary and the New Evangelicalism* (Grand Rapids, MI: William B. Eerdmans, 1987), 48.

12. The retrenchment of evangelicals during this time is documented, for instance, in George M. Marsden, *Fundamentalism and American Culture: The Shaping of Twentieth-Century Evangelicalism, 1870–1925* (New York: Oxford University Press, 1980), 3–48, 141–57; Joel A. Carpenter, *Revive Us Again: The Reawakening of American Fundamentalism and Mass Culture, 1920–1940* (New York: Oxford University Press, 1997); and Virginia Lieson Brereton, *Training God's Army: The American Bible School, 1880–1940* (Bloomington: Indiana University Press, 1990), 26–38.

13. Dudley Clendinen, "'Christian New Right's Rush to Power," *New York Times*, August 18, 1980. For other timelines that date evangelical political activism to the 1960s or later, see for instance James Davison Hunter, *American Evangelicalism: Conservative Religion and the Problem of Modernity* (New Brunswick, NJ: Rutgers Uni-

versity Press, 1983); Walter H. Capps, *The New Religious Right: Piety, Patriotism, and Politics* (Columbia, SC: University of South Carolina Press, 1990); Linda Kintz, *Between Jesus and the Market: The Emotions that Matter in Right-Wing America* (Durham, NC: Duke University Press, 1997); Michael Lienesch, *Redeeming America: Piety and Politics in the New Christian Right* (Chapel Hill: University of North Carolina Press, 1993); and D. Michael Lindsay, *Faith in the Halls of Power: How Evangelicals Joined the American Elite* (New York: Oxford University Press, 2007).

14. For insight, see for instance Grant Wacker, *Heaven Below: Early Pentecostals and American Culture* (Cambridge, MA: Harvard University Press, 2001), 268; and D. G. Hart, *That Old-Time Religion in Modern America: Evangelical Protestantism in the Twentieth Century* (Chicago: Ivan R. Dee, 2002), 110–11.

15. This rise-and-fall pattern in twentieth-century US religion and politics is noted in Jon Butler, "'Jack-in-the-Box Faith: The Religion Problem in Modern American History," *Journal of American History* 90 (March 2004): 1357–78. The rise-and-fall timeline and apolitical nature of fundamentalism in the interwar years has been challenged by an emerging historical literature, which emphasizes continuity and engagement in evangelical political action during the first half of the twentieth century. See especially Barry Hankins, *Jesus and Gin: Evangelicalism, the Roaring Twenties, and Today's Culture Wars* (New York: Palgrave Macmillan, 2010); Matthew Avery Sutton, *American Apocalypse: A History of Modern Evangelicalism* (Cambridge, MA: Belknap, 2014); and Daniel K. Williams, *God's Own Party: The Making of the Christian Right* (New York: Oxford University Press, 2010).

16. See especially Kim Phillips-Fein, *Invisible Hands: The Making of the Conservative Movement from the New Deal to Reagan* (New York: W. W. Norton, 2009); George H. Nash, *The Conservative Intellectual Movement in America since 1945* (Wilmington, DE: Intercollegiate Studies Institute, 1996), 1–21; and Gregory Eow, "Fighting a New Deal: Intellectual Origins of the Reagan Revolution, 1932–1952" (PhD diss., Rice University, 2007).

17. On contestations of religion and labor, and corporate Christian leaders' involvement in the suppression of a labor mandate, see for instance Richard J. Callahan Jr., *Work and Faith in the Kentucky Coal Fields: Subject to Dust* (Bloomington: Indiana University Press, 2008); Christopher D. Cantwell, Heath W. Carter, and Janine Giordano Drake, eds., *The Pew and the Picket Line: Christianity and the American Working Class* (Champaign: University of Illinois Press, 2016); Ken Fones-Wolf and Elizabeth Fones-Wolf, *Struggle for the Soul of the Postwar South: White Evangelical Protestants and Operation Dixie* (Champaign: University of Illinois Press, 2015); Erik S. Gellman and Jarod Roll, *The Gospel of the Working Class: Labor's Southern Prophets in New Deal America* (Champaign: University of Illinois Press, 2011); Alison Collis Greene, *No Depression in Heaven: The Great Depression, the New Deal, and the Transformation of Religion in the Delta* (New York: Oxford University Press, 2016); and Jarod Roll, *Spirit of Rebellion: Labor and Religion in the New Cotton South* (Champaign: University of Illinois Press, 2010).

18. Kevin M. Kruse, *One Nation Under God: How Corporate America Invented Christian America* (New York: Basic Books, 2015); Bethany Moreton, *To Serve God and Wal-Mart: The Making of Christian Free Enterprise* (Cambridge, MA: Harvard Univer-

sity Press, 2009). See especially Darren Grem, *The Blessings of Business: How Corporations Shaped Conservative Christianity* (New York: Oxford University Press, 2016). As he himself notes, Grem's interests and scholarship were shaped and enriched by Sarah Hammond's dissertation on Christian business, which was completed at the same time Darren was finishing his. Sarah Hammond benefited equally from this exchange. See Grem, *The Blessings of Business*, 240n8.

19. Lewis, *Babbitt*, 195.

20. R. G. LeTourneau, "From the Chairman," *Contact: The Magazine for Christian Business Men*, (hereafter *Contact*) September–October 1946, 10.

21. The "inconsistencies" evident in LeTourneau's relationship with the state are carefully documented in a study of prominent southwestern boosters: Elizabeth Tandy Shermer, *Sunbelt Capitalism: Phoenix and the Transformation of American Politics* (Philadelphia: University of Pennsylvania Press, 2013).

22. Roland Marchand, *Advertising the American Dream: Making Way for Modernity, 1920–1940* (Berkeley: University of California Press, 1986), 324.

23. Vernon W. Patterson, "Unique Position of the Layman," *Christian Workers*, December 1941, 3.

24. References here are to Matthew 22:21 and Mark 12:17.

25. On evangelical nationalism during World War I, see Marsden, *Fundamentalism and American Culture*, 150–53.

26. Description of Taylor's glasses stems from Sarah Hammond's conversation with William G. Enright, November 1, 2009.

CHAPTER ONE

1. Erik Barnouw, *The Golden Web: A History of Broadcasting in the United States, 1933–1953* (New York: Oxford University Press, 1958), 58.

2. Transcript for "Robert 'Believe It or Not' Ripley Presents . . . God Rewards Faith and Service, Broadcast September 27, 1940." 2–3 To avoid confusion, ellipses that signal dramatic pauses in the original transcript have been omitted in this text.

3. Ibid.

4. See, for instance, Marsden, *Fundamentalism and American Culture*, and Joel A. Carpenter, *Revive Us Again*.

5. Bob Considine, *Ripley: The Modern Marco Polo* (Garden City, NY: Doubleday, 1961), 47, 83.

6. On the problematic categories of "religion" and the "secular," see Wilfred Cantwell Smith, *The Meaning and End of Religion* (New York: Macmillan, 1963; reprint, Minneapolis: Fortress, 1991), 15–50; Talal Asad, *Formations of the Secular: Christianity, Islam, Modernity* (Palo Alto, CA: Stanford University Press, 2003); José Casanova, *Public Religions in the Modern World* (Chicago: University of Chicago Press, 1994); Jonathan Z. Smith, *Map Is Not Territory: Studies in the History of Religions* (Chicago: University of Chicago Press, 1993); and David Chidester, *Savage Systems: Colonialism and Comparative Religion in Southern Africa* (Charlottesville: University Press of Virginia, 1996).

7. On Christian capitalism and manhood, see Michael Kimmel, *Manhood in Amer-*

ica: A Cultural History (New York: Free Press, 1996); and Anthony Rotundo, *American Manhood: Transformations in Masculinity from the Revolution to the Modern Era* (New York: Basic Books, 1993). On the role of risk and fate in LeTourneau's Christian capitalist order, see Timothy Gloege, *Guaranteed Pure: The Moody Bible Institute, Business, and the Making of Modern Evangelicalism* (Chapel Hill: University of North Carolina Press, 2015); and B. M. Pietsch, "Lyman Stewart and Early Fundamentalism," *Church History* 82 (September 2013): 617–46.

8. A note on spelling: modern usage of "businessman/businessmen" will, for the sake of consistency, be adopted here, even though earlier autobiographical and biographical accounts of LeTourneau and his peers separated the terms "business man" and "business men."

9. Albert W. Lorimer, *God Runs My Business: The Story of R. G. LeTourneau, Farmhand, Foundry Apprentice, Master Molder, Garage Mechanic, Laborer, Inventor, Manufacturer, Industrialist, Christian Business Man, and Lay Evangelist* (New York: Fleming H. Revell, 1941), 45, 46–47; Donald F. Ackland, *Moving Heaven and Earth: The Story of R. G. LeTourneau; Inventor, Designer, Manufacturer, Preacher* (New York: Iverson Ford Associates, 1949), 62–63.

10. R. G. LeTourneau, *Mover of Men and Mountains*: *The Autobiography of R. G. LeTourneau* (New York: Prentice Hall, 1960), 135; Lorimer, *God Runs My Business*, 111.

11. Despite his flaws as a historian, Max Weber's insight into post-Reformation Christian economics still stands: "[S]ince the success of work is the surest symptom that it pleases God, capitalist profit is one of the most important criteria for establishing that God's blessing rests on the enterprise." Max Weber, *Economy and Society: An Outline of Interpretive Sociology*, ed. Guenther Roth and Claus Wittich (New York: Bedminster, 1968; reprint, Berkeley: University of California Press, 1978), 1200. See also Max Weber, *The Protestant Ethic and the Spirit of Capitalism*, trans. Talcott Parsons (New York: Scribner, 1958). On the nineteenth-century forms of evangelical businessmen's contractual theology, see John Corrigan, *Business of the Heart: Religion and Emotion in the Nineteenth Century* (Berkeley: University of California Press, 2002), 187, 227–30.

12. Transcript for "Ripley Presents," 3–4.

13. LeTourneau, *Mover of Men and Mountains*, 109–10. See also Ackland, *Moving Heaven and Earth*, 55–56, and Lorimer, *God Runs My Business*, 40–41.

14. Lorimer, *God Runs My Business*, 49–52, 63, 67, 91; Robert W. Babson, "The Need of the Hour," *The King's Business*, August 1931, 345. On evangelical businessmen's contractual theology, see Corrigan, *Business of the Heart*, 187, 207–30. See also David M. Kennedy, *Freedom from Fear: The American People in Depression and War, 1929–1935* (New York: Oxford University Press, 2005), 85–92.

15. Phillips-Fein, *Invisible Hands*, 3–9.

16. LeTourneau, *Mover of Men and Mountains*, 209–10.

17. On the relationship of prominent businessmen to Charles Finney, see Charles E. Hambrick-Stowe, *Charles G. Finney and the Spirit of American Evangelicalism* (Grand Rapids, MI: W. B. Eerdmans, 1996), 129–40; Robert H. Abzug, *Cosmos Crumbling: American Reform and the Religious Imagination* (New York: Oxford University Press, 1994), 107–11; and Bertram Wyatt-Brown, *Lewis Tappan and the Evangelical War*

against Slavery (Cleveland: Case Western Reserve University Press, 1969; reprint, Baton Rouge: Louisiana State University Press, 1997).

18. Transcript for "Ripley Presents," 4.

19. LeTourneau, *Mover of Men and Mountains*, 5–7.

20. Paul Boyer, *When Time Shall Be No More: Prophecy Belief in Modern American Culture* (Cambridge, MA: Belknap, 1994), 86–93; Marsden, *Fundamentalism and American Culture*, 51–71. For fuller examination of premillennial dispensationalism in modern American religious and political culture, see Ernest R. Sandeen, *The Roots of Fundamentalism: British and American Millenarianism, 1800–1930* (Chicago: University of Chicago Press, 1970); and, more recently, Sutton, *American Apocalypse*.

21. On the modernist Protestant imperative, see William R. Hutchison, *The Modernist Impulse in American Protestantism* (Durham, NC: Duke University Press, 1992); and Ronald C. White and C. Howard Hopkins, *The Social Gospel: Religion and Reform in a Changing America* (Philadelphia: Temple University Press, 1976). For fresh insight into the ways modernist impulses crossed and obscured liberal-conservative designations within late nineteenth-century evangelicalism, see Matthew Bowman, *The Urban Pulpit: New York City and the Fate of Liberal Evangelicalism* (New York: Oxford University Press, 2014).

22. Marsden, *Fundamentalism and American Culture*, 32–39.

23. Boyer, *When Time Shall Be No More*, 87.

24. LeTourneau, *Mover of Men and Mountains*, 7, 12.

25. Ibid., 23.

26. Ibid., 7–8, 11.

27. Ibid., 22.

28. Ibid., 19.

29. Walter Nugent, *Into the West: The Story of Its People* (New York: Random House, 1999), 77–78, 132; LeTourneau, *Mover of Men and Mountains*, 52.

30. LeTourneau, *Mover of Men and Mountains*, 22.

31. Ibid., 29.

32. Ibid.. Hill's foundry was shifting from casting iron to steelmaking, using alloys such as copper and manganese, a process developed in midcentury Britain and popularized in the United States by Andrew Carnegie. See Paul Krause, "Iron and Steel Industry," in *The Oxford Companion to United States History*, ed. Paul S. Boyer (New York: Oxford University Press, 2001), 394–96.

33. LeTourneau, *Mover of Men and Mountains*, 33. As with many of LeTourneau's stories, facts vary from version to version without harming the message. One biographer, quoting from LeTourneau's speeches, describes a conventionally melodramatic moment: "Then I cried out in desperation to God, 'Lord, save me or I perish!' Right there something happened. The glory of the Lord broke over me and the full reality of salvation came into my soul." Lorimer, *God Runs My Business*, 30.

34. LeTourneau, *Mover of Men and Mountains*, 35.

35. Ibid., 44.

36. William R. Hutchison, *An Errand to the World: American Protestant Thought and Foreign Missions* (Chicago: University of Chicago Press, 1987), 112.

37. On American missions to China, see Alvyn Austin, "Blessed Adversity:

Henry W. Frost and the China Inland Mission," in *Earthen Vessels: American Evangelicals and Foreign Missions, 1880–1890*, ed. Joel A. Carpenter and Wilbert R. Shenk (Grand Rapids, MI: William B. Eerdmans, 1990), 57, 64–64. See also Donald MacGillivray, *A Century of Protestant Missions in China, 1807–1907: Being the Centenary Conference Historical Volume* (Shanghai: American Presbyterian Mission, 1907); and Lynn E. Bodin and Christopher Warner, *The Boxer Rebellion* (Oxford: Osprey, 1979), 3–6.

38. LeTourneau, *Mover of Men and Mountains*, 86–87.

39. Ibid., 41.

40. See White and Hopkins, *The Social Gospel*, 246–47. White and Hopkins distinguish between Christocentric "evangelical liberalism" and humanistic "modernistic liberalism," suggesting as well the fluid boundaries separating the two forms of social Christianity.

41. Hutchison, *An Errand to the World*, 112–24.

42. LeTourneau, *Mover of Men and Mountains*, 250–51.

43. Ibid., 126.

44. Ibid., 58–59; R. T. Sloss, *The Book of the Automobile: A Practical Volume Devoted to the History Construction [sic], Use and Care of Motor Cars and to the Subject of Motoring in America* (New York: D. Appleton, 1905), 17.

45. LeTourneau, *Mover of Men and Mountains*, 67–68, 78–79, 83–86, 91–92, 102; Nugent, *Into the West*, 181.

46. LeTourneau, *Mover of Men and Mountains*, 92, 79.

47. Ibid., 131.

48. Ibid., 127.

49. Ibid., 79.

50. Lorimer, *God Runs My Business*, 169.

51. LeTourneau, *Mover of Men and Mountains*, 87–88; Albert Edward Thompson, *The Life of A. B. Simpson* (Brooklyn: Christian Alliance, 1920), 1–3, 41; Allan Anderson, *An Introduction to Pentecostalism* (Cambridge: Cambridge University Press, 2004), 29–31; Grant Wacker, *Heaven Below*, 3, 148. Simpson was selective in his embrace of Pentecostal teachings. For instance, while he experimented with speaking in tongues, he quickly rejected the practice.

52. LeTourneau, *Mover of Men and Mountains*, 88–89.

53. Ibid., 111, 118, 135–37, 162.

54. Ibid., 135.

55. Ibid., 180.

56. Ibid., 143–48; Mark S. Foster, "Giant of the West: Henry J. Kaiser and Regional Industrialization, 1930–1950," *Business History Review* 59 (Spring 1985): 3.

57. "Business: Piety & Profits," *Time*, March 25, 1940, 78; Lorimer, *God Runs My Business*, 58–61.

58. William Russell Haycraft, *Yellow Steel: The Story of the Earthmoving Equipment Industry* (Urbana: University of Illinois Press, 2002), 72.

59. LeTourneau, *Mover of Men and Mountains*, 170.

60. Ibid., 174; Foster, "Giant of the West," 304; Haycraft, *Yellow Steel*, 72.

61. LeTourneau, *Mover of Men and Mountains*, 174–75, 181–83.

62. Lorimer, *God Runs My Business*, 63. Although different factors in calculations make for an inexact comparison, LeTourneau's loss in 1931 matched overall manufacturing trends, while his 1932 profit bucked an even worse year. T. J. Kreps, "Dividends, Interest, Profits, Wages, 1923–35," *Quarterly Journal of Economics* 49 (August 1935): 577.

63. "Caterpillar, Inc.—Company History," *International Directory of Company Histories*, vol. 63 (London: St. James, 2004), http://www.fundinguniverse.com/company-histories/caterpillar-inc-history/, accessed November 10, 2015.

64. Ibid.; LeTourneau, *Mover of Men and Mountains*, 162, 169, 199–201.

65. John C. Teaford, *Cities of the Heartland: The Rise and Fall of the Industrial Midwest* (Bloomington: Indiana University Press, 1993), 253. On Chicago's surpassing of Philadelphia as America's "second city," see A. J. Liebling, *Chicago: The Second City* (New York: Knopf, 1952), 10.

66. Peoria Chamber of Commerce, "Facts about the Nation's Bright Spot," n.d., box F10, folder 12, Papers of R. G. LeTourneau, LeTourneau University, Longview, Texas (hereafter LTP); *Fifteenth Census of the United States—1930—Population*, vol. 1 (Washington, DC: US Government Printing Office, 1931), 279. Second-generation immigrants like LeTourneau would have been included in the "native born" total, so there was more cultural diversity than the percentage suggests.

67. Peoria Historical Society, *Peoria's History*, "Industry," http://www.peoriahistoricalsociety.org/!/History-Of-Peoria/Industry, accessed November 10, 2015.

68. "Caterpillar, Inc."; Federal Writers' Project, *Illinois: A Descriptive and Historical Guide* (Chicago: A. C. McClurg, 1939), 573–74; Haycraft, *Yellow Steel*, 66, 118, 166–67, 198.

69. LeTourneau, *Mover of Men and Mountains*, 35.

70. Ibid., 54, 98, 209.

71. Ibid., 203.

72. Rinehart J. Swensen, "The Chamber of Commerce and the New Deal," *Annals of the American Academy of Political and Social Science* 179 (May 1935): 136–43.

73. LeTourneau, *Mover of Men and Mountains*, 203.

74. Ibid.

75. Ibid., 40.

76. "Sermon Notes, R. G. LeTourneau," 1938–42, box J1P, folder 2, LTP. LeTourneau repeated himself often enough that some titles must date to the Peoria period.

77. Ibid.; Lorimer, *God Runs My Business*, 107. Even in this pre–Cold War period, anticommunism was a central theme of American political discourse and for fundamentalist Protestants especially an important means through which they could escape marginalization and capture legitimate status in the political mainstream.

78. Ackland, *Moving Heaven and Earth*, 164.

79. Ibid., 163; "Plant Life," *NOW*, October 15, 1937, 4; "Plant Life," *NOW*, August 20, 1937, 4; "Plant Life," *NOW*, November 11, 1936, 4; "Girls Have Their Own Shop Meeting," *NOW*, January 11, 1937, 1; "Plant Life," *NOW*, January 11, 1937, 4; "Plant Life," *NOW*, February 12, 1937, 4.

80. "Peoria Plant," box J5J, LTP.

81. Sean Wilentz, *Chants Democratic: New York City and the Rise of the American Working Class, 1788–1850* (1986; reprint, New York: Oxford University Press, 2004), 299–323.

82. Boyer, *When Time Shall Be No More*, 156–57.

83. LeTourneau, *Mover of Men and Mountains*, 151–52; Brereton, *Training God's Army*, xiii–xix, 87–100; Louis S. Bauman, "Present-Day Fulfillment of Prophecy," *The King's Business*, June 1933, 181. For a fuller picture of premillennialism's ties to anti–New Deal politics, see Matthew Avery Sutton, "Was FDR the Antichrist? The Birth of Fundamentalist Antiliberalism in a Global Age," *Journal of American History* 98 (March 2012): 1052–74.

84. Patrick Allitt, *The Conservatives: Personalities throughout American History* (New Haven, CT: Yale University Press, 2009), 145–48.

85. George Wolfskill, *The Revolt of the Conservatives: A History of the American Liberty League, 1934–1940* (Boston: Houghton Mifflin, 1962), 49–55.

86. Ibid., 94–97, 64.

87. Ibid., 150–54; Robert A. Slayton, "Al and Frank: The Great Smith-Roosevelt Feud," in *FDR, the Vatican, and the Roman Catholic Church in America, 1933–1945*, ed. David B. Woolner and Richard G. Kural (New York: Palgrave Macmillan, 2003), 55–56; Alonzo L. Hamby, *For the Survival of Democracy: Franklin Roosevelt and the World Crisis of the 1930s* (New York: Free Press, 2004), 318, 320–22.

88. Alan Brinkley, *Voices of Protest: Huey Long, Father Coughlin and the Great Depression* (New York: Vintage Books, 1982), 114–15, 153–56, 252–59, 265–68. Initially, Coughlin placed himself in the Catholic social justice tradition, which tried to steer a middle way between the individualism and inequality of capitalism and the forced equality and atheism of communism. His hatred of "international bankers," which had populist roots and potentially, though not necessarily, anti-Semitic implications, led him to fear the private economic sector more than the tyrannical state—except when the latter, in his eyes, began to resemble the former by concentrating power and wealth in a few hands. See also Anthony Burke Smith, "John A. Ryan, the New Deal, and Catholic Understandings of the Culture of Abundance," in *FDR, the Vatican, and the Roman Catholic Church in America, 1933–1945*, ed. David B. Woolner and Richard G. Kural (New York: Palgrave Macmillan, 2003), 47–53; Kevin E. Schmiesing, *Within the Market Strife: American Catholic Economic Thought from* Rerum Novarum *to Vatican II* (Lanham, MD: Lexington Books, 2004), 15–18, 37–39, 41–45.

89. Hugh R. Monro, "Has the Church Failed Socially? A Travel Experience," *The King's Business*, June 1931, 252–54.

90. Wolfskill, *The Revolt of the Conservatives*, 244–45, 122–23.

91. Quoted in M. J. Heale, *American Anti-Communism: Combatting the Enemy Within, 1830–1970* (Baltimore: Johns Hopkins University Press, 1990), 116.

92. LeTourneau, *Mover of Men and Mountains*, 208.

93. Lisabeth Cohen, *Making a New Deal: Industrial Workers in Chicago, 1919–1939* (Cambridge: Cambridge University Press, 1990), 160–83; Richard E. Holl, *From the Boardroom to the War Room: America's Corporate Liberals and FDR's Preparedness Program* (Rochester, NY: University of Rochester Press, 2005), 9–21.

94. Lorimer, *God Runs My Business*, 102; Ackland, *Moving Heaven and Earth*, 166.

95. "R. G. LeTourneau Talks on Status of Employees," *NOW*, February 26, 1937, 2–3.

96. LeTourneau, *Mover of Men and Mountains*, 208.

97. Ackland, *Moving Heaven and Earth*, 157–58. By 1939, one million Olson tracts were distributed from the Peoria plant each month. See "Acts 16:30 and 31," *NOW*, November 17, 1939, 1.

98. "Questions Preaching at LeTourneau Plant," *NOW*, February 5, 1937, 3.

99. See "Plant Life" in the following issues of *NOW*: October 16, 1936, 4; October 23, 1936, 4; October 30, 1936, 4; November 6, 1936, 4; November 13, 1936, 4; January 15, 1937, 4. For broader context of these and other features of welfare capitalism, see Cohen, *Making a New Deal*, 164.

100. "Union Pledges Loyalty to R. G. LeTourneau," *NOW*, June 18, 1937, 3.

101. "Plant Life," *NOW*, January 20, 1939, 4.

102. See, for example, "19 Men Preach from One Motorcycle," *NOW*, June 16, 1939, 3.

103. [Tom Olson], "Coal Mine Fire Burning 51 Years," "Wins Prize for Naming Most Horrible Sin," and "President's Voice Used to 'Prove Broken Pledge,'" *NOW*, September 24, 1937, 3.

104. [Tom Olson], "Wins Prize for Naming Most Horrible Sin," and "President's Voice Used to 'Prove Broken Pledge,'" *NOW*, September 24, 1937, 3.

105. [Tom Olson], "President's Popularity Sliding, Says Writer," *NOW*, September 24, 1937, 3.

106. [Tom Olson], "President's Proposal Resembles Jethro's," *NOW*, January 29, 1937, 3; "Partial Quotation Twists Hughes' Words," *NOW*, April 9, 1937, 2–3; "Press Told How to Use Remarks of President," *NOW*, August 20, 1937.

107. [Tom Olson], "Millions Listen When Hitler, Mussolini Speak," *NOW*, May 7, 1937, 3; [Olson], "Britain Compromises on Jew, Arab Promises," *NOW*, July 30, 1937, 3.

108. Lorimer, *God Runs My Business*, 185–86; Ackland, *Moving Heaven and Earth*, 157–58.

109. Charles R. Morris, *The Tycoons: How Andrew Carnegie, John D. Rockefeller, Jay Gould, and J. P. Morgan Invented the American Supereconomy* (New York: Henry Holt, 2005), 192–94.

110. Kathleen D. McCarthy, *Noblesse Oblige: Charity & Cultural Philanthropy in Chicago, 1849–1929* (Chicago: University of Chicago Press, 1982), 53.

111. Reference here is to Luke 12:48 (King James Version).

112. Lorimer, *God Runs My Business*, 128.

113. Judith Sealander, *Private Wealth and Public Life: Foundation Philanthropy and the Reshaping of American Social Policy from the Progressive Era to the New Deal* (Baltimore: Johns Hopkins University Press, 1977), 11–27, 39.

114. Ilana H. Eisenstein, "Keeping Charity in Charitable Trust Law: The Barnes Foundation and the Case for Consideration of Public Interest in Administration of Charitable Trusts," *University of Pennsylvania Law Review* 151 (2002–3): 1754; Robert Hamlett Bremner, *American Philanthropy* (Chicago: University of Chicago Press, 1988), 100–115.

115. Lorimer, *God Runs My Business*, 187–88.

116. Donald M. Taylor to W. A. Dyer, January 30, 1947, box J3F, folder 75, LTP; LeTourneau, *Mover of Men and Mountains*, 204–5.

117. William R. Glass, *Strangers in Zion: Fundamentalism in the South, 1900–1950* (Macon, GA: Mercer University Press, 2001), xvii.

118. LeTourneau, *Mover of Men and Mountains*, 205–7, 211–12; Lorimer, *God Runs My Business*, 74; Ackland, *Moving Heaven and Earth*, 157–58.

119. Lorimer, *God Runs My Business*, 67.

120. Lorene Moothart, *Achieving the Impossible with God: The Life Story of Dr. R. A. Forrest* (1956; reprint, Toccoa Falls, GA: Toccoa Falls College Press, 1996), 84–96.

121. LeTourneau, *Mover of Men and Mountains*, 219–22; Lorimer, *God Runs My Business*, 84–87; Moothart, *Achieving the Impossible with God*, 142–46, 165–66.

122. Troy Damon, *A Tree God Planted: The Story of Toccoa Falls College* (1982; Toccoa Falls, GA: Toccoa Falls College Press, 1996), 68.

123. Ibid., 70–71.

124. David M. Kennedy, *Freedom from Fear: The American People in Depression and War, 1929–1945* (New York: Oxford University Press, 2005), 148–49; Robert Rodgers Korstad, *Civil Rights Unionism: Tobacco Workers and the Struggle for Democracy in the Mid-Twentieth Century South* (Chapel Hill: University of North Carolina Press, 2003), 5–6.

125. Kennedy, *Freedom from Fear*, 344–45; "Troubles of South Typify World's Woes," *NOW*, September 9, 1938, 2–3.

126. "G.O.P. Win Changes Legislative Outlook," *NOW*, November 25, 1938, 3.

127. Lorimer, *God Runs My Business*, 95.

128. Ackland, *Moving Heaven and Earth*, 72.

129. "An Then 5,000 People Were Fed," *NOW*, July 21, 1939, 1.

130. "Another Factory Revival," *NOW*, July 21, 1939, 2, 4.

131. Lamar Q. Ball, "Toccoa Factory is Dedicated to Principles of Christianity," *Atlanta Constitution*, July 12, 1939, 2.

132. "Another Factory Revival," 2, 5.

133. Lorimer, *God Runs My Business*, 168–69; LeTourneau, *Mover of Men and Mountains*, 203.

CHAPTER TWO

1. Paul H. Heidebrecht, *God's Man in the Marketplace: The Story of Herbert J. Taylor* (Downers Groves, IL: Intervarsity, 1990), 39.

2. Herbert J. Taylor, *The Herbert J. Taylor Story* (Downers Grove, IL: Intervarsity, 1968), 48.

3. Unless otherwise noted, information about the meeting comes from "First Meeting of Heads of Groups Cooperating in the Charles Fuller Revival Meeting," February 5, 1942, box 11, folder 22, Papers of Herbert J. Taylor (hereafter HJT), Billy Graham Center Archives, Wheaton College, Wheaton, IL (hereafter BGCA).

4. Bruce J. Evenson, *God's Man for the Gilded Age: D. L. Moody and the Rise of Mass Evangelism* (New York: Oxford University Press, 2003), 96. On John Wanamaker, the Philadelphia department store owner who, like Taylor, backed men like Moody because they wanted to bridge religion and business, see William Leach, *Land of Desire:*

Merchants, Power, and the Rise of a New American Culture (New York: Pantheon Books, 1993), 194–202.

5. "Vaughn Shoemaker; Created John Q. Public," *New York Times*, August 22, 1991, D2, http://query.nytimes.com/gst/fullpage.html?res=9D0CE4D6143AF931A1575BC0A967958260, accessed January 8, 2016.

6. M. A. Henderson, *Sowers of the Word: A 95-Year History of Gideons International, 1899–1994* (Nashville: Gideons International, 1995), 1–5.

7. "Mrs. Philip D. Armour Dies," *Kansas City Times*, September 1, 1950, 7.

8. Upton Sinclair, "Mr. Sinclair Would Be Sued; Asks J. Ogden Armour to Give Him a Chance to Prove His Charges," *New York Times*, May 4, 1906, http://query.nytimes.com/mem/archive-free/pdf?_r=1&res=9F0DE3D8113EE733A25757C0A9639C946797D6CF, accessed January 12, 2016; "Philip Armour and the Packing Industry," *Encyclopedia of Chicago*, http://www.encyclopedia.chicagohistory.org/pages/1724.html, accessed January 12, 2016; "People & Events: Philip Danforth Armour (1833–1901)," American Experience website, *Chicago: City of the Century*, http://www.pbs.org/wgbh/amex/chicago/peopleevents/p_armour.html, accessed January 12, 2016.

9. "Philip D. Armour Is Dead," *New York Times*, January 7, 1901, http://query.nytimes.com/mem/archive-free/pdf?_r=1&res=9406E3DA1138E733A25754C0A9679C946097D6CF, accessed January 14, 2016; Rev. John Evans, "Illinois Tech Outgrowth of '1,000,000 Sermon,'" *Chicago Tribune*, February 20, 1944, 4; Walter Hendricks, "Armour Institute: Historical Sketch of Armour Institute of Technology," Illinois Institute of Technology Archives, http://archives.iit.edu/armour/, accessed January 14, 2016.

10. Annual Report of the Christian Workers Foundation, July 1, 1941–June 30, 1942, 2, box 11, folder 1, HJT.

11. Herbert Taylor to V. Raymond Edman, September 18, 1942, box 11, folder 22, HJT.

12. H. L. Mencken, "Bryan," *Baltimore Evening Sun*, July 27, 1925.

13. Marsden, *Fundamentalism and American Culture*, 48.

14. Herbert Taylor to George Corwin, July 29, 1939, box 11, folder 25, HJT.

15. Glen Gough, Harold Taylor, and Harvey Blair, "Pickford Centennial," Pickford Area Historical Society, http://www.rootsweb.ancestry.com/~mipahs/Pickford_Centennial.html, accessed September 19, 2016; Daniel Morrison, *A History of Pickford Area Pioneer Families* (n.p., 1973), 1, 138.

16. David W. Bebbington, *The Dominance of Evangelicalism: The Age of Spurgeon and Moody* (Downers Grove, IL: InterVarsity, 2005), 11–20.

17. Heidebrecht, *God's Man in the Marketplace*, 23.

18. Herbert J. Taylor with Robert Walker, *God Has a Plan for You* (New York: Revell, 1968), 25. For a description of the merged grocery and shoe store as a Pickford economic and social center in 1912, see "On Pickford Main St . . . 1912" and "Pickford," Pickford Area Historical Society, http://www.rootsweb.ancestry.com/~mipahs/Taylor_Grocery_1912.html, accessed September 19, 2015.

19. Morrison, *A History of Pickford Area Pioneer Families*, 139.

20. Heidebrecht, *God's Man in the Marketplace*, 25.

21. Taylor, *God Has a Plan for You*, 28.

22. Ibid., 27.

23. Ibid., 25.

24. Richard Rabinowitz, *The Spiritual Self in Everyday Life: The Transformation of Personal Religious Experience in Nineteenth-Century New England* (Boston: Northeastern University Press, 1989), 228.

25. Richard Carwardine, "Charles Sellers's 'Antinomians' and 'Arminians': Methodists and the Market Revolution," in *God and Mammon: Protestants, Money, and the Market, 1790–1860*, ed. Mark A. Noll (New York: Oxford University Press, 2001), 80–86.

26. Jay Pridmore, *Northwestern University: Celebrating 150 Years* (Evanston, IL: Northwestern University Press, 2000), 11–14.

27. Harold F. Williamson and Payson S. Wild, *Northwestern University: A History, 1850–1975* (Evanston, IL: Northwestern University Press, 1976), 111–19; Laurence R. Veysey, *The Emergence of the American University* (Chicago: University of Chicago Press, 1965), 50–56; Frederick Rudolph, *The American College and University: A History* (1962; Athens, GA: University of Georgia Press, 1990), 355–72.

28. Taylor, *God Has a Plan for You*, 94–95.

29. Heidebrecht, *God's Man in the Marketplace*, 25; "Technical Men in Advertising Firms," *Printers' Ink* 99, no. 1 (April 5, 1917): 98; "Electrical Trade Publishing Company Organized," *Printers' Ink* 110, no. 11 (March 11, 1920): 82.

30. Williamson and Wild, *Northwestern University*, 125; Nathan D. Showalter, *The End of a Crusade: The Student Volunteer Movement for Foreign Missions and the Great War* (Lanham, MD: Scarecrow, 1998), 46–47; Chu Hsing, *Baptized in the Fire of Revolution: The American Social Gospel and the YMCA* (Cranbury, NJ: Associated University Presses, 1996), 25–43.

31. Marsden, *Fundamentalism and American Culture*, 178, 119–20.

32. Taylor, *God Has a Plan for You*, 21.

33. Ibid., 22.

34. Quoted in Pridmore, *Northwestern University*, 113.

35. "ANBHF Herbert Taylor," American National Business Hall of Fame, http://anbhf.org/laureates/herbert-taylor/, accessed September 29, 2008; Maurice Karker to Herbert J. Taylor, March 26, 1943, box 11, folder 5, HJT.

36. Taylor, *God Has a Plan for You*, 22.

37. Ibid.

38. Ibid., 30; "Pauls Valley, Oklahoma" http://www.citytowninfo.com/places/oklahoma/pauls-valley, accessed September 28, 2015.

39. Dan T. Boyd, "Oklahoma Oil: Past, Present, and Future," *Oklahoma Geology Notes* 62 (Fall 2002): 98; "Native American Tribes of Oklahoma," http://www.native-languages.org/oklahoma.htm, accessed September 28, 2015.

40. Sinclair Oil Corporation: Sinclair History, 2008, https://www.sinclairoil.com/history/1910.html accessed February 2, 2017; Taylor, *God Has a Plan for You*, 30.

41. Taylor, *God Has a Plan for You*, 30.

42. Ibid.

43. Ibid., 31.

44. Ibid., 30–33; David B. Wolcott, *Cops and Kids: Policing Juvenile Delinquency in Urban America, 1890–1940* (Columbus: Ohio State University Press, 2005); Susan

Magarey, "The Invention of Juvenile Delinquency in Early Nineteenth-Century England," *Labour History* 34 (May 1978): 11–27.

45. Taylor, *God Has a Plan for You*, 32.

46. Ibid., 32–33. Taylor cites the *Daily Oklahoman* of December 28, 1924.

47. Taylor, *God Has a Plan for You*, 33.

48. Paul P. Harris, *The Founder of Rotary* (Chicago: Rotary International, 1928), 93, 94–97.

49. Jeffrey A. Charles, *Service Clubs in American Society: Rotary, Kiwanis, and Lions* (Urbana: University of Illinois Press, 1993), 3.

50. Ibid., 4, 42.

51. Ibid., 40.

52. Ibid., 51n175.

53. Taylor, *God Has a Plan for You*, 33.

54. Ibid.; Heidebrecht, *God's Man in the Marketplace*, 28.

55. Marsden, *Fundamentalism and American Culture*, 117.

56. Heidebrecht, *God's Man in the Marketplace*, 54.

57. Sydney E. Ahlstrom, *A Religious History of the American People* (New Haven, CT: Yale University Press, 1972), 455–58.

58. Miller, *City of the Century*, 15–17.

59. Cohen, *Making a New Deal*, 17.

60. Miller, *City of the Century*, 461–64.

61. Taylor, *God Has a Plan for You*, 34.

62. "About Park Ridge," http://www.parkridge.us/about/about.aspx, accessed January 18, 2016; Kenneth T. Jackson, *Crabgrass Frontier: The Suburbanization of the United States* (New York: Oxford University Press, 1987), 87–115.

63. Heidebrecht, *God's Man in the Marketplace*, 30–31.

64. Amanda Seligman, "Near North Side," *Encyclopedia of Chicago*, http://www.encyclopedia.chicagohistory.org/pages/876.html, accessed January 8, 2016.

65. Alice O'Connor, *Poverty Knowledge: Social Science, Social Policy, and the Poor in Twentieth-Century U.S. History* (Princeton, NJ: Princeton University Press, 2001), 45–49.

66. Taylor, *God Has a Plan for You*, 48.

67. Ahlstrom, *A Religious History of the American People*, 778–79, 802–4.

68. Kennedy, *Freedom from Fear*, 58–59.

69. Taylor, *God Has a Plan for You*, 38.

70. Percy Livingston Parker, ed., *The Journal of John Wesley* (Chicago: Moody, 1951), Christian Classics Ethereal Library, http://www.ccel.org/ccel/wesley/journal.vi.ii.xvi.html, accessed January 18, 2016; Taylor, *God Has a Plan for You*, 38–39.

71. Taylor, *God Has a Plan for You*, 39–40.

72. Heidebrecht, *God's Man in the Marketplace*, 35–38; "Club Aluminum Loss at $332,846: Utensil Company's Showing Compares with $321,941 Deficit in Preceding Fiscal Year," *Wall Street Journal*, August 31, 1932; "National Home Service, Inc. History of the Board of Directors," box 7, folder 20, HJT; Susan Porter Benson, *Counter Cultures: Saleswomen, Managers, and Customers in American Department Stores, 1890–1940*

(Champaign: University of Illinois Press, 1986), 290; Sean Silverman, interview with Walter A. Friedman, "The Return of the Salesman," Harvard Business School Working Knowledge, http://hbswk.hbs.edu/item/6150.html, accessed September 10, 2015.

73. Heidebrecht, *God's Man in the Marketplace*, 39–41.

74. Kennedy, *Freedom from Fear*, 218, 130–52.

75. See, for example, Herbert Taylor to the National Republican Party of Cook County, Illinois, giving ten dollars to the congressional campaign of Ralph E. Church, March 29, 1940; and William J. Balmer, Chairman of the National Progressive Republican Organization, to Herbert Taylor, May 24, 1939, referencing donations made to "enhance the welfare of those Americans, whose problems can best be remedied by strong concerted action and . . . a national policy in government," both in box 1, folder 28, HJT. The Christian Workers Foundation also funded Republicans. See Heidebrecht, *God's Man in the Marketplace*, 67.

76. Holl, *From the Boardroom to the War Room*, 4–5.

77. The 4-Way Test Association, http://www.4waytest.org/, accessed September 10, 2015.

78. Taylor, *God Has a Plan for You*, 40–41.

79. Reference here is to 1 Corinthians 12:12 (King James Version).

80. Taylor, *God Has a Plan for You*, 40–41.

81. Ibid., 52.

82. William F. McDermott, "Broke in 1933; On Top in 1941," *Rotarian*, March 1942, 34.

83. Taylor, *God Has a Plan for You*, 41–42, 45.

84. Heidebrecht, *God's Man in the Marketplace*, 54.

85. Ibid., 54.

86. McDermott, "Broke in 1933," 36.

87. Ibid.

88. Heidebrecht, *God's Man in the Marketplace*, 49–52.

89. McDermott, "Broke in 1933," 36.

90. Quoted in ibid., 36.

91. Kennedy, *Freedom from Fear*, 151, 298–308.

92. Cohen, *Making a New Deal*, 174–79.

93. Mary G. Godner, "Notes on Christian Endeavor," *The King's Business*, August 1932, 366.

94. Quoted in Morrell Heald, "Business Thought in the Twenties: Social Responsibility," *American Quarterly* 13 (Summer 1961): 128; see also Leo P. Ribuffo, *The Old Christian Right: The Protestant Far Right from the Great Depression to the Cold War* (Philadelphia: Temple University Press, 1983), 10–13.

95. Quoted in Heald, "Business Thought in the Twenties," 132–33.

96. Roger W. Babson, *Religion and Business* (New York: Macmillan, 1921), 86; Bruce Barton, *The Man Nobody Knows* (1925; reprint, New York: Collier Books, 1952), 16; Richard M. Fried, *The Man Everybody Knew: Bruce Barton and the Making of Modern America* (Chicago: Ivan R. Dee, 2005).

97. Babson, *Religion and Business*, 210.

98. Gabriel Kolko, *The Triumph of Conservatism: A Reinterpretation of American History, 1900–1916* (New York: Free Press, 1963), 1–6.

99. Clayton Sinyai, *Schools of Democracy: A Political History of the American Labor Movement* (Ithaca, NY: Cornell University Press, 2006), 65–68.

100. Alex Baskin, "The Ford Hunger March—1932," *Labor History* 13 (Summer 1972): 355.

101. Quoted in Bellamy Foster, "The Fetish of Fordism—Henry Ford's Economic Ideas," *Monthly Review*, March 1988, 5.

102. Kennedy, *Freedom from Fear*, 352.

103. Ibid., 292; "Swope Plan," *Time*, September 28, 1931, http://content.time.com/time/magazine/article/0,9171,742325-1,00.html, accessed September, 2015.

104. Kennedy, *Freedom from Fear*, 83–84.

105. Quoted in "Chicagoans Ask U.S. Aid to Form Building-Loan," *Chicago Daily Tribune*, September 6, 1933, 30.

106. "First Chicago Federal Loan Group Starts," *Chicago Daily Tribune*, January 28, 1934, 20.

107. Louis S. Bauman, "Present-Day Fulfillment of Prophecy," *The King's Business*, June 1933, 181.

108. James L. Baughman, *Henry Luce and the Rise of the American News Media* (1987; reprint, Baltimore: Johns Hopkins University Press, 2001), 57–58.

109. Taylor, *God Has a Plan for You*, 40.

110. Ibid., 44.

111. Clyde Smith to Herbert Taylor, June 19, 1939, box 1, folder 18, HJT; Taylor, *God Has a Plan for You*, 48.

112. Robert Walker, "Report of Activities of the Christian Workers Foundation, July 1, 1940–June 30, 1941," 1–2, box 11, folder 1, HJT.

113. On Taylor's pivotal role in Young Life, which follows the same pattern as his dominance in the Inter-Varsity Christian Fellowship—identifying a gifted religious entrepreneur and not only funding but collaborating on (or commandeering) his vision—see David B. Hunsicker, "The Rise of the Parachurch Movement in American Protestant Christianity during the 1930s and 1940s: A Detailed Study of the Beginnings of the Navigators, Young Life, and Youth for Christ International" (PhD diss., Trinity Evangelical Divinity School, 1998), 283–307. Taylor also supported the California-based Navigators, which ministered principally to servicemen, and Youth for Christ. See, for instance, Judy Carlson to Herbert Taylor, September 6, 1946, box 1, folder 3, HJT). For Hi-Y, see Walker, "Report of Activities of the Christian Workers Foundation," 2. For Fuller Theological Seminary, see Herbert Taylor to Charles Fuller, December 19, 1944, box 33, folder 19, HJT. For the Kentucky mission, see Nellie DeWar to Paul Westburg, July 27, 1939, box 55, folder 11, HJT.

114. Marsden, *Fundamentalism and American Culture*, 142–53.

115. Walker, "Christian Workers Foundation Annual Report," 2.

116. Carpenter, *Revive Us Again*, 177, 182.

117. A. Donald MacLeod, *C. Stacey Woods and the Evangelical Rediscovery of the University* (Downers Grove, IL: IVP Academic, 2007), 80.

118. Keith Hunt and Gladys M. Hunt, *For Christ and the University: The Story of InterVarsity Christian Fellowship-USA, 1940–1990* (Downers Grove, IL: InterVarsity, 1992), 77–87, 99, 59, 64–67.

119. During the 1939–40 school year, there were twenty-two IVCF chapters in the United States: nine were in Washington or Oregon, and eight were in Chicago or the upper Midwest. See "List of United States Colleges and Universities in Which Fellowship Groups Were Officially Meeting at Close of Year 1939–1940," box 60, folder 24, HJT.

120. Hunt and Hunt, *For Christ and the University*, 86–89, 99–103.

121. "The International Fellowship of Evangelical Students," n.d., box 60, folder 29, HJT.

122. Quoted in MacLeod, *C. Stacey Woods and the Evangelical Rediscovery of the University*, 80.

123. Herbert Taylor to J. F. Stormbeck, September 24, 1940, box 12, folder 6, HJT.

124. Herbert Taylor to Stacey Woods, July 1, 1941, box 60, folder 24, HJT; MacLeod, *C. Stacey Woods and the Evangelical Rediscovery of the University*, 60.

CHAPTER THREE

1. Edward E. Ham, *50 Years on the Battle Front with Christ: A Biography of Mordecai F. Ham* (1950; reprint, n.p.: Larry Harrison, 2005), 13–14.

2. Ahlstrom, *A Religious History of the American People*, 381; Evenson, *God's Man for the Gilded Age*, 22, 25–29.

3. Vernon Patterson and other BMEC/CMC leaders, "Ham-Ramsay Meeting, Charlotte, N.C., Aug. 30th–Nov. 25th, 1934," 1, collection 5, box 1, folder 1, Vernon W. Patterson Papers (hereafter VWP), BGCA.

4. Quoted in Ham, *50 Years on the Battle Front with Christ*, 17–19; Billy Graham, *Just as I Am: The Autobiography of Billy Graham* (San Francisco: Harper, 1997), 22; Marshall Frady, *Billy Graham: A Parable of American Righteousness* (Boston: Little, Brown, 1979), 80–81; "Ham-Ramsay Meeting General Committee," and Vernon W. Patterson, "Prayer Preparation for Revival," December 1, 1972, 1–2, collection 9, box 1, folder 1, VWP.

5. Graham, *Just as I Am*, 25–26; "Ham Wins Word-Battle with City Officials," *Charlotte News*, November 12, 1934, n.p.; affidavit of Walter Waitt, State of North Carolina, County of Mecklenburg, November 14, 1934; A. W. Russell to Vernon Patterson, November 15, 1934, collection 9, box 1, folder 1, VWP.

6. Graham, *Just as I Am*, 26–30; Ham, *50 Years on the Battle Front with Christ*, 23–24.

7. Graham, *Just as I Am*, 26–30.

8. Carpenter, *Revive Us Again*, 116.

9. Nathan D. Showalter, *The End of a Crusade: The Student Volunteer Movement for Foreign Missions and the Great War* (Lanham, MD: Scarecrow Press, 1998), 2; Hutchison, *Errand to the World*, 118–24.

10. Showalter, *The End of a Crusade*, 120–46; Hutchison, *Errand to the World*, 180–90.

11. "White-collared": R. G. LeTourneau quoting Arnold Grunigen, "Notes from the Chairman," *Contact*, September–October 1946, 22. For further context see Robert Wiebe, *The Search for Order, 1877–1920* (New York: Hill and Wang, 1967), 112–13, 127–29.

12. Geoffrey Perrett, *Days of Sadness, Years of Triumph: The American People, 1939–1945* (Baltimore: Penguin Books, 1973), 72.

13. On this process see Richard W. Pointer, "Philadelphia Presbyterians, Capitalism, and the Morality of Success," in *God and Mammon: Protestants, Money, and the Market, 1790–1860*, ed. Mark Noll (New York: Oxford University Press, 2001), 171–91.

14. For wider context see also James Hudnet-Beumler, *In Pursuit of the Almighty's Dollar: A History of Money and American Protestantism* (Chapel Hill: University of North Carolina Press, 2007), 57, 60–72.

15. Use of the much-criticized "separate spheres" trope here is not because of disagreement with the critics but because the men in this study took male and female domains for granted, even as they challenged them in a religious context. See Linda K. Kerber, "Separate Spheres, Female Worlds, Woman's Place: The Rhetoric of Women's History," *Journal of American History* 75 (June, 1988): 9–39. On women's numerical dominance and volunteer labor in the church, see David D. Hall, *Worlds of Wonder, Days of Judgment: Popular Religious Belief in Early New England* (Cambridge, MA: Harvard University Press, 1989), 14; and Bebbington, *The Dominance of Evangelicalism*, 221–22.

16. William Bond, Minutes of the Christian Laymen's Crusade Meeting Held at the Benjamin Franklin Hotel, November 1, 1941, box J4J, folder F19, LTP.

17. C. J. W.-L. Wee, "Christian Manliness and National Identity: The Problematic Construction of a Racially 'Pure' Nation," in *Muscular Christianity: Embodying the Victorian Age*, ed. Donald E. Hall (Cambridge: Cambridge University Press, 1994), 73; Norman Vance, *The Sinews of the Spirit: The Ideal of Christian Manliness in Victorian Literature and Thought* (Cambridge: Cambridge University Press, 1985), 53–55; Michael Kimmel, *Manhood in America: A Cultural History* (New York: Free Press, 1996), 60; Andrew Carnegie, *The Gospel of Wealth and Other Timely Essays* (1889; reprint, Cambridge, MA: Belknap, 1962), esp. 14–49; Barton, *The Man Nobody Knows*, esp. 1–17, 56–59.

18. Edgar Guest, "The Layman," *Christian Worker*, November 3, 1938, 3, in collection 5, box 2, folder 2, VWP. The *Christian Worker* was "the official organ of the Association of Business Men's Evangelistic Clubs," the parent organization of the Charlotte BMEC/CMC. The poem also appeared in the LeTourneau Evangelistic Institute's *Joyful News*, October 1946, 3.

19. David Enlow, "Tenth Annual Convention," *Contact*, November–December 1947, 14.

20. Henderson, *Sowers of the Word*, 19.

21. On "the male culture of the workplace," including all-but-required networking through leisure activities that were anathema to evangelicals, see Rotundo, *American Manhood*, 194, 196–205.

22. Jeffrey A. Charles, *Service Clubs in American Society: Rotary, Kiwanis, and Lions* (Urbana: University of Illinois Press, 1993), 9–10.

23. Henderson, *Sowers of the Word,* 23–24, 37, 376–77. Professionals were allowed membership in the Gideons after 1960.

24. The "camp" was deliberate reference to a passage in the Old Testament, Judges 7:21: "And they stood every man in his place around the camp."

25. Henderson, *Sowers of the Word,* 7, 9, 24, 48, 371.

26. J.M.G. [James M. Gray], "Mr. Leaman Goes into Evangelism," *Moody Bible Institute Monthly,* May 1932, 466; Gene Johnson, "God in the World of Business," fortieth anniversary paper for the CBMCI, courtesy of the CBMCI, in author's possession.

27. David Enlow, *Men Aflame: The Story of the Christian Business Men's Committee International* (Grand Rapids, MI: Zondervan, 1962), 18.

28. Kathryn Long, *The Revival of 1857–58: Interpreting an American Religious Awakening* (New York: Oxford University Press, 1998), 81–92, 137–38.

29. Gail Bederman, "'The Women Have Had Charge of the Church Work Long Enough': The Men and Religion Forward Movement of 1911–1912 and the Masculinization of Middle-Class Protestantism," *American Quarterly* 41 (September 1989): 432–65.

30. C. B. Hedstrom, *"Pay-Day—Some Day" with Other Sketches from Life and Messages from the World,* 2d ed. (Grand Rapids, MI: Zondervan, 1938), 12, 17.

31. Enlow, *Men Aflame,* 18.

32. "Vaughn Shoemaker, Created John Q. Public."

33. Ernest D. Christie, "Evangelistic and Bible Conference Fields," *Moody Monthly* 38 (June 1938): 543.

34. Ernest D. Christie, "Evangelistic and Bible Conference Fields," *Moody Bible Institute Monthly* 32 (August 1932): 602; *Who? Why? What? The Christian Business Men's Committee of Change,* 1938 pamphlet, courtesy of CBMCI, in author's possession.

35. On the "religious depression" of the 1930s, see for instance Robert T. Handy, "The American Religious Depression, 1925–1935," in *Religion in American History: A Reader,* ed. Jon Butler and Harry S. Stout (New York: Oxford University Press, 1997): 370–83; and especially Collis Greene, *No Depression in Heaven.*

36. Tom Glasgow, "A Plea for a Christian Organization," *Charlotte News,* February 24, 1932; "The Appeal of Mr. Glasgow," *Charlotte News,* February 24, 1932.

37. Henderson, *Sowers of the Word,* 24–25.

38. Ibid., 25; J.M.G., "Mr. Leaman Goes into Evangelism." According to the latter account, Leaman left his twelve-year position at Moody Bible Institute "on faith," without a source of income, to evangelize at the Century of Progress fairs in 1933 and 1934. See Richard Hughes Seager, *The World's Parliament of Religions: The East/West Encounter, Chicago, 1893* (Bloomington: Indiana University Press, 1995), on why world fairs such as the Century of Progress fairs were considered ripe evangelical mission fields.

39. Paul Rood, "Around the King's Table," *The King's Business,* March 1936, 82; Enlow, *Men Aflame,* 17.

40. Arnold Grunigen Jr., "Golden Gate Exposition Is Gospel Territory," *Moody Monthly* 39 (March 1939): 576.

41. *14 Prominent Business Men Look at Life,* souvenir ed., Golden Gate International Exposition, Treasure Island, San Francisco, 1940, box J4J, folder 23, LTP.

42. For wider context on this and other radio-reliant outreach attempts by twentieth-century evangelicals, see Tona J. Hangen, *Redeeming the Dial: Radio, Religion and Popular Culture in America* (Chapel Hill: University of North Carolina Press, 2002).

43. Quoted in Randall Balmer and Lauren S. Winner, "Moody, Dwight Lyman (1837–1899)," *Protestantism in America* (New York: Columbia University Press, 2002), 236.

44. Paul Rood, "Around the King's Table," *The King's Business*, March 1936, 82; Rood, "Around the King's Table," *The King's Business*, April 1936, 122.

45. Claes Wyckoff, "With Him It's Stocks & Bonds: Our Vice-Chairman, Arnold Grunigen, Jr.," *Contact*, March–April 1946, 1–5; Lorimer, *God Runs My Business*, 73–76.

46. "The Heaven and Earth Man: Our Chairman, R. G. LeTourneau," *Contact*, January–February 1946, 6–7. This article credits LeTourneau with serving as a noonday speaker in the "early days" of the Chicago CBMC, but he was not in the area during the founding. No other source puts him in the CBMC until the late 1930s.

47. Enlow, *Men Aflame*, 13–14.

48. CBMC USA, "75 Years of Ministry" (2006), 3, pamphlet in author's possession.

49. Ernest D. Christie, "Evangelistic and Bible Conference Fields," *Moody Bible Institute Monthly* 32 (June 1932): 507.

50. Christian Business Men's Committee International brochure, n.d. [between 1939 and 1942], collection 20, box 11, folder 9, HJT; Enlow, *Men Aflame*, 19.

51. Joan H. Wise, "Yours for Souls—Charles E. Gremmels," *Contact*, May–June 1946, 4–8; Enlow, *Men Aflame*, 19.

52. Jon Butler, *Awash in a Sea of Faith: Christianizing the American People* (Cambridge, MA: Harvard University Press, 1990), 1–5, 285–86; R. Laurence Moore, *Selling God: Religion in the Marketplace of Culture* (New York: Oxford University Press, 1994), 3–10; Stephen Prothero, *American Jesus: How the Son of God Became a National Icon* (New York: Farrar, Straus, and Giroux, 2003), 3–7; William Leach, *Land of Desire: Merchants, Power, and the Rise of the New American Culture* (New York: Pantheon Books, 1993), 191–224. In opposition to Leach's and other historians' declension narrative of consumer capitalism and cultural demise, see Joyce Oldham Appleby, "The Vexed Story of Capitalism Told by American Historians," *Journal of the Early Republic* 21, no. 1 (Spring 2001): 1–18.

53. Alan Trachtenberg, *The Incorporation of America: Culture and Society, 1865–1893* (New York: Hill and Wang, 1982), 1–10.

54. Quoted in Michael Kazin, *A Godly Hero: The Life of William Jennings Bryan* (New York: Anchor Books, 2007), 60.

55. In a phrase that historians have applied retroactively ever since, Franklin D. Roosevelt Supreme Court appointee William O. Douglas complained in an antitrust case that "a nation of shopkeepers" had become "a nation of clerks." See William O. Douglas, *Democracy and Finance: The Addresses and Public Statements of William O. Douglas as Member and Chairman of the Securities and Exchange Commission*, ed. James Allen (London: H. Milford, 1940), 15. See also Gail Bederman, *Manliness and Civilization: A Cultural History of Gender and Race in the United States, 1800–1917* (Chicago: University of Chicago Press, 1995), 84–88.

56. There is little biographical information about Jepson, except details of his professional degree. "High School Graduation Rates in Washington and the United States: A Long-Run View" (2005), Washington State Institute for Public Policy, 1. For context see Claudia Golden and Lawrence F. Katz, "Human Capital and Social Capital: The Rise of Secondary Schooling in America," *Journal of Interdisciplinary History* 29 (Spring 1999): 683–723.

57. LeTourneau, *Mover of Men and Mountains*, 202, 209.

58. Ibid., 44–45; "History of Apprenticeship," Washington State Department of Labor and Industries, http://www.lni.wa.gov/TradesLicensing/Apprenticeship/About/History/, accessed January 6, 2016.

59. Amy Johnson Frykholm, *Rapture Culture: Left Behind in America* (New York: Oxford University Press, 2004), 17.

60. Sydney Ahlstrom, *The Religious History of America* (New Haven, CT: Yale University Press, 1972), 848–50, 916–17.

61. *Evangelistic Club Handbook: The Association of Business Men's Evangelistic Clubs, 1921–1929*, 2, reports 131 clubs in 6 states; *Program: Association of Business Men's Evangelistic Clubs, Eleventh Annual Convention* (1931); "Lay Evangelists Hold Sessions Here," *Harrisonburg (VA) Daily News Record*, June 15, 1936, all in collection 5, box 2, folder 1, VWP.

62. C. C. Goen, *Broken Churches, Broken Nation: Denominational Schisms and the Coming of the American Civil War* (Macon, GA: Mercer University Press, 1985), 66–139.

63. Ibid., 9–10.

64. David W. Blight, *Race and Reunion: The Civil War in American Memory* (Cambridge, MA: Belknap, 2001), 248, 3–5.

65. Charles Reagan Wilson, *Baptized in Blood: The Religion of the Lost Cause, 1865–1920* (Athens: University of Georgia Press, 1980), 62–68. Wheaton College president J. O. Buswell gave a keynote address to the Charlotte BMEC/CMC, which also welcomed a representative from the Moody Bible Institute Extension Department. "Patterson Again Head of Evangelistic Clubs," *Charlotte News*, June 21, 1936. Southern educator Bob Jones Sr. had ties to Wheaton and Moody and a history of evangelism in the North. See Mark Taylor Dalhouse, *An Island in a Lake of Fire: Bob Jones University, Fundamentalism, and the Separatist Movement* (Athens: University of Georgia Press, 1996), 7, 21–51.

66. "President Hargraves Visits the North," *Christian Workers*, November 1936, 3.

67. Having introduced the CBMCI, I will keep using the acronym even when the "I" does not apply (that is, to the CBMC before the 1938 convention or local committees at any time).

68. "Columbus, Ohio Meeting Planned," *Christian Workers*, October 1936, 3; Henderson, *Sowers of the Word*, 71, 104.

69. "President Hargraves Visits the North," 3. For broader context on what Hargraves encountered, see Jill Watts, *God, Harlem U.S.A.: The Father Divine Story* (Berkeley: University of California Press, 1992), 131–43.

70. Bishop W. A. Chandler, "America Is a Money Mad Nation," *Christian Workers*, December 1936, 2, 4.

71. Quoted in Watts, *God, Harlem U.S.A.*, 106.

72. "For God's Glory," *Christian Workers*, November 1936, 4.

73. "Convention Secretary," *Christian Workers*, August 1940, 3; "Religion: The New Evangelist," *Time*, October 25, 1954, 5.

74. LeTourneau first heard and began supporting R. A. Forrest, the founder of Toccoa Falls Institute, in 1936. Lorimer, *God Runs My Business*, 84–85.

75. Willis G. Haymaker, "Big Business and the Real Gospel," *Christian Workers*, January 1937, 1–4.

76. Ibid.

77. Ibid.

78. *Program—Association of BMEC's in Eleventh Annual Convention*, August 14–16, 1931, collection 5, box 2, folder 1, VWP.

79. Boyd Hargraves to Vernon W. Patterson, January 1, 1933, and July 8, 1932, collection 5, box 2, folder 1, VWP.

80. Vernon W. Patterson, "Unique Position of the Layman," *Christian Workers*, December 1941, 3.

81. Minutes of the 21st Annual Convention of the National Association of Business Men's Evangelistic Clubs, August 14–17, 1941, collection 20, box 2, folder 1, VWP.

82. Vernon Patterson to R. G. LeTourneau, June 11, 1940, box J4J, folder F19, LTP.

83. LeTourneau to Patterson, June 12, 1940, box J4J, folder F19, LTP; "20th Annual Convention Very Outstanding," *Christian Workers*, September 1940, 1.

84. "The Conference of Christian Laymen," *Christian Workers*, November 1940, 1, 4.

85. R. G. LeTourneau to the CBMCI Board, April 30, 1940, box J3F, folder 42, LTP.

86. Paul Fischer to Boyd Hargraves, June 30, 1940, box J3F, folder 42, LTP.

87. Carpenter, *Revive Us Again*, 119.

88. "Emergency Called Conference of Business and Professional Men," October 23–24, 1940, 1–4, collection 20, box 11, folder 9, HJT.

89. Arnold Grunigen, "Chairman's Report," *Monthly News Letter Christian Business Men's Committee San Francisco Region*, October 1940, 1, collection 20, box 11, folder 9, HJT.

90. "The Conference of Christian Laymen," *Christian Workers*, November 1940, 4.

91. R. G. LeTourneau to potential CLC financiers, December 9, 1940, collection 20, box 11, folder 9, HJT.

92. "Christian Laymen's Crusade," *Christian Laymen's Crusade Bulletin*, May 1941, 1, collection 20, box 11, folder 2, HJT.

93. R. G. LeTourneau to Vernon Patterson, June 12, 1940, box J4J, folder F19, LTP.

94. *Christian Laymen's Crusade Bulletin*, May 1941, 2, collection 20, box 11, folder 3, HJT.

95. R. G. LeTourneau to potential CLC financiers, December 9, 1940; Vernon Patterson to R. G. LeTourneau, November 1, November 5, November 7, November 23, and December 16, 1940, all box J4J, folder 10, LTP. On C. B. Nordland's clerical status, see "Borbeck-Grosser Wedding Takes Place in Illinois," *Westfield Leader*, April 1, 1943, 12.

96. Vernon Patterson to R. G. LeTourneau, January 13, 1941, box J4J, folder 19, LTP.

97. Pan-American Bus Lines is a case in point of how business leaders antagonistic

to Roosevelt took advantage of the very regulation they deplored. Pan-American and other large transportation companies secured a virtual monopoly on the industry in 1936 with the blessing of the Interstate Commerce Commission. See "Pan-American Bus Lines Operation," 1 M.C.C., 190, 203 [1936].

98. "A Country Schoolmaster Stirs the World," *Popular Science Monthly*, August 1925, 27; Vernon Patterson to R. G. LeTourneau, January 14, 1941, box J4J, folder 19, LTP.

99. Gary Wills, *Under God: Religion and American Politics* (New York: Simon and Schuster, 1990), 100–107; Tracy Fessenden, "The Nineteenth Century Bible Wars and the Separation of Church and State," *Church History* 74 (December 2005): 807. Besides Tennessee, the states were Pennsylvania, Delaware, Alabama, Georgia, Maine, Kentucky, Florida, Ohio, and Arkansas.

100. Vernon Patterson to R. G. LeTourneau, January 14, 1941, box J4J, folder 19, LTP.

101. Henderson, *Sowers of the Word*, 103.

102. Lorimer, *God Runs My Business*, 157–58.

103. Ibid., 162–63.

104. Paul Henry Packard, D.D., "The Bible or Revolution," *Christian Workers*, September 1941, 1.

105. Reverend Arvid E. Nygren, "The Challenge for the Church," *Moody Monthly* 35 (September 1941): 12–13.

106. "Revival Today?," *Moody Monthly* 35 (September 1941): 4.

107. "Christian Men in High Office," *Christian Workers*, June 1941, 2.

108. "21st Convention Best in History," *Christian Workers*, September 1941, 3.

109. For a jaded view of the dollar-a-year men's effectiveness, see Milton Mayer, "Washington Goes to War," *Life*, January 5, 1942, 60.

110. "Report of Proceedings at 21st Annual Convention," National Association of Business Men's Evangelistic Clubs, Held at Lake Louise Conference Grounds, August 14–17, 1941, collection 5, box 2, folder 1, VWP.

111. Henderson, *Sowers of the Word*, 104, 115–16, 120; Brian Waddell, "Corporate Influence and World War II: Resolving the New Deal Political Stalemate," *Journal of Policy History* 11 (Fall 1999): 233–39; Holl, *From the Boardroom to the War Room*, 6–8, 33. Pietsch's father, William Pietsch, was active in the CBMCI and gave them radio time in his weekly broadcast.

112. Carpenter, *Revive Us Again*, 170–71; Matthew Avery Sutton, *Aimee Semple McPherson and the Resurrection of Christian America* (Cambridge, MA: Harvard University Press, 2007), 258–66.

113. "Annual Convention Was the Best in the History of Our Clubs," *Christian Workers*, September 1942, 4. The antiliquor campaign was widespread, encompassing several denominations and the liberal *Christian Century*. See Gerald L. Sister, *A Cautious Patriotism: The American Churches and the Second World War* (Chapel Hill: University of North Carolina Press, 1997), 199–200.

114. "Pres. Roosevelt Appreciates Prayers," *Christian Workers*, December 1942, 3.

115. Rolan Stoker, "Christ or Chaos," *Christian Workers*, January 1943, 3.

116. "Pray for Peace," *Christian Workers*, November 1943, 2.

CHAPTER FOUR

1. Hangen, *Redeeming the Dial*, 37–112, 81–91.

2. J. Elwin Wright, *The Old-Fashioned Revival Hour and the Broadcasters* (Boston: Fellowship, 1940), 55–84; Hangen, *Redeeming the Dial*, 95.

3. Philip Goff, "We Have Heard the Joyful Sound: Charles E. Fuller's Radio Broadcast and the Rise of Modern Evangelicalism," *Religion and American Culture* 9 (Winter 1999): 71–72. Hangen appears unaware of Taylor's vital role in the expansion of the *Old Fashioned Revival Hour* in the 1940s. For example, she credits Charles and Grace Fuller with creating "Revival Hour Night" films for churches, a project conceived and executed by Taylor and his assistant Robert Walker. Neither Taylor nor the Christian Workers Foundation appear in her chapter on Fuller, and she attributes all of Fuller's fund-raising to ordinary listeners who responded to his weekly please for money. See Hangen, *Redeeming the Dial*, 96, 109; "Radio Artists Films to Be Shown Here," n.d., box 33, folder 27, HJT.

4. See Hangen, *Redeeming the Dial*, 104.

5. Herbert Taylor to Will H. Houghton, March 8, 1942; Will H. Houghton to Herbert Taylor, March 10, 1942, both box 11, folder 22, HJT.

6. Robert Van Kampen, Minutes of the Committee for Nominating Various Officers and Committee Chairmen for the Proposed Charles Fuller Revival Meeting, February 5, 1942, box 11, folder 22, HJT.

7. Herbert Taylor, "Proposed Chas. Fuller Revival Meeting Agenda," n.d., box 11, folder 22, HJT.

8. Herbert Taylor to V. Raymond Edman, September 18, 1942, box 11, folder 22, HJT.

9. Tim Stafford, "Imperfect Instrument: World Vision's Founder Led a Tragic and Inspiring Life," *Christianity Today*, February 24, 2005, http://www.christianitytoday.com/ct/2005/march/19.56.html, accessed November 10, 2015.

10. David Enlow, "Tenth Annual Convention," *Contact* (November–December 1947): 14.

11. "Soviet Victory Formula: Moscow Paper Stresses Maximum Action and Production," *New York Times*, April 7, 1942, F9.

12. Associated Press, "U.S. 'Hustle' in Australia Builds Base in 12 Hours," *New York Times*, April 7, 1942, F9; LeTourneau, *Mover of Men and Mountains*, 230–31.

13. It should be emphasized that Roosevelt's "corporate liberal" allies in the 1930s laid the groundwork by supporting the New Deal, smoothing its radical edges, and making business "hustle" indispensable to mobilization for war. See Holl, *From the Boardroom to the War Room*, 1–8; Jennifer Klein, *For All These Rights: Business, Labor, and the Shaping of America's Public-Private Welfare State* (Princeton, NJ: Princeton University Press, 2005), 9–10.

14. Meg Jacobs, *Pocketbook Politics: Economic Citizenship in Twentieth-Century America* (Princeton, NJ: Princeton University Press, 2005), 192–220.

15. "Boeing Bombers Get Credit for U.S. Army Successes," *Chicago Tribune*, April 7, 1942, 1–2.

16. "ASKS 'COMMANDOS' TO SPUR BUSINESS; Morris L. Cooke Would Set Up an Industrial Front to Bring in the Small Producers QUICK ACTION IS SOUGHT Former REA

Head Stresses Need for Making Every Possible Weapon Now," *New York Times*, April 7, 1942, 16.

17. Lewis Wood, "Strike Aboard Ship Held to Be Mutiny Even if It Is in Port," *New York Times*, April 7, 1942, F9.

18. "Moves 660 Japanese from San Francisco," *New York Times*, April 7, 1942, F9.

19. "American Mother of 42 Has 13 Children and Job," *Chicago Daily Tribune*, April 7, 1942, 1.

20. United Press International, "Services on Bataan Most Impressive: Men Attend Easter Rites While Enemy Bombers Threaten," *New York Times*, April 7, 1942, F9.

21. "J. N. Pew: A Biographical Sketch," *Our Sun*, 1961, 11, Sun Oil—75th Anniversary, box 55, 1961 folder, Sun Oil Company Papers (hereafter SOC), Hagley Museum and Library (hereafter HML), Wilmington, DE; August W. Giebelhaus, *Business and Government in the Oil Industry: A Case Study of Sun Oil, 1876–1945* (Greenwich, CT: JAI Press, 1980), 6–8, 59–61.

22. Giebelhaus, *Business and Government in the Oil Industry*, 59–61. "The Story of Sun," *Our Sun*, 1961, 30–31, box 55, 1961 folder, SOC.

23. On Pew's and business's assault on the New Deal, see Phillips-Fein, *Invisible Hands*.

24. Giebelhaus, *Business and Government in the Oil Industry*, 249–62; "Sun Ship's 30 Years," *Our Sun*, July–August 1946, 4–6; "Sun Shipbuilding," *Fortune*, February 1941, 54; "Billionth Gallon," *Our Sun*, February 1945, 15; memos dated March 17 and March 31, 1941, box 5, J. Howard Pew Papers, HML.

25. Quoted and referenced in Stephen J. Randall, *United States Foreign Oil Policy since World War II: For Profits and Security* (Kingston, ON: McGill-Queen's University Press, 2005), 172–73, 197.

26. Quoted in Giebelhaus, *Business and Government in the Oil Industry*, 218; "The Creed We Work By: A Statement of Principles," *Our Sun*, 1961, 20, Sun Oil—75th Anniversary, box 55, 1961 folder, SOC; J. Howard Pew, "Management and the Free Market," May 17, 1950, in Binder marked "Speeches & Remarks by J. Howard Pew," #54–89, SOC; Roger M. Olien and Diana Davids Olien, *Oil and Ideology: The Cultural Creation of the American Petroleum Industry* (Chapel Hill: University of North Carolina Press, 2000), 204; Receipt for Pew donation in box 1, Pew Family Collection, HML; "An Album of Sun Memories," *Our Sun*, 1961, 34, Sun Oil—75th Anniversary, box 55, 1961 folder, SOC. This discussion borrows from Darren Dochuk, "Prairie Fire: The New Evangelicalism and the Politics of Oil, Money, and Moral Geography," in *American Evangelicals and the 1960s*, ed. Axel R. Schäfer (Madison: University of Wisconsin Press, 2013), 43–47.

27. Jacob Bos to R. G. LeTourneau, November 18, 1940, quoting *Newsweek*, November 11, 1940, 50, box J4J, folder 38, LTP.

28. Kennedy, *Freedom from Fear*, 41–42, 387–88.

29. Dan Gilbert, "Views and Reviews of Current News," *The King's Business*, December 1938, 406. The same column echoed the complaint of fiscal conservatives that programs such as Social Security were swelling the deficit beyond sustainability.

30. Malcolm W. George to R. G. LeTourneau, December 31, 1940, box J4J, folder 38, LTP.

31. Florence D. Baile to R. G. LeTourneau, December 23, 1940, box J4J, folder 38, LTP.

32. Alfred W. Swan to R. G. LeTourneau, December 8, 1940, box J4J, folder 38, LTP.

33. Louie and Ted Snyder to R. G. LeTourneau, January 17, 1941, box J4J, folder 38, LTP.

34. R. G. LeTourneau to John Kalsheek, April 8, 1941, box J4J, folder 38, LTP.

35. E. R. Galvin to All District Representatives, July 7, 1941, box F1U, folder 1, LTP.

36. Ackland, *Moving Heaven and Earth*, 115–29.

37. LeTourneau, *Mover of Men and Mountains*, 230–32, 239.

38. Marsden, *Fundamentalism and American Culture*, 6–7, 68, 210; Sacvan Berkovitch, *The American Jeremiad* (Madison: University of Wisconsin Press, 1978), 7–8.

39. "CIO Disowns John Lewis," *Joyful News*, May–June 1943, 3; Korstad, *Civil Rights Unionism*, 4–5.

40. "Georgia Plant Targeted by Ambitious CIO Organizers: CIO Out to Communize LeTourneau Company," *Joyful News*, May–June 1943, 4.

41. "Editor's Explanation," *Joyful News*, May–June 1943, 1.

42. "Georgia Plant Targeted by Ambitious CIO Organizers," 4.

43. "Whose World Is This?," *Joyful News*, May–June 1943, 3.

44. "Bible Declares the Rights of Capital and Labor," *Joyful News*, May–June 1943, 4.

45. Ibid.

46. Ackland, *Moving Heaven and Earth*, 140.

47. *An Invitation to Attend a Tri-State Patriotic Rally in Connection with the Dedication of the Vicksburg Plant of the LeTourneau Company of Mississippi, Saturday, November 28, 1942*, 1, box F1U, folder 39, LTP.

48. J. S. McCain to R. G. LeTourneau, February 8, 1943, box J4J, folder 24, LTP.

49. *An Invitation to Attend a Tri-State Patriotic Rally*, 2.

50. Hangen, *Redeeming the Dial*, 21–22, 37–111.

51. Cort Vitt, "The Hour of Charm," *Radio Recall*, February 2008, http://www.mwotrc.com/rr2008_02/charm.htm, accessed September 15, 2015; Robert Walker to Charles Fuller, October 31, 1946, box 33, folder 19, HJT.

52. Robert Walker to Charles Fuller, October 31, 1946, box 33, folder 19, HJT; "Light of the World," *Time*, March 25, 1940, http://www.time.com/time/magazine/article/0,9171,763750,00.html, accessed September 15, 2015.

53. Heidebrecht, *God's Man in the Marketplace*, 44.

54. Mel Larson, *Young Man on Fire: The Story of Torrey Johnson and Youth for Christ* (Chicago: Youth Publications, 1945), 65.

55. Don Cusic, *The Sound of Light: A History of Gospel and Christian Music* (Milwaukee: Hal Leonard, 2002), 182–83; J. Elwin Wright Scrapbook, 1944, BGCA; Lewis Sperry Chafer, *Systematic Theology* (1947; reprint, Grand Rapids, MI: Kregel, 1993), iii.

56. Larson, *Young Man on Fire*, 80–81.

57. Hunsicker, "The Rise of the Parachurch Movement in American Protestant Christianity," 371–74.

58. George Beverly Shea to Robert Walker, March 27, 1945, box 13, folder 1, HJT.

59. George Beverly Shea to Herbert J. Taylor, January 15, 1945, box 13, folder 1, HJT.

60. George Beverly Shea to Robert Walker, January 22, 1945, box 13, folder 1, HJT.

61. "Returns from 'Club Time' Radio Program," n.d. (June 14–21, 1944), box 13, folder 1, HJT.

62. Ibid.

63. "Returns from 'Club Time' Radio Program," n.d. (July 15–August 2, 1944), box 13, folder 1, HJT.

64. George F. Drake to Robert Walker, n.d., box 8, folder 17, HJT. A survey of *Hymns of All Churches* listeners included in this correspondence found the audience to be "practically identical to other daytime programs . . . women between the ages of 35 and 50 years, who are housewives with families. Otherwise it would never pay them to continue the program, advertising breakfast foods, cake flour, and other foods."

65. George Beverly Shea to Robert Walker, March 27, 1945, box 13, folder 1, HJT.

66. George Beverly Shea to Robert Walker, January 22, 1945, box 13, folder 1; Shea to Walker, July 31, 1945, and "Club Time, Tuesday, August 7, 1945," box 15, folder 12, HJT.

67. Herbert Taylor to All Company Personnel, October 16, 1945, box 15, folder 12, HJT.

68. Ibid.

69. George F. Drake, "Talk Delivered before Club Aluminum Sales Conference," December 17, 1945, box 8, folder 19, HJT.

70. "The Story Behind the 'Favorite Hymns' Promotion," n.d. (1947), box 10, folder 2, HJT.

71. Drake, "Talk Delivered before Club Aluminum Sales Conference."

72. "The Story Behind the 'Favorite Hymns' Promotion"; "Schedule of Famous People," box 10, folder 2, HJT; "Listening in with Don Foster," *Chicago Sunday Times*, April 27, 1947, 47.

73. Chuck Doty to George T. Drake, n.d., newspaper clipping of *Club Time* advertisement, box 10, folder 12, BGCA.

74. Mrs. Wilhelmina Kraus to Club Aluminum Products of the Housewife, March 17, 1947, box 6, folder 26, HJT.

75. Robert Walker to Advertising Manager, January 15, 1947, box 15, folder 26, HJT.

76. Edward G. Smith to Robert Walker, January 27, 1947, box 15, folder 26, HJT.

77. E. R. Borroff to Herbert Taylor, January 20, 1947, box 6, folder 3, HJT.

78. *Printers' Ink*, September 19, 1947, excerpt dated in Taylor's handwriting with typed comments above, box 10, folder 2, HJT.

79. "'Club Time' (For Thy Good Cheer)," April 7, 1947, box 6, folder 3, HJT.

80. The LeTourneau Foundation heavily subsidized the CBMCI. See "The Heaven and Earth Man: Our Chairman R. G. LeTourneau," *Contact*, January–February 1946, 7. To offer another example, Charles Gremmels, the shipping magnate, and lawyer Paul Fischer each contributed one hundred dollars to the CBMCI in 1940 to "bridge the gap." See Charles Gremmels to Arnold Grunigen, May 20, 1940, box J4J, folder 23, LTP.

81. "Haymaker Wants His Back Salary," *Christian Workers*, March 1942, 1; C. P. Pelham, "A Special Message from Our Secretary," *Christian Workers*, February 1942, 1, 3; A. J. Jefferson, "Our Pocketbooks vs. Our Religion," *Christian Workers*, April 1942, 1, 3.

82. "Special Statement by President Hargraves," *Christian Workers*, June 1942, 3.

83. Vernon Patterson to David Enlow, May 18, 1962, collection 5, box 2, folder 4, VWP.

84. "The National Convention Plans Enlarged Program," *Christian Workers*, September 1944, 4.

85. See, for instance, Lisa McGirr, *Suburban Warriors: The Origins of the New American Right* (Princeton, NJ: Princeton University Press, 2001), 24–26, 30–39. Kevin Phillips coined the term "Sunbelt" in his 1969 political classic *The Emerging Republican Majority* (New York: Arlington House, 1969).

86. For broader assessment of this transformation see Darren Dochuk, *From Bible Belt to Sunbelt: Plain-Folk Religion, Grassroots Politics, and the Rise of Evangelical Conservatism* (New York: W. W. Norton, 2011).

87. George Sweeting, *The Jack Wyrtzen Story: The Personal Story of the Many, His Message, and His Ministry* (Grand Rapids, MI: Zondervan House, 1960), 38, 54–56.

88. Larry Eskridge summons the image of "Graham, resplendent in the flashy suits, hand-painted ties, and bright 'glo-sox' that characterized the YFC style"—neither the first nor the last self-conscious and slightly awkward evangelical appropriation of popular culture. "'One Way': Billy Graham, the Jesus Generation, and the Idea of an Evangelical Youth Culture," *Church History* 67 (March 1988): 85.

89. Mel Larson, *Youth for Christ: Twentieth-Century Wonder* (Grand Rapids, MI: Zondervan, 1947), 52.

90. Ibid., 53.

91. Larson, *Young Man on Fire*, 4–5, 80–81.

92. Larson, *Youth for Christ*, 56–57.

93. Larson, *Young Man on Fire*, 84, 89.

94. Larson's *Youth for Christ* begins with a litany of conversion stories. See especially *Youth for Christ*, 11–18.

95. Ibid., 53, 58.

96. YFC's own statistics suggest this interpretation. Of the estimated 70,000 attendees of the 1945 Memorial Day rally at Soldier Field, 1,800 came forward to accept Christ and 5,000 Christians vowed to become missionaries if God called them. That's .03 percent and .07 percent, respectively, with the already saved having the clear edge. The same numbers held true at smaller YFC rallies. In the fall of 1945, Pittsburgh had 2,300 attendees and 50 conversions (less than .02 percent) and LaSalle, Illinois, claimed 3,000 attendees and "over 50" conversions. This reflects the in-group nature of mass evangelism in general, not just YFC. Also, by evangelical reckoning, every saved soul is infinitely valuable. See Torrey Johnson, "Pressing on in YFC," July 22, 1946, 4, Minutes of Second Annual Convention of Youth For Christ International, Inc.; Youth for Christ International, Inc., Board of Directors' Meeting, October 8–9, 1945, box 9, folder 4, Records of Youth for Christ/USA, BGCA.

97. Larson, *Youth for Christ*, 25.

98. Ibid., inside cover.

99. Carpenter, *Revive Us Again*, 172.

100. Larson, *Youth for Christ*, 59.

101. Torrey Johnson and Robert Cook, *Reaching Youth for Christ* (Chicago: Moody, 1944), 22.

102. Rita Fitzpatrick, "60,000 Youths Swing Out at Religious Fest," *Chicago Daily Tribune*, May 31, 1945, 1; Clyde Dennis, "I Witnessed the Greater Soldier Field Rally," *Contact*, May–July 1945, 4–5.

103. Carpenter, *Revive Us Again*, 172.

104. "The Story of Youth for Christ and How CBMCs Are Co-Operating," *Contact*, March–April 1945, 1–5.

105. Larson, *Young Man on Fire*, 73–74.

106. "The Story of Youth for Christ and How CBMCs Are Co-Operating," 13, 33; Graham, *Just as I Am*, 95.

107. "The USO—Home Away from Home," Nebraska Studies, http://www.nebraskastudies.org/0800/frameset_reset.html?http://www.nebraskastudies.org/0800/stories/0801_0124.html, accessed January 26, 2016.

108. Betty Lee Skinner, *Daws: The Story of Dawson Trotman, Founder of the Navigators* (Grand Rapids, MI: Zondervan, 1974), 12, 58, 89–90, 143, 158, 194, 210–11.

109. "CBMC Service Work," *Contact*, January–February 1945, 17.

110. "Hear Our Every Friday Radio Broadcast Direct from the CBMC Service Men's Center," January 1945, in author's possession, courtesy of Phil Wade, Christian Business Men's Committee International, Chattanooga, TN.

111. Clyde Wycoff scrapbook, n.d., 11, 35, In author's possession, courtesy of Phil Wade, Christian Business Men's Committee International, Chattanooga, TN.

112. For the more standard daily meal plus gospel and Saturday night worship schedule of servicemen's evangelism, not always in its own "center," see "New CBMC's in Canada," *Contact*, May–July 1945, 15; "Here and There among the Committees," *Contact*, August–October 1945, 6–7.

113. Glass, *Strangers in Zion*, xiv–xix; Frank Eades, "Request for Prayer," *Christian Workers*, October 1944, 1; "Ex. Committee Has Special Meeting," *Christian Workers*, November 1944, 2; "Patterson Elected President—The Best Convention Yet," *Fishers of Men*, September 1946, 1.

114. "Macon, GA, Great Christian Center," *Fishers of Men*, December 1944, 1.

115. "Ex. Committee Has Special Meeting," 2.

116. Eugene Steele, "Toccoa Club Launches Youth for Christ," *Fishers of Men*, November 1945, 1.

117. Carpenter, *Revive Us Again*, 158–59, 214; Larson, *Youth for Christ*, 76.

118. Larson, *Youth for Christ*, 146–48. Southern Baptist preacher Robert G. Lee, who keynoted the first St. Louis YFC rally, also gave the closing sermon at the National Association of Evangelicals' organizational meeting. See Larson, *Youth for Christ*, 52.

119. See Rolan Stoker, "Reports on YFC Conferences," *Fishers of Men*, December 1945, 1; Stoker, "Secretary Stoker Speaks," *Fishers of Men*, December 1945, 3.

120. "President's Report—State Convention" (draft), BMEC/CMC, Charlotte, 1942," box 2, folder 1, VWP. On BMEC/CMC placement of forty-seven hundred copies of "Story of the Bible" in schoolrooms, see *Charlotte Observer*, February 19, 1944. Also "Report Made by Resolutions Committee," *Christian Workers*, October 1944, 2; J. P. McCallie, "The National Convention Plans Enlarged Program," *Christian Workers*, October 1942, 1; R. R. Stoker, "Ladies' Auxiliaries," *Fishers of Men*, December 1944, 1.

121. Quoted in Enlow, *Men Aflame*, 23.

122. Carpenter, *Revive Us Again*, 211–32.

123. Kennedy, *Freedom from Fear*, 770–71.

124. Paul Fischer, "Lake Louise Conference of National Christian Laymen's Evangelistic Association," *Contact*, May–July 1945, 20; "Minutes of Joint Committee Meeting," *Fishers of Men*, January 1946, 2. The lineage of the "Billy Sunday clubs" and personnel remained the same—Stoker, Patterson, and Walter Anderson led the change—and the most important, but symbolic, shift was to the word "National" in the name. See Minutes of the Meeting of the Incorporation of the National Laymen's Evangelistic Association, Inc., October 6, 1945, in author's possession, courtesy of Phil Wade, Christian Business Men's Committee International, Chattanooga, TN.

125. "The Laymen's Evangelistic Association is on the March, Going Forward," *Fishers of Men*, January 1946, 3.

126. Quoted in Perrett, *Days of Sadness, Years of Triumph*, 196–97.

127. Ibid., 196.

128. "Europe Turning to Religion," *Christian Workers*, January 1943, 2.

129. "A Day of Prayer for Our Country," *Christian Workers*, October 1943, 3.

130. Perrett, *Days of Sadness, Years of Triumph*, 411–12.

131. "Editorially Speaking," *The King's Business*, June 1945, 207.

132. See, for instance, Friends of Israel Relief Committee, Inc., "A Thanksgiving Message," *Moody Monthly*, November 1941, inside cover.

133. Robert H. Glover, M.D., "Coming Revival," *Contact*, May–July 1945, 29–30.

134. For wider context, see Richard Pierard, "*Pax Americana* and the Evangelical Mission Alliance," in *Earthen Vessels: American Evangelicals and Foreign Missions, 1880–1990*, ed. Joel A. Carpenter and Wilbert R. Shenk (Grand Rapids, MI: William B. Eerdmans, 1990): 155–79.

135. "Unaccustomed As I Am—Here Are Some Memorable Quotes from Seattle," *Contact*, November–December 1946, 30.

136. Clyde Dennis, "Reporting the Convention," *Contact*, November–December 1946, 8–9.

137. "Here and There among the Committees," *Contact*, May–June 1945, 18.

138. Henderson, *Sowers of the Word*, 55, 219; MacArthur to the Southern Baptist Convention, December 13, 1947, quoted in Pierard, "*Pax Americana* and the Evangelical Mission Alliance," 174–75. MacArthur was, of course, a slippery character, and Pierard shows both how eager evangelicals were to reduce his complex views on religion to their own and how easy he made it for them to do so.

139. Dennis, "Reporting the Convention," 6.

140. V. R. Edman to R. G. LeTourneau, May 19, 1947, box J3F, folder 76, LTP.

141. In 1938, LeTourneau opened an earthmoving company in Australia, which soon supplied earthmoving equipment to the Pacific Front. See LeTourneau, *Mover of Men and Mountains*, 230–31.

142. "Seeing Strange Sights in Stockton," *Joyful News*, December 1946, 1; "A Remarkable Man from Illinois," *Evangelical News*, October 18, 1946, n.p., clipping in box F10, folder 17, LTP.

143. Syd Jackson, "It's 'Mass Produce or Bust' at Stockton!," *Evening Gazette*, October 23, 1946, 2.

144. "Millionaire Preacher in Edinburgh," *Evangelical News*, October 20, 1946, n.p., box F10, folder 17, LTP.

145. "God's Business Man, R. G. LeTourneau, Goes Global," *Joyful News*, November 1946, 4.

146. Graham, *Just as I Am*, 94.

147. Larson, *Youth for Christ*, 70–71.

148. Graham, *Just as I Am*, 108.

149. Harold Strathearn, "READ! REJOICE! PRAY!," *Joyful News*, February–March 1947, 1.

150. "A Call for Special Prayer," *Contact*, March–April 1947, 9.

151. The evangelical press followed China closely and hailed Madame Chiang Kai-Shek as something close to a Protestant saint. See, for instance, Louis T. Talbot, D.D., "I Saw China's Need," *The King's Business*, November 1947, 10–11, 14; L. P. Liu, "Mme. Chang Kai-Shek's Father Was a Missionary," *Moody Monthly*, December 1941, 202–3.

152. George Sirgiovanni, *An Undercurrent of Suspicion: Anti-Communism in America during World War II* (New Brunswick, NJ: Transaction, 1990), 47–72, 147–74; Richard Gid Powers, *Not without Honor: The History of American Anticommunism* (New Haven, CT: Yale University Press, 1998), 44–57.

153. Rolan Stoker to Billy Graham, June 3, 1947, box 1, folder 4, VWP.

154. Vernon Patterson to "Christian Friend," n.d., invitation to Preliminary Rally, box 1, folder 4, VWP.

155. Billy Graham to Ed Darling, November 17, 1947, box 1, folder 4, VWP.

156. Donald Enlow, "Tenth Annual Convention," *Contact*, November–December 1947, 14–15.

CHAPTER FIVE

1. James MacDonald, "Paris District Bombed Again; Big Force Hammers Cologne," *New York Times*, April 7, 1942, F9.

2. "Nazis over Malta in Big-Scale Air Raid," *New York Times*, April 7, 1942, F9.

3. "MacArthur Hailed as Symbol of Spirit That'll Beat Japs," *Los Angeles Times*, April 7, 1942, 1, 8.

4. "Church Group Warns against Totalitarianism," *St. Louis Post-Dispatch*, April 7, 1942. Scrapbook of J. Elwin Wright, BGCA.

5. The *Post-Dispatch* did not cover Ockenga but referred to "speakers," plural, concerned about totalitarianism. The quote is in Carpenter, *Revive Us Again*, 147.

6. See "Church Group Warns against Totalitarianism." Wright's scrapbook also includes postconference coverage, which focuses on the organizational outcome rather than the early speeches: "Unity Body Votes to Organize Now," *St. Louis Globe-Democrat*, April 9, 1942; "New Church Unit Decides to Ignore Both Councils," *Washington Evening Star*, April 9, 1942; "Evangelicals Discuss Stand on Councils," *St. Louis Post-Dispatch*, n.d.; "Group of Churchmen Plan Another National Council," *United Presbyterian*, April 23, 1942; "New Fundamental Association," *Alliance Weekly*, May 16, 1942, all in Scrapbook of J. Elwin Wright, BGCA. See also J. Howard Murch, *Cooperation without Compromise: A History of the National Association of Evangeli-*

cals (Grand Rapids, MI: W. B. Eerdmans, 1956), 48–61; Bruce L. Shelley, *Evangelicalism in America* (Grand Rapids, MI: W. B. Eerdmans, 1967), 80–83.

7. "Religious Aims of U.S. Council Attacked Here," *Chattanooga News–Free Press*, January 13, 1942, Scrapbook of J. Elwin Wright, BGCA.

8. "Church Group Warns against Totalitarianism"; Carpenter, *Revive Us Again*, 137–48; Douglas A. Sweeney, "The Essential Evangelicalism Dialectic: The Historiography of the Early Neo-Evangelical Movement and the Observer-Participant Dilemma," *Church History* 60 (March 1991): 78.

9. "Church Group Warns against Totalitarianism."

10. J. Elwin Wright, "Report of the Promotional Director," in *United We Stand: A Report of the Constitutional Convention of the National Association of Evangelicals*, May 3–6, 1943, 8, box 65, folder 20, HJT.

11. Paul R. Gorman, *Left Intellectuals and Popular Culture in Twentieth-Century America* (Chapel Hill: University of North Carolina Press, 1996), 152.

12. Nash, *The Conservative Intellectual Movement in America since 1945*, 3, 30–49. Hayek's book *The Road to Serfdom* was published in 1944.

13. Marchand, *Advertising the American Dream*, 324.

14. The full name was originally National Association of Evangelicals for United Action.

15. J. Elwin Wright to Herbert Taylor, November 24, 1941, box 11, folder 22, HJT; Minutes of the Executive Committee of the National Association of Evangelicals for United Action, May 11, 1942, box 65, folder 16, HJT.

16. Wright to Taylor, Nov. 24, 1941.

17. National Association of Evangelicals, "About Us," http://nae.net/about-nae/history/, accessed September 15, 2015.

18. "Policy upon Witness," n.d., labeled "St. Louis Meeting of Evangelicals" by Herbert Taylor, box 65, folder 16, HJT.

19. On the history of the FCC, see Robert A. Schneider, "Voice of Many Waters: Church Federation in the Twentieth Century," in *Between the Times: The Travail of the Protestant Establishment in America*, ed. William R. Hutchison (Cambridge: Cambridge University Press, 1989), 101–16. Martin E. Marty, among others, shows that the FCC and conservative Protestants were united in viewing Catholicism as a political, theological, and existential threat. See Martin E. Marty, "The Twentieth Century: Protestants and Others," in *Religion and American Politics: From the Colonial Period to the 1980s*, ed. Mark A. Noll (New York: Oxford University Press, 1990), 330.

20. Carpenter, *Revive Us Again*, 145–55.

21. Ibid., 142.

22. A Catholic priest selected "Cooperation without Compromise" for the Naval Chaplaincy School, established in 1943. See William A. Wildhack III, CHC, USNR, "Navy Chaplains at the Crossroads: Navigating the Intersection of Free Speech, Free Exercise, Establishment, and Equal Protection," *Naval L. Rev* 51 (2005): N126.

23. "'Cooperation without Compromise': Highlights of the Seventh Annual Convention," 1949, 1, box 66, folder 23, HJT.

24. Elizabeth Fones-Wolf and Ken Fones-Wolf, "Shirtsleeve Religion: Business and the Post-war Industrial Chaplain Movement," 2–4, 8–14. Paper presented at the Business

History Conference Annual Meeting, Sacramento, April 2008. Cited with authors' permission. The Ethics and Spirituality in the Workplace program at Yale Divinity School has pushed for a mainline Protestant renaissance of the industrial chaplaincy in the 2000s. See David Miller, *God at Work: The History and Promise of the Faith at Work Movement* (New York: Oxford University Press, 2006).

25. Eckard Vance Toy Jr., "The National Lay Committee and the National Council of Churches: A Case Study of Protestants in Conflict," *American Quarterly* 21 (Summer 1969): 120–209; Toy, "Ideology and Conflict in American Ultraconservatism, 1945–1960," (PhD diss., University of Oregon, 1965); Phillips-Fein, *Invisible Hands*, 26–86; Carol V. R. George, *God's Salesman: Norman Vincent Peale and the Power of Positive Thinking* (New York: Oxford University Press, 1993), 103–27, 170–74. See also Steven P. Miller, *Billy Graham and the Rise of the Republican South* (Philadelphia: University of Pennsylvania Press, 2009).

26. Carpenter, *Revive Us Again*, 142–43.

27. Ibid., 143.

28. Ibid.

29. Margaret Lamberts Bendroth, *Fundamentalists in the City: Conflict and Division in Boston's Churches, 1885–1950* (New York: Oxford University Press, 2005), 170–76.

30. Carpenter, *Revive Us Again*, 144–45.

31. Marsden, *Reforming Fundamentalism*, 148–53.

32. Carpenter, *Revive Us Again*, 158.

33. See Charles A. Foster, *An Errand of Mercy: The Evangelical United Front, 1790–1837* (Chapel Hill: University of North Carolina Press, 1960).

34. Reprinted in Clarence H. Benson, "Our Monthly Potpourri," *Moody Bible Institute Monthly*, January 1936, 260.

35. "Christian Duty," Editorial Notes, *Moody Monthly*, October 1940.

36. Dr. Paul W. Rood, "Biola Hall of Fame," Biola University, http://100.biola.edu/index.cfm?pageid=33, accessed December 15, 2015.

37. Carpenter, *Revive Us Again*, 7, 26, 37–38, 142.

38. "Annual Meeting: The World's Christian Fundamentals Association," advertisement, *The King's Business*, January 1937, inside cover, 14.

39. J. Elwin Wright to Herbert Taylor, November 24, 1941, box 11, folder 22, HJT.

40. Wright, "Report of the Promotional Director," 6.

41. "Religious Aims of U.S. Council Attacked Here."

42. Minutes, Meeting of Committee for United Action among Evangelicals, January 19, 1942, 1, Scrapbook of J. Elwin Wright, BGCA.

43. Harry S. Stout, *The Divine Dramatist: George Whitefield and the Rise of Modern Evangelism* (Grand Rapids, MI: W. B. Eerdmans, 1991), 44–46.

44. Hangen, *Redeeming the Dial*, 68.

45. Charles Fuller to Herbert Taylor, September 12, 1940, box 11, folder 22, HJT; Quentin Schultze, "Evangelical Radio and the Electronic Church, 1921–1948," *Journal of Broadcasting and Electric Media* 32 (Summer 1988): 301. McIntire's battle with broadcasting regulations would be lifelong. In the early 1970s, he was the first and only broadcaster to lose his license based on the Fairness Doctrine of equal time for oppos-

ing views. See Heather Hendershot, "God's Angriest Man: Carl McIntire, Cold War Fundamentalism, and Right-Wing Broadcasting," *American Quarterly* 59 (June 2007): 373–96.

46. Schultze, "Evangelical Radio and the Electronic Church, 1921–1948," quoting the National Association of Broadcasters, 298.

47. Sydney E. Ahlstrom and David D. Hall, *A Religious History of the American People* (1972; reprint, New Haven, CT: Yale University Press, 2004), 1106; Executive Committee Meeting, NAE, June 17, 1943, 4, box 65, folder 19, HJT.

48. Hangen, *Redeeming the Dial*, 117.

49. Daniel P. Fuller, *Give the Wind a Mighty Voice: The Story of Charles E. Fuller* (Waco, TX: Word Books, 1972), 152–53.

50. US National War Labor Board Records, 1944. See Guide to the NWLB Arbitration Regarding Electrical Transcription Manufacturers and American Federation of Musicians, collection no. 5315, Kheel Center for Labor-Management Documentation and Archives, Cornell University Library, Ithaca, New York, http://rmc.library.cornell.edu/EAD/htmldocs/KCL05315.html, accessed December 18, 2015.

51. Wright, "Report of the Promotional Director," 6.

52. Committee for United Action among Evangelicals, November 10, 1941, Scrapbook of J. Elwin Wright, BGCA.

53. "Government: Great Game of War Contract," *Time*, November 16, 1942, http://www.time.com/time/magazine/article/0,9171,932899,00.html, accessed December 17, 2015.

54. Taylor, *The Herbert J. Taylor Story*, 41.

55. Jeffrey A. Charles, *Service Clubs in American Society: Rotary, Kiwanis, and Lions* (Urbana: University of Illinois Press, 1993), 40–47, 138.

56. Herbert Taylor to J. Elwin Wright, June 12, 1943, box 65, folder 16, HJT; C. Lawrence Christenson, "Economic Implications of Renegotiation of Government Contracts," *Journal of Political Economy* 52 (March 1944): 71n51.

57. See Guide to Papers of Herbert Taylor, BGCA, http://www.wheaton.edu/bgc/archives/GUIDES/020.htm, accessed December 17, 2015; Robert Walker to J. Elwin Wright, April 27, 1943, box 65, folder 16, HJT.

58. Joy Elmer Morgan, "Review: Education by Radio Begins a New Epoch," *School Review* 39 (September 1931): 547–48; Cindy C. Welch, "Broadcasting the Profession: The American Library Association and the National Children's Radio Hour" (PhD diss., University of Illinois, 2009), 69–70.

59. Quoted in Fuller, *Give the Wind a Mighty Voice*, 154–55.

60. Christopher H. Sterling, *The Museum of Broadcast Communications Encyclopedia of Radio* (New York: Fitzroy Dearborn, 2004), 1214. See Brinkley, *Voices of Protest*, 82, 175–79.

61. Quoted in Fuller, *Give the Wind a Mighty Voice*, 152.

62. Murch, *Cooperation without Compromise*, 74.

63. Albeit unreliably. Ibid., 154. Fuller describes an "Elwin Wright delegation" swooping in and flexing evangelical muscle, a version that no contemporary sources confirm.

64. Wright, "Report of the Promotional Director," 8.

65. Reference here is to Matthew 15:14 and Luke 6:39.

66. Otto D. Tolischus, "Challenge of a Master Propagandist," *New York Times*, July 28, 1940.

67. Dr. Harold J. Ockenga, "Christ for America," in *United We Stand: A Report of the Constitutional Convention of the National Association of Evangelicals*, May 3–6, 1943, 10–12, box 65, folder 20, HJT.

68. Wright, "Report of the Promotional Director," 7.

69. Ibid., 1–2; Herbert Taylor to [blank], November 1942, "According to our records you kindly pledged ____," box 65, folder 16, HJT.

70. J. Elwin Wright to Herbert Taylor, January 27, 1943, box 65, folder 16, HJT.

71. Robert Walker to J. Elwin Wright, December 28, 1942, box 65, folder 16, HJT; Herbert Taylor to Charles Fuller, February 2, 1943, box 13, folder 11, HJT.

72. Ockenga, "Christ for America," 16.

73. J. Elwin Wright to Herbert Taylor, November 24, 1942 (NEF stationery), box 11, folder 22, HJT; J. Elwin Wright to General Lucius D. Clay, n.d., box 15, folder 20, HJT.

74. A. D. Weir to Herbert J. Taylor, April 28, 1940, box 12, folder 18, HJT; Minutes of the Executive Committee of the National Association of Evangelicals for United Action, May 11, 1942, box 65, folder 16, HJT. On Weyerhaeuser see Stewardship Foundation, http://stewardshipfdn.org/applying-for-funding/submitting-an-applicationproposal/our-founder/, accessed January 5, 2017. The Frederick K. Weyerhaeuser professorship at the Yale School of Forestry is named after Weyerhaeuser's father.

75. *United Evangelical Action*, May 4, 1943, 2.

76. "R. G. LeTourneau's Speaking Schedule," *NOW*, April 3, 1942, back page; "R. G. LeTourneau's Speaking Schedule," *NOW*, April 23, 1943, LTP.

77. A. Donald MacLeod, *C. Stacey Woods and the Evangelical Rediscovery of the University* (Downers Grove, IL: InterVarsity, 2007), 195.

78. Dr. John Bradbury, "Cooperation among Evangelicals," in *United We Stand: A Report of the Constitutional Convention of the National Association of Evangelicals*, May 3–6, 1943, 22, box 65, folder 20, HJT.

79. Carpenter, *Revive Us Again*, 191–92, 195.

80. Executive Committee Meeting, National Association of Evangelicals, June 17–18, 1943, 5, box 65, folder 19, HJT; *In the Light*, Canadian IVCF pamphlet, 1941–42, box 60, folder 2, HJT.

81. Executive Committee Meeting, National Association of Evangelicals, June 17–18, 1943, 5; "To Be Present," n.d. [1942?], box 33, folder 27, HJT.

82. Executive Committee Meeting, National Association of Evangelicals, June 17–18, 1943, 5; Ted Benson to Herbert Taylor, November 30, 1940, box 11, folder 7, HJT.

83. "Archives—Presidents of the National Association of Realtors, 1957—Kenneth Keyes," https://dev.nar.realtor/bios/kenneth-keyes, accessed January 30, 2017; Executive Committee Meeting, National Association of Evangelicals, June 17–18, 1943, 2.

84. J. Elwin Wright, "Report of the Field Secretary to the Board of Administration, September 21, 1943," Board of Administration Meeting, National Association of Evangelicals, September 21–22, 1943, 6, box 65, folder 19, HJT.

85. "Report of the Treasurer," ibid., 8.

86. Carpenter, *Revive Us Again*, 152.

87. Ibid., 158–59.

88. J. Elwin Wright, "Report of the Temporary Field Secretary to the Executive Committee," May 20, 1943, box 65, folder 19, HJT; Minutes of the Meeting of the Commission on Missions, September 17, 1943, 10, box 65, folder 21, HJT. The Committee on Missions met in the Chicago CBMCI's Victory Center for servicemen.

89. Oral interview, T3 Transcript, Torrey Johnson Collection, BGCA, http://www.wheaton.edu/bgc/archives/trans/285t03.htm, accessed January 5, 2016.

90. Herbert Taylor to J. Elwin Wright, October 10, 1943, and Wright to Herbert Taylor, October 13, 1943, both box 65, folder 21, HJT.

91. Unsigned, n.d., draft invitation to November 16, 1943, dinner on Hager's church stationery, box 65, folder 21, HJT.

92. Rollin Severance to Herbert Taylor, November 8, 1943, box 65, folder 21, HJT.

93. Typed, annotated list of Chicago NAE dinner invitees, n.d. (November 1943), 3, box 65, folder 21, HJT.

94. Stacey Woods to Herbert Taylor, September 30, 1941, box 60, folder 24, HJT; Herbert Taylor to Mr. and Mrs. George Beverly Shea, February 6, 1945, box 24, folder 26, HJT; J. F. Strombeck to Herbert Taylor, May 20, 1941, box 60, folder 24, HJT.

95. See Guide to Papers of Robert C. Van Kampen, BGCA, http://www.wheaton.edu/bgc/archives/GUIDES/313.htm, accessed January 4, 2016.

96. Herbert Taylor to J. Elwin Wright, November 10, 1943, box 65, folder 21, HJT.

97. Robert Walker to J. Elwin Wright, July 16, 1943, box 65, folder 21, HJT. On the importance of color to advertising "style" and high class, see Marchand, *Advertising the American Dream*, 120–28.

98. Gertrude Clark to Robert Walker, October 19, 1943, quoting Wright, box 65, folder 21, HJT. On Good News Publishing's history with the CWF, see "Report of Activities of the Christian Workers Foundation," 3. The motto is on various iterations of its stationery.

99. Taylor ended the CWF's ties to Good News in 1945, accusing publisher Clyde Dennis of "getting ahead of the Lord's plans" with repeated expansions despite company debt. Nevertheless, Dennis and Good News continued to thrive in the world of evangelical publishing. The current company history omits Taylor's name, influence, and $17,500 from the tale of Dennis's ascent. Herbert Taylor, "Reasons for Severing Relationship between the Christian Workers Foundation and the Good News Publishing Co.," April 3, 1945, 3, box 13, folder 4, HJT; "The Good News Story: Celebrating Sixty Years of God's Faithfulness," https://www.crossway.org/about/history/, accessed January 16, 2016.

100. J. Elwin Wright to Robert Walker, November 1, 1943, box 65, folder 21, HJT.

101. Minutes, Committee for United Action Among Evangelicals, October 27–28, 1941, 2, Scrapbook of J. Elwin Wright, BGCA.

102. "Religious Aims of U.S. Council Attached Here," *Chattanooga News–Free Press*, January 14, 1942.

103. D. Shelby Corlett, Nazarene Publishing House, to General Superintendents, May 12, 1943, box 65, folder 16, HJT.

104. Quoted in Carpenter, *Revive Us Again*, 153.

105. Pasi Falk, "The Genealogy of Advertising," in David B. Clarke, Marcus A. Doel, and Kate M. L. Housiaux, *The Consumption Reader* (London: Routledge, 2003), 187–89.

106. Taylor, *The Herbert J. Taylor Story*, 41.

107. Marchand, *Advertising the American Dream*, 2.

108. Ibid., 117–32.

109. "The St. Louis Convention," *Sunday School Times*, June 20, 1942, 493–94, 498–99.

110. J. Elwin Wright to "Gentlemen" of *Sunday School Times*, n.d. (1942), box 65, folder 16, HJT.

111. Herbert Taylor to J. Elwin Wright, July 6, 1942, box 65, folder 16, HJT.

112. "Notes on Open Letters: The National Association," *Sunday School Times*, August 8, 1942, 626.

113. Leslie R. Marston to Herbert Taylor, May 24, 1944, box 65, folder 24, HJT.

114. J. Elwin Wright [Robert Walker], *Flash Sheet*, July 14, 1944, box 65, folder 25, HJT; "David Toong, 1895–1998," *Biographical Dictionary of Chinese Christianity*, http://www.bdcconline.net/en/stories/t/toong-david.php, accessed September 15, 2015.

115. Leslie R. Marston to J. Elwin Wright, October 20, 1944, box 65, folder 24, HJT.

116. J. Elwin Wright to Rev. J. Roswell Flower, January 23, 1945, box 65, folder 4, HJT.

117. On the circular relationship between local indifference and the NAE's perpetual financial crises, see R. L. Decker to Carl Gunderson, October 21, 1947, box 6, folder 14, HJT.

118. Leslie Marston to Herbert Taylor, December 1944, box 65, folder 26, HJT.

119. J. Elwin Wright to Herbert Taylor, February 2, 1945, box 65, folder 26, HJT.

120. Herbert Taylor to J. Elwin Wright, February 7, 1945, box 65, folder 26, HJT; Gertrude Clark to Herbert Taylor, February 13, 1945, box 65, folders 25, HJT.

121. Herbert Taylor to J. Elwin Wright, January 16, 1945, box 65, folder 26, HJT.

122. Leslie Marston to Herbert Taylor, October 23, 1944, box 65, folder 24, HJT; Herbert Taylor to J. Elwin Wright, January 16, 1945, box 65, folder 26, HJT.

123. Herbert Taylor to T. Roland Phillips, March 27, 1945, box 65, folder 26, HJT.

124. Leslie Marston to Herbert Taylor, February 14, 1945, and Herbert Taylor to Rev. Neville O. Hatcher, March 15, 1945, both box 65, folder 24, HJT.

125. Gertrude Clark to J. Roswell Flower, November 19, 1947, NAE Correspondence, folder 4, Flower Pentecostal Heritage Center Archives, Springfield, MO, courtesy of Molly Worthen.

126. Carl F. H. Henry, NAE press release, May 1, 1945, box 65, folder 28, HJT; Frank D. Lombar to Herbert Taylor, February 1, 1945, box 65, folder 26, HJT.

127. J. Elwin Wright to Herbert Taylor, February 2, 1945, box 65, folder 26, HJT.

128. J. Elwin Wright to Herbert Taylor, February 16, 1945, box 65, folder 26, HJT; Kenneth Keyes to Leslie Marston, February 16, 1945, box 65, folder 24, HJT.

129. Dr. R. L. Decker, "An Evangelical 'Over-All Strategic Concept,'" in *Action: Program of the Fourth Annual Convention of the National Association of Evangelicals and Associated Organizations*, April 24–May 2, 1946, 39–42, box 66, folder 3, HJT.

130. Herbert Taylor to J. Elwin Wright, February 22, 1946, box 66, folder 5, HJT; Kenneth Keyes to Herbert Taylor, February 25, 1946, box 66, folder 3, HJT.

131. Kenneth Keyes to Herbert Taylor, April 16, 1946, box 66, folder 3, HJT.

132. J. Elwin Wright to R. L. Decker, July 1, 1946, box 66, folder 11, HJT.

133. R. L. Decker to Herbert Taylor, June 29, 1946, box 66, folder 3, HJT.

134. Kenneth Keyes to R. L. Decker, October 15, 1946, box 6, folder 11, HJT.

135. Herbert Taylor to J. Elwin Wright, November 14, 1946, box 66, folder 11, HJT.

136. R. L. Decker to Herbert Taylor, June 18, 1946, box 66, folder 3, HJT.

137. R. L. Decker to Herbert Taylor, May 1, 1947, box 66, folder 11, HJT.

138. S. A. Rohrer to Herbert Taylor, Aug. 26, 1947, box 66, folder 20, HJT.

139. R. L. Decker to Carl Gunderson, October 21, 1947, box 66, folder 14, HJT.

140. Leslie Marston to Herbert Taylor, October 23, 1944, box 65, folder 24. Depending on the date, the commission is sometimes called the committee.

141. Carl Henry, "Ntl. Assn. of Evangelicals," May 1, 1945, 1–2, box 65, folder 28, HJT.

142. Ibid.; Wright to Herbert Taylor, June 16, 1944, box 65, folder 24, HJT; Jeremy Brecher, "The World War II and Post-War Strike Wave," excerpted in *Strike!*, rev. and updated ed., South End Press Classics Series (New York: South End, 1999), excerpt at http://libcom.org/history/world-war-ii-post-war-strike-wave, accessed September 15, 2015.

143. The New Jersey Stoker Company is described in 290F.2d 675, United Court of Appeals Third Circuit, 1961, http://bulk.resource.org/courts.gov/c/F2/290/290.F2d.675.13391.13392.html, accessed September 13, 2015.

144. The masthead is on p. 11 of *Industrial Chaplain* (1945), box 15, folder 10, HJT.

145. "Rollin Severance, Michigan Governor Candidate, 1966," http://www.prohibitionists.org/History/votes/Rollin-Severance_Bio.htm, accessed September 16, 2015.

146. Henderson, *Sowers of the Word*, 49; Albert Muchka, *West Allis* (Charleston, SC: Arcadia, 2003), 39.

147. Gustav Sætra, "Torrey Mosvold—Elaboration," *Norwegian Biographical Encyclopedia*, in translation, http://www.snl.no/.nbl_biografi/Torrey_Mosvold/utdypning, accessed January 16, 2010; Larson, *Young Man on Fire*, 12–13.

148. Herbert Taylor to Dr. Stephen W. Pain, December 9, 1948, box 66, folder 23, HJT. See also Carl Henry, "Ntl. Assn. of Evangelicals," May 1, 1945, 2, box 65, folder 28, HJT.

149. Fones-Wolf and Fones-Wolf, "Shirtsleeve Religion," 3. For more extensive treatment by these coauthors see Ken Fones-Wolf and Elizabeth A. Fones-Wolf, *Struggle for the Soul of the Postwar South: White Evangelical Protestants and Operation Dixie* (Urbana: University of Illinois Press, 2015).

150. J. Elwin Wright [Robert Walker], "Latest News from the Front Lines," *Flash Sheet* November 1944, box 65, folder 24, HJT.

151. Elizabeth A. Fones-Wolf, *Selling Free Enterprise: The Business Assault on Labor and Liberalism, 1945–60* (Urbana: University of Illinois Press, 1994), 218–54.

152. Fones-Wolf and Fones-Wolf, "Shirtsleeve Religion," 5; "History of the McGill Clubhouse" (Nevada copper mill with YMCA presence), http://mcgillclubhouse.com/

blank.html, accessed September 20, 2015; Richard Wightman Fox, *Reinhold Niebuhr: A Biography* (New York: Pantheon Books, 1985), 88–103.

153. LeTourneau, *Mover of Men and Mountains*, 210; Fones-Wolf, *Selling Free Enterprise*, 224.

154. "Plant Life," *NOW*, October 3, 1941, foldout.

155. "Plant Life," *NOW*, March 28, 1941, 4.

156. Tom Olson, "Around the Clock around the Calendar and around the World," *NOW*, April 17, 1942, foldout.

157. Fones-Wolf and Fones-Wolf, "Shirtsleeve Religion," 8.

158. Ibid., 6–8.

159. A. H. Armerding, "The Post-War Industrial Problem," *Industrial Chaplain* (1945), 12, box 15, folder 10, HJT.

160. Ibid.

161. A. H. Armerding, "A Need and Its Remedy," *Industrial Chaplain* (1945), 2, box 15, folder 10, HJT.

162. H. C. Fraser, "The Chaplain in Industry," *Army-Navy Chaplain*, January–February 1945, reprinted in *Industrial Chaplain* (1945), 7, box 15, folder 10, HJT.

163. Armerding, "A Need and Its Remedy."

164. Walter Block, "To Whom It May Concern," *Industrial Chaplain* (1945), 10, box 15, folder 10, HJT.

165. Ford News Bureau, "Good Friday Services at Ford Motor Co. March 30, 1945," and "Religious Activities at the Ford Motor Company," *Industrial Chaplain* (1945), 5–6, box 15, folder 10, HJT; Brecher, "The World War II and Post-War Strike Wave"; Stephen Meyer, "An Economic 'Frankenstein': UAW Workers' Response to Automation at the Ford Brook Park Plant in the 1950s," *Automobile in American Life and Society* (2004), http://www.autolife.umd.umich.edu/Labor/L_Casestudy/L_casestudy3.htm, accessed September 18, 2015.

166. [A. H. Armerding], "Foreword," *Industrial Chaplain*, 1, box 15, folder 10, HJT.

167. John E. Mitchell Jr., "To Whom It May Concern," *Industrial Chaplain* (1945), 4, box 15, folder 10, HJT.

168. Ernest L. Chase to Herbert Taylor, October 29, 1945, box 15, folder 10, HJT.

169. Irwin McLean to Herbert Taylor, September 5, 1945, box 15, folder 10, HJT.

170. A. H. Armerding to Herbert Taylor, February 4, 1946, box 15, folder 10, HJT; Brecher, "The World War II and Post-War Strike Wave."

171. Commission for Industrial Chaplains, "Announcing a Six-Weeks Seminar for Industrial Chaplains and Candidates," n.d. (Spring 1945), box 15, folder 10, HJT.

172. A. H. Armerding, "Report of Chaplain Counselors for Industry, Inc.," *United Evangelical Action*, n.d., 53–55, clipping in box 15, folder 10, HJT. Armerding attributed the three nonhires to "age and other handicaps," which, if true, reflected poorly on the commission's screening process.

173. A. H. Armerding to Brethren in Christ, November 5, 1946, box 15, folder 20, HJT.

174. V. R. Edman to Herbert Taylor, February 14, 1947, box 15, folder 39, HJT.

175. Chaplain Counselors for Industry, Inc., "'Chaplain Counselors' for Industry:

A Scientific Development in Counseling for Industrial Workers," n.d. (1947), 8, box 15, folder 45, HJT.

176. Ibid., 8–10.

177. A. H. Armerding, "Brief Report to Trustees for Year 1947," n.d., box 15, folder 45, HJT.

178. A. H. Armerding, "Underwriting Proposed for One Year Only," September 29, 1947; A. H. Armerding to Herbert Taylor, October 29, 1947, and December 18, 1947; A. H. Armerding, "Brief Report to Trustees for Year 1947," all box 15, folder 45, HJT.

179. A. H. Armerding to Stephen Paine, March 22, 1949, box 66, folder 23, HJT.

180. Ernest L. Chase, "Report of Commission on Industrial Chaplaincies," in *United—In the Faith, Sixth Annual Convention, National Association of Evangelicals*, May 3–6, 1948, 21, box 66, folder 23, HJT.

CONCLUSION

1. Stuart James, "The Man Who Can Move Mountains," *Popular Mechanics*, July 1966, 99–100.

2. Quoted in "Rowan Companies Marks 50th Anniversary of Landmark LeTourneau Jackup," *Drilling Contractor* (September–October 2005), 34–36.

3. Quoted in "LeTourneau Is Sued," *New York Times*, May 12, 1958.

4. James, "The Man Who Can Move Mountains," 176.

5. Ibid., 177.

6. Nels E. Stjernstrom, "Epilogue to the 1967 Edition," in LeTourneau, *Mover of Men and Mountains*, 281.

7. *Industrial Missionary Enterprises of the LeTourneau Foundation*, n.d., 1, box J2Z, folder 25-2, LTP. On Ford's blend of industry and cultural outreach see Greg Grandin, *Fordlandia: The Rise and Fall of Henry Ford's Forgotten Jungle City* (New York: Metropolitan Books / Henry Holt, 2009).

8. *Industrial Missionary Enterprises of the LeTourneau Foundation*, 3.

9. Stjernstrom, "Epilogue," 280.

10. "Tournavista Days," http://www.facebook.com/profile.php?v=wal&id=100000220876427.

11. Nels E. Stjernstrom, "In Memoriam," in LeTourneau, *Mover of Men and Mountains*, 286.

12. "About LeTourneau Technologies," http://www.rowan.com/our-company/history/default.aspx, accessed January 6, 2016.

13. "Mission Statement," LeTourneau University, http://letu.edu/opencms/opencms/_Other-Resources/_Community-and-Media/about-letourneau/mission-and-vision.html, accessed January 6, 2016.

14. "Christian Leadership," LeTourneau University, http://www.letu.edu/opencms/opencms/_Student-Life/leadership/, accessed January 6, 2016.

15. Heidebrecht, *God's Man in the Marketplace*, 73–74, 79–80.

16. Biographical details offered here are drawn from Heidebrecht, *God's Man in the Marketplace*, 75, 78, 89 [quote], 91–92.

17. Ibid., 81.

18. "Rotary President Taylor: 50 Years to the Good," *Newsweek*, February 28, 1955.

19. Heidebrecht, *God's Man in the Marketplace*, 85.

20. Ibid., 85; George, *God's Salesman*, 108.

21. Heidebrecht, *God's Man in the Marketplace*, 85.

22. Graham, *Just as I Am*, 288.

23. Miller, *Billy Graham and the Rise of the Republican South*, 75–84, 97–102; Heidebrecht, *God's Man in the Marketplace*, 93–94.

24. Heidebrecht, *God's Man in the Marketplace*, 102.

25. Ibid., 104.

26. Ibid., 107–9.

27. "Guiding Principles," Rotary, Inc., https://www.rotary.org/myrotary/en/learning-reference/about-rotary/guiding-principles, accessed January 6, 2016.

28. Joan Giangrasse Kates, "Robert Walker: 1912–2008: Trailblazing Christian Journalist magazine Founder Guided by Spirituality," *Chicago Tribune*, March 14, 2008, http://articles.chicagotribune.com/2008-03-14/news/0803130874_1_strang-communications-christian-publishing-stephen-strang, accessed January 30, 2017.

29. McGirr, *Suburban Warriors*, 24–26.

30. Christian Business Men's Committee International Directory, 1948, 4, box J4S, folder 47, LTP. Although the first meeting of the Full Gospel Business Men's Fellowship was in 1951, the formal founding date was 1952. See R. Marie Griffith, *God's Daughters: Evangelical Women and the Power of Submission* (Berkeley: University of California Press, 1997), 30. On merger see CBMC USA, "75 Years of Ministry," 10.

31. Miller, *Billy Graham and the Rise of the Republican South*, 125.

32. William H. Frey, "The Electoral College Moves to the Sunbelt," Brookings Institution research brief, May 2005, 1.

33. Ibid., 11, 14.

34. Henderson, *Sowers of the Word*, 168.

35. "Operation Timothy," http://www.operationtimothy.com/whatisot, accessed January 8, 2016.

36. CBMC USA, "75 Years of Ministry," 14, 20, 22.

37. These developments are detailed in Marsden, *Reforming Fundamentalism*.

38. Grem, *The Blessings of Business*, 166.

39. See guide for "Ephemera of James Elwin Wright—Collection 564," BGCA, http://wheaton.edu/bgc/archives/GUIDES/565.html, accessed January 6, 2016.

40. This account is indebted to Fones-Wolf and Fones-Wolf, "Shirtsleeve Religion," 24–28.

41. Ibid., 20.

42. Heale, *American Anti-Communism*, 148–50.

43. Fones-Wolf, *Selling Free Enterprise*, 7–8, 22–26.

44. Ibid., 42–44, 22 (quote).

45. Ibid., 224.

46. A. H. Armerding, "Report of Chaplain Counselors for Industry, Inc.," *United Evangelical Action*, n.d., 54, clipping in box 15, folder 10, HJT.

47. See especially Moreton, *To Serve God and Wal-Mart*, 100–111, 125–44.

48. Carl F. H. Henry, *The Uneasy Conscience of Modern Fundamentalism* (Grand Rapids, MI: William B. Eerdmans, 1947), 32.

49. Marsden, *Reforming Fundamentalism*, 167–68.

50. William Martin, *A Prophet with Honor: The Billy Graham Story* (New York: William Morrow, 1991), 218–24, 239–40. On the complex alliances in white American Protestantism in the early Cold War, see Thomas C. Berg, "'Proclaiming Together?': Convergence and Divergence in Mainline and Evangelical Evangelism, 1945–1967," *Religion and American Culture* 5 (Winter 1995): 49–76.

51. Henry, *The Uneasy Conscience of Modern Fundamentalism*, 78.

52. Anniversary Prayer, Anniversaries, box 639, Sun and Oil Industry folder, SOC; "Pioneering Petroleum Progress: A 75th Anniversary Address by Robert G. Dunlop, President, Sun Oil Company," 7, 9–11, 14, box 55, Sun Oil—75th Anniversary 1961 folder, SOC.

53. Waldemar A. Nielsen, *Golden Donors: A New Anatomy of the Great Foundations* (New Brunswick, NJ: Transaction, 2002), 169, 174.

54. Grem, *The Blessings of Business*, 49–51.

55. Billy Graham, "God before Gold," *Nation's Business*, September 1954, 34–35, 55–56.

56. This article and general overview of Graham's relationship to big business in the 1950s are discussed and analyzed at length in Grem, *The Blessings of Business*, 57–59.

INDEX